CORPORATIONS™

Authors:
Mark Arsenault and Geoff Berman

Editor/Developer: Bruce Harlick

Project Specific Contributions:
Art Direction: Jessica Ney-Grimm;
Cover Graphics: Coleman Charlton
Pagemaking: Blackhawk Typestting
Layout: Nick Morawitz;
Editorial Contributions: Coleman Charlton, Sean Fannon, Ray Greer, Steve Peterson, Maggi Perkins, W.D. Robinson
Series Editor: Bruce Harlick

Cover Art: Storn Cook

Interior Illustrations: Storn Cook, Fredd Gorham, Greg Smith

ICE Staff — *Sales Manager:* Deane Begiebing;
Managing Editor: Coleman Charlton;
President: Peter Fenlon; *CEO:* Bruce Neidlinger;
Editing, Development, & Production Staff: John Curtis, Bruce Harlick, Jessica Ney-Grimm, Nick Morawitz;
Sales, Customer Service & Operations Staff: Heike Kubasch, Dave Platnick;
Shipping Staff: Dave Morris, Daniel Williams.

DEDICATION

Special thanks to Steven Long and Sean Patrick Fannon; their feedback and input helped shape this book and keep continuity within the CHAMPIONS Universe. Thanks also to the rest of the folks who gave their suggestions and otherwise contributed to this project, directly or indirectly: Michael Adams, Glen Bailey, Scott Bennie, Theron Bretz, Carl Cravens, Amy Crittenden, Paul Games, Ray Greer, Karl Griffin, Bruce Harlick, Matt Iskra, Damien Johnson, Stan Mitchell, Marty Nix, Ken Pryde, Wayne Shaw, Allen Varney, Eric Weber, Mike Weber, Jessica at Viking Hobby.

Dedicated to Alice Bawolski, in loving memory.

Printed in U.S.A., First Printing 1994

STOCK #: 434

Produced & Distributed by Iron Crown Enterprises, Inc., the exclusive manufacturer of Hero Games.

ISBN 1-55806-208-4

TABLE OF CONTENTS

INTRODUCTION

Tahashi Yoshida and his security man entered the huge boardroom, pausing momentarily in the doorway to ensure that everyone could observe his entrance. Standing behind each of the twenty chairs surrounding the farther three sides of the oak table was an executive, each one a division head of the United States division of Yoshida Corporation. Each felt the tension as Yoshida-san, the President of their powerful international corporation, looked over them. Each man could feel himself being scrutinized by Yoshida-san's gaze.

After a brief moment that felt like an eternity, Yoshida-san seated himself at the large, leather high-back chair at the head of the table. Ozeki Honda, Yoshida-san's chief security man, stood slightly behind Yoshida-san's chair, hands crossed behind his back. Once Yoshida-san was seated, the other executives did the same. Yoshida-san continued looking straight ahead, out the boardroom window, as if lost in some kind of trance. Chiro Takamura, seated to Yoshida's right, greeted him in Japanese, bowing as deeply as he could while seated at the mirror-finished table.

"Greetings, honorable Yoshida-san," Chiro started. "You honor us with your presence here in America. I trust you have found everything to be in order?" Yoshida simply nodded, acknowledging Chiro's comments without honoring him with a spoken word. "I have prepared a report of our progress for this quarter. "Chiro opened the report binder before Yoshida. "As you can see, our productivity is up three percent over last quarter," Chiro said with feigned enthusiasm. He knew what was coming next.

"What about our shipments?" Yoshida asked, his gravelly voice accentuating his obvious displeasure. "Why have two of our shipments from Korea not arrived in our New York warehouses?"

"Yoshida-san," Chiro's voice was wavering now, "I apologize, but our shipments were delayed at customs. There were..." Chiro looked around the room at his fellow executives, hoping for someone to say something to help him. But the others simply looked downward or aside, averting Chiro's pleading eyes. "There were complications," he finally completed.

"What?" Yoshida-san looked at Chiro, his bushy black eyebrows furled. Yoshida made a fist with one hand. Ozeki instinctively reached under his coat and gripped his wakazashi, drawing it ever so little from its scabbard. Beads of sweat were now visible on Chiro's forehead.

"Superheroes delayed the shipments, Yoshida-san — both of them. We sent our Yakuza to safeguard the second shipment, but the heroes overpowered them. Even now our company is under investigation by the American Justice Department for trying to smuggle Asian computer parts without paying tariffs. I failed, honorable lord." Again Chiro bowed, his forehead touching the $80,000 table.

With an almost imperceptible motion of his head, Yoshida-san signaled Ozeki. With blinding speed, Ozeki withdrew his wakazashi. With a loud yell, he plunged the Japanese short sword through Chiro's neck and deep into the table. Everyone in the room jerked slightly at the sudden noise and violence, but not a word was said. Ozeki stepped back into his previous place behind Yoshida, his hands once again crossed in front of him. The pool of blood continued to expand around Chiro as the last bits of life flowed out of him. Yoshida stood, followed immediately by the others. As he spoke, Yoshida-san looked at each executive in the room, as if to signify that they, too, could suffer as grisly a fate if their orders were not carried out.

"These American heroes have disrupted our production too many times. I have ordered Ozeki to bring his contingent of warriors and remain in the United States to help counter the problem of these so-called heroes. Until then, I want our legal department to obtain a retraining order against these heroes. I do not want them coming within a hundred yards of any of our facilities or employees. If you cannot find legal grounds for a restraining order, then create grounds. Use whatever means you have at hand, including our friends and associates in the local Tongs and street gangs. They have sworn loyalty to us — let them now display that loyalty."

"Hai!" was the response, yelled in unison by the remaining executives as they bowed. Ozeki opened the board-room doors in preparation for Yoshida-san's departure.

"Do not fail me again, gentlemen. I have another CEO coming to take Takamura-sama's place as director of the American division of Yoshida Corp. The appropriate press releases have already been circulated. Kaizen, gentlemen. Improvement is what I expect to see."

With that, Yoshida-san and his security man exited the boardroom, unaware of the person outside the window, clinging precariously to the wall, just out of sight....

HOW TO USE THIS BOOK

Corporations are mentioned in every comic book universe. There are companies owned by armored heroes, companies owned by villains and companies that serve as fronts to certain evil organizations with obligatory cliché acronyms. Corps are often major players in the politics of the "world" in which they operate. They fund scientific and medical research, investigate strange occurrences, employ literally thousands of potential paranormals (not to mention DNPCs) and often interact with hero teams or governments in one capacity or another.

We decided that the best way to present the corporations was to provide thorough backgrounds and descriptions for each company, along with adventure seeds and campaign ideas. The HERO System was written to allow maximum flexibility for GMs and players alike. Therefore, rather than writing a lengthy description of each company's role in the CHAMPIONS Universe, each company has been written with both an "official" and an optional background. The optional background is presented to give the GM some flexibility in adding the company to his campaign. With two versions presented for each company, any players who also own this book (and we're confident there will be lots of you)won't know for sure which version the GM is using. This allows the GM to customize each company while maintaining an element of mystery for the players.

CHAMPIONS UNIVERSE

Some of the companies in this book will become a part of the official CHAMPIONS Universe. They may be mentioned in future products, such as *The Ultimate Powered Armor* source book. These companies will be indicated by Defender's smiling face. The official version of the company is the main version written into each company's background, not the alternate version. As always, however, the reader has the final say on how each corporation will fit into his campaign.

Suggested scenarios are also given for each company, providing the reader with a large number of pre-designed adventures to use. With all things considered, *Corporations* provides fully detailed reference sections on corporations and the securities market, ideas on running corporations, additional vehicles, new equipment and dozens of ready-made companies and scenarios to add to your campaign!

The descriptions of the various corporations come first, followed by the "What is a Corporation" section. If you encounter a term or concept that you don't understand while reading the corporation write-ups, please refer to the second part of this book.

THE CORPORATE ROSTER

The following section contains a number of fully detailed corporations for use in your campaign. Each of the companies has the following information listed:

ABBREVIATION

This is the corporations stock exchange abbreviation code, used for identifying the corporation on the NYSE (or Hudson City Stock Exchange, in the case of those using *Dark Champions*). An abbreviation is listed for every public company; that is, any company which sells common stock on a stock exchange. Privately held corporations will not have this item listed.

PRIMARY OPERATIONS

This indicates the corporation's chief product (in the case of manufacturing companies), service or function. It is not always indicative of the company's entire capabilities, but rather the business most commonly associated with that company.

WORTH

This indicates the corporation's net worth, or total value. This amount is derived by adding the value of all of the corporations assets (equipment, real estate, securities, investments, and so on) and subtracting its total liabilities (debts). The result is the company's net worth. Many corporations in this book will have a seemingly outrageous net worth. This was done intentionally to reflect their increased importance in the CHAMPIONS Universe (in comparison to similar companies in the real world).

HQ LOCATION

This is the city in which the corporation's main headquarters or administrative offices can be found. While many companies have executive offices in many different cities, this is where the company's Board of Directors meets and where the President can usually be found.

HEAD

This is the most important person in the corporation. The person will be listed by name, followed by their position. Most often their position will be either President or CEO, or both. While many larger corporations will have a person filling each position, only one was listed for each company in the book (with the exception of LKT). In these cases, the person listed is the most often associated with the corporation or has the most public exposure. The GM is free to create additional NPCs for the positions not listed for each company.

HUNTED/WATCHED

The point values shown were derived by considering each corporation's ability, willingness and likelihood of undertaking the appropriate actions for each Disadvantage. For example, Armbruster Industries has no point value as a Hunted; Armbruster Industries simply does not hunt people. They do Watch people, however, and are worth 5 pts as a monitor.

In addition, the point values listed assume an 11- appearance roll. This was chosen as a standard roll for each of the corporations. GMs and players should modify the point values appropriately for a Hunted or Watched roll that is higher (14-) or lower (8-). Use the rules for Hunteds in ***Champions***, pg. 122.

PRIMARY COMPETITORS

This is the name of the main competitor(s) of the given corporation. No company has a monopoly in their area of operations, and rivalries are very important for the dynamic use of corporations in a ***Champions*** campaign.

ALLIED BRITAIN CHEMICALS

ABBREVIATION: AllBrCh

PRIMARY OPERATIONS: Chemical research & application

PRIMARY COMPETITORS: Fordham ChemTech; Dew Chemical Company

WORTH: $700 Million

HQ LOCATION: London, England

HEAD: Brynn Tucker

HUNTED/WATCHED: 15 Pts (Less Pow, NCI, 11-) / 10 Pts (As Pow, NCI, 11-)

BACKGROUND/DESCRIPTION: Allied Britain Chemicals was created in the early 50s. The company was unique in that it was founded by the merger of four separate companies, each based in a different part of Great Britain. The companies and their Presidents were James Monday of Monday Plastics (of England), Steven Tucker of Tucker Chemicals (in Scotland), Morgan Pryde from Pryde Industries (a Welsh corporation) and Ian McClean of ChemEire (based in Ireland). Shortly after the four company heads decided to merge into one large chemical company, all of the companies merged their stock and holdings. After the reorganizing, Allied Britain Chemicals voted to buy back as much stock as it could. As of 1993, Allied Britain owns fully 50% of its own stock. The Tucker family owns 13% of the stock, The Pryde family owns 13%, the McClean family owns 12%, and the Monday family owns 12%.

Brynn Tucker took over the company in 1987, after Morgan stepped down from the presidency. The four families have since intermarried, and taking control from them is nearly impossible. Brynn has expanded ABC worldwide. They have plants in New York City, Singapore, Mexico City, and L.A.

Although always a good, strong company, ABC was, at one point, infiltrated by a master spy. The "mole" acquired a great deal of valuable information. News of unsafe chemical storage and leaking containers at the domestic plants was leaked to investors. As a result, the information was picked up by the media and spread across the airwaves. Allied Britain's stock value plummeted. The ABC Board of Directors took swift action and fired the executive they thought was responsible.

It has taken years to get over the negative impact of the incident, and Allied Britain Chemicals is continuing an aggressive advertising campaign to win over the hearts of the American citizens and their elected officials. However, in 1988, ABC got an unexpected windfall. James Dandy, leader of the supervillain team, the Corporate Raiders, made a secret deal with Brynn. Brynn paid Dandy $200,000 for innumerable secret files of Briar Chemicals. With this information, Brynn was able to put Briar Chemicals out of business through a cleverly directed media and public relations campaign (along with a few calls to influential members of the U.S. Senate).

Allied has contracts with both Henderson Electronics and Eye-Tech Identification Systems, Inc. to provide security equipment. Allied purchases most of the weapons for its security force from B.L.A.D.E. Inc. and SimCorp. They are currently setting up new security measures at all of their plants, under the expert direction of Malcolm Dowell, the company's chief of security.

Brynn is, for the most part, a scrupulously honest businessman. ABC obeys all applicable laws, especially those pertaining to the storage and handling chemicals. ABC has tightened its internal safety and security policies, as well, since the earlier "incidents" involving its American plants. It is well known that anyone caught breaking the laws will be fired, sued for damages to the business, and turned over to the authorities. Although ABC has plants in some lesser developed countries, they police themselves and uphold the various laws and regulations governing their activities. Allied Britain maintains the same standards at all of its plants. This makes them less objectionable to environmentalists than some other chemical companies, although ABC still remains among those companies that those groups seek to shut down. One ultra left-wing environmentalist group based in Canada, Green Earth, uses terrorist threats and sabotage in an attempt to impede ABC's production of chemicals.

Allied Britain Chemicals thrives in the European chemical market and controls a lion's share of that market. Its chief competitors in Europe (who, together, make up a respectable 46% of chemical sales in Western Europe) manage to keep Allied Britain's advertising and marketing departments very busy in order that the company may maintain its position in chemical and sales. Interestingly, Allied Britain Chemicals does not have the distinction of being the largest producer of chemicals. That title goes to the Dew Chemical Co., who's production to meet the North American demand for chemical products exceeds even Europe's.

OPTIONAL VERSION: Brynn is unscrupulous and dishonest; he's real pond scum. The reason behind Allied Britain Chemicals's worldwide expansion efforts was simply to construct production plants in lesser-regulated countries. Brynn was more than glad when James Dandy sold him the information from Briar Chemicals. Brynn had planned to destroy Briar anyway — Dandy's information gave Brynn an edge in his plans against Briar Chemicals.

Brynn is psychotic and feels that people are out to get him (he never says exactly who it is that is after him; just "them"). He has only a handful of friends, and he is quick to believe the worst of them. ABC is Brynn's private playground. Brynn has chemical tests conducted on animals and is rumored to have experimented on people. ABC has devised some of the worst nerve gases in the world. Allied Britain Chemicals has even sold chemical compounds, necessary for the production of nerve gas, to countries such as Iraq and Awad (before the current economic sanctions were in place, of course). If an ABC plant were to catch fire it is possible that everything in a 10 mile square area would become uninhabitable. That's why Brynn lives in France, hundreds of miles away from the nearest ABC plant.

CAMPAIGN USE: Researching a deadly chemical substance uncovered in a villain's lab ("Gee, Mr. Macho, what does Dr. Stein's Absurdium P-20 do?"), a visit to the local Allied Britain Chemicals labs is recommended. Origins anyone? How about the classic: John Dexterous slips on his shoelace and falls into a vat of stretcho-plastic (patent pending), becoming Stretch Armlong.

A hero might own shares of ABC stock, making him more than just a little curious when he hears rumors of ABC chemicals showing up in criminal's hands. For a change of pace, how about making ABC the employer of a main campaign villain? "How does Dr. Stein keep getting these rare chemical components"

DNPCs can get into plenty of trouble at a chemical plant they work at. For that matter, so can PCs. Combine these elements, and you have a ready-made campaign: George Macho works with Frank Stein. Unknown to either of them, they are arch enemies in their super IDs — Mr. Macho and the nefarious Dr. Stein.

SLOGAN: "We follow the ABCs of safety."

SCENARIO IDEA: ABC has just developed "Stretcho-plastic," a plastic that is liquid until mixed with a special hardener. Genocide has gotten wind of it and plans to make use of it themselves. Genocide plans to use the plastic compound to destroy mutants. Genocide gathers an assault team to raid the ABC plant (conveniently located near, but not in, the Campaign City) with instructions to steal the compound and all related research data. ABC has relatively good security at all of its plants so Genocide assigns the following agents to the raid: 2 Knights, 1 Rook and 10 pawns.

ABC will be able to mobilize 10 guards in recently-purchased Turtle Armor. As soon as the attack occurs, ABC will deploy its security force and send out a distress call for help. The PCs will either hear of the distress call or receive it directly. When the heroes arrive, it will be obvious that the security guards are outmatched and are losing ground to the better-equipped Genocide agents.

Can our intrepid heroes save the day? If the PCs get knocked out of the fight, the Genocide agents will pull out, having retrieved the needed data and plastic samples. Genocide can't afford protracted fire fights. It gives their enemies too much time to mobilize. If the opportunity presents itself, the Genocide agents will capture a mutant hero. (Note: this scenario is well-suited for bringing a group of PCs together for the first time.)

ARMBRUSTER INDUSTRIES

ABBREVIATION: ArmBr

PRIMARY OPERATION: Computer engineering and robotics

PRIMARY COMPETITORS: Henderson Electronics; Kirashi Robotics; Yoshida Corporation

WORTH: $46.7 Billion

HQ LOCATION: Campaign City

HEAD: Matthew Armbruster, President/CEO

HUNTED/WATCHED: — / 5 Pts (Less Pow, 11-)

BACKGROUND/DESCRIPTION: Anthony Armbruster worked hard to keep food on his family's table and to instill a sense of pride and hope in his son, Matthew. After years of hard work he saved money enough to send Matthew to college. It was Matthew's first time away from home and he was reluctant to leave. Still, he had always loved designing things and studying for an engineering degree seemed the most logical thing to do. Matthew boarded the plane, full of pride and hope. "I'll do it," Matthew promised his father. "I'll make you proud." With that Matthew gave his mother a hug, shook his father's hand and was off. When he arrived in New York Matthew's life was irrevocably changed. His parents, on their way home from the airport, had been involved in a terrible pileup on the freeway — they were dead.

From that day on, Matthew has harbored a deep feeling of guilt, thinking that had he not left for college his parents might still be alive today. Matthew carried on, however, like he knew his father would have wanted him to. Matthew graduated from the university with honors and a Master's Degree in computer engineering. With his inheritance, Matthew founded Armbruster Industries. It wasn't long before Matthew had made numerous contacts within the government. In short time, Armbruster Industries landed several government contracts to provide computer chips and circuit boards, as well as advanced robotics designs.

One such design was the XA-600 (for Experimental Armbruster). Dubbed the Advanced Robotic Reconnaissance Unit (or ARC), this device contained a near-artificially intelligent computer "brain" and a super-tough titanium alloy chassis and was designed for dangerous reconnaissance work in enemy territory. While the project was eventually scrapped due to Pentagon budget cuts, Armbruster nevertheless maintained a reputation among Pentagon and State Department officials as a top notch robotics designer.

Matthew's most "infamous" creation, however, remains the robotic device known to the world as Mechanon. While its programming had been altered by Senator Helms and SAT technicians, Matthew still has the unwelcome reputation as Mechanon's creator. Matthew swears, however, that Mechanon's original design was error-free. Matthew has had all files relating to the Mechanon project stored away in a classified location and all references to the project have been erased from the company's main computer systems (Computer Programming roll at -3 to locate them in a subsystem). Matthew intends that no one else (especially the military, which he mildly distrusts) be allowed access to the files, lest another Mechanon be created.

Today, Armbruster Industries has over 8,000 employees at various plants and research facilities across the country. AI has also recently opened a plant in Canada, a deal made more appealing to the Canadian government after the passage of NAFTA. The company specializes in computer and robotics systems research, with three specialized divisions. The Military Systems Research Division (jokingly referred to as "Misread" by the staff) develops military weaponry, specifically "smart weapons," such as the Arrowhawk cruise missile which performed with great success during the Persian Gulf War. The Domestic Applications Division (DAD) is responsible for designs intended to facilitate general operations in fields such as agriculture (with automated combines), medical care (through computerized vital sign monitors) and corrections (with the robotic guards used in Stronghold). The Aeronautical Research Division specializes in aeronautical engineering and aircraft design. While it sometimes works side-by-side with the Military division, the ARD's primary focus is the design of safer, more efficient commercial aircraft and flight systems. One of the division's most famous designs is the AI-454 passenger jet (employed almost exclusively by Intercon Airlines).

The sometimes eccentric President and CEO of the company loves his wife, Congresswoman Shanna Armbruster, very much and is not afraid to show it in public. The two get along like newlyweds even though they have been married for more than 12 years now. Matthew attributes much of his zest for life to her. Matthew still finds time to run his company, of course, but he is as likely to show up to a board meeting in an oily racing suit as a pinstripe suit. He has also been known to call board meetings at the local country club and park (Matthew loves the outdoors). His good nature and relaxed attitude (not to mention his healthy Christmas bonuses) have earned him the respect of all of his employees.

While Armbruster Industries maintains an active Research & Development division, Matthew Armbruster is often more involved in his leisure activities to dictate aggressive marketing policies to keep his company ahead of the competition. His management staff works doubly hard to assure that the company stays on the cutting edge of technology, but it seldom makes substantial progress ahead of the company's rivals. Henderson Electronics remains their biggest competitor in the field of electrical engineering. Kirashi and Yoshida represent Armbruster's chief competitors in the development of robotics and microelectronics, respectively.

CAMPAIGN USE: Armbruster Industries is a giant in the robotics field. Any character with a background in robotics engineering will have at least heard of AI and may even be employed by Armbruster Industries. The advanced technologies being worked on by AI will undoubtedly attract the attention of certain villains and organizations, like Master Control, Doc Digital (*High Tech Enemies*), VIPER or The Corporate Raiders. A breakthrough in robotics could make the company the target of a raid to steal that technology.

Matthew Armbruster also does quite a bit of charity work and work to help underprivileged youths. Someone may believe Armbruster to be just another racist making himself look good by giving handouts to minorities. This individual could plan an attack on Matthew, or a series of harassing incidents, to intimidate him. If Matthew feels his life threatened, or if his wife hears of it, the PCs can be called in to help.

PCs who have a base with robot servants or security, or even an advanced monorail, may purchase the equipment from AI. In such a case, Matthew himself will come out to the heroes' base, not just to supervise the installation but to help with it. (Note: For additional information on Matthew and Shanna Armbruster see *Normals Unbound*, pgs. 27 & 85.)

SLOGAN: "Because life's too short for imperfection."

OPTIONAL VERSION: Matthew Armbruster is a very intense and unhappy man. His relationship with his wife fell apart years ago when she asked him for a divorce. All of his freewheeling boyish antics had caused them to grow apart, she claimed. He begged her not to leave him and she agreed, on the condition that he transfer half of all the family's fortunes (current and future) to a separate account in her name. Furthermore she told him that if he ever did anything to embarrass her publicly, she would destroy him.

Matthew knows that in order to keep most of his regular customers, he needs to keep up appearances. Shanna is becoming increasingly difficult to appease, however. The fact of the matter is that Shanna is having an affair with none other than her own godfather, Senator Jeremiah Relm. Matthew is currently unaware of their relationship. Nonetheless, Senator Relm is becoming worried that they will be found out. Relm has been making plans to have Shanna take over control of Armbruster Industries in the event that Matthew should have an "accident."

SCENARIO IDEA: Former Representative Jasperson has been brooding for years, ever since he lost the election to Shanna Armbruster. Jasperson was thrown into prison after being convicted of conspiracy to commit murder. While in prison, he kept in contact with the VIPER nest through an agent who worked in the prison kitchen. Jasperson convinced the local nest leader that eliminating Rep. Armbruster would be in the organization's best interest, as she is a member of the Joint Committee on Metahuman Activities and a strong advocate of metahuman rights. Her removal could pave the way for a new introduction of the Metahuman Registration Act, effectively tying the hands of many of VIPER's greatest foes in one fell swoop!

VIPER has organized an elaborate plan to kidnap Shanna Armbruster. They plan to use a team of mercenary villains dressed up as the PCs. Matthew Armbruster will make no public statement about the incident, except to denounce the action by the "heroes," for fear of angering her captors. Once the PCs prove their innocence to the authorities, or otherwise investigate the kidnapping, they should end up at one of Armbruster Industries' plants near the campaign city, with Matthew secretly following them. Inside they will confront the kidnappers, as well as some VIPER reinforcements. The PCs should be very careful how they handle this encounter. Should any harm come to Shanna or Matthew, Shanna may be convinced to side with Senator Relm regarding the Metahuman Registration Act. In addition, the heroes would be subjected to incredible amounts of negative press, easily resulting in new Reputations or Hunteds for the PCs.

AVERY FOODS, INC.

ABBREVIATION: AveryF

PRIMARY OPERATION: Fast Food/Grocery store chain

PRIMARY COMPETITORS: Shop Smart; Food 4 Less; Kernoggs Corporation

WORTH: $3 Billion

HQ LOCATION: Vancouver, B.C.

HEAD: Maurice Chaney, President

HUNTED/WATCHED: — / 3 Pts (Less Pow, Lim, 11-)

BACKGROUND/DESCRIPTION: Quenton Avery was the best idea man on Madison avenue. He knew it — why didn't anyone else? After all, it was he who came up with the slogan for the Granny Grain cereal company: "If it's good enough for Granny, it's good enough for you." For years, however, the Rond group had been passing him over for promotion.

Using his life savings and every bit of credit he could muster, he started Avery Foods, Inc. in 1980. As soon as he could, he bought up controlling interest in the Count Savings food store chain. Using his advertising skills, Quenton produced 8 different commercials which contributed to a rise in consumer confidence and boosted sales. Avery grew stronger every year with Quenton at the helm.

By 1983 Quenton was ready to take Avery public. He used the revenue from the sales of common stock to buy Twain Foods, owner of two fast food franchise chains. Once again he revitalized the businesses. He posted no profits the first quarter due to the enormous amounts of money spent improving the quality of food served. By 1985 Speed-"E" Pizza and Swift-"T" Chicken were household names, and mini chicken and pizza franchises were opened in each of the Count Savings Food stores.

Then, in 1991, disaster struck. The Rond group took an interest in Avery Foods Inc. and attempted a hostile take-over. Moving fast, Rond bought 30% of the stocks and persuaded 2 other major shareholders to vote with them to remove Quenton Avery. Maurice Chaney, a yes man for the Rond Group, was installed as President of the company, overseeing the board of directors.

Although Quenton was removed as President he still owns 47% of Avery Foods' common stock. The Rond Group owns 30%, Colleen Simmons (of SimCorp) has 12%, and Yoshida Corp. has 9%. The remaining shares are owned by various individual investors. For 2 years Rond, Simmons and Yoshida have voted as a block to keep control of Avery Foods, much to Quenton's displeasure.

Several unusual events have occurred in Quenton's life since the takeover. Messages left on his telephone answering machine, notes left on his car and letters with no return address all posing vague threats against Quenton unless he sells his shares of Avery Stock. Quenton suspects that one (if not all) of the other major shareholders is behind the harassment, but he has so far steadfastly defied all of the threats.

Quenton was planning to retire anyway, however, and he realizes that a takeover of Avery Foods is inevitable. All the take-over means to him is that he retires earlier than he had planned (assuming he can stay alive long enough to collect his pension and cash in on his stock options!). Quenton's chief concern is the future of Avery Foods. While viewed as just another asset to the major controlling shareholders, Quenton would like to see Avery Foods continue as a family business and be passed on to his heir. Quenton's immediate goals are to find a way that he can buyback a majority share of Avery Foods stock

Avery Foods continues to provide customers with the best possible prices on commercial food products. The sheer size of its Count Savings grocery store chain allows the company to keep its everyday prices at extremely competitive rates. Avery also maintains its own distribution centers and fleet of trucks, making it one of the country's largest self-distributing food store chains in the country. One of the more common tactics used by Avery's competitors is the use of allegations of illegal chemical use and poor sanitation procedures in the production and packaging of its foods. These allegations occasionally make headlines, raising consumer concern as well as getting the attention of the FDA.

CAMPAIGN USE: Avery Foods is a good company for "name-dropping," allowing the GM to toss in several of the company's products to add flavor to the game.

While it owns several fast food chains, Avery Foods is best known by the public for its popular Count Savings supermarket chain. Count Savings stores can be found in nearly every major city throughout the U.S. There is a good chance that no matter where the heroes' base is located, there is a Count Savings supermarket not far away.

PCs with any level of Streetwise will be familiar with the chain, and low-powered heroes, such as the 4th Street Protector(s), are especially likely be familiar with the company — or at least the Count Savings store in their own neighborhood. Many other heroes may shop at the store in their secret IDs, or eat at any of its fast food chains while on patrol.

Avery Foods also makes a good "business under siege", due to the strife between Quenton Avery and the other major owners of the company. Quenton Avery is frustrated by his lack of influence over the company, not to mention the threats against him.

The fact is that the president of the Rond Group is behind the not-so-subtle threats. He wants to buy Quenton's shares of Avery stock to secure his control over Avery Foods. With Quenton's shares added to their own, The Rond Group would control Avery outright and they would no longer need SimCorp or Yoshida. The president will continue his harassment against Quenton, eventually resorting to hiring thugs or even villains to intimidate Quenton into selling.

The GM is encouraged to play up Quenton Avery as the stereotypical nice guy so that the PCs are sympathetic to his dilemma.

SLOGAN: "Quality since day one!"

OPTIONAL VERSION: Quenton is very upset with being kicked out of the company that he helped make great. As a result he is planning something rash. No one is going to scare him into selling his shares of Avery, no matter how many threats are made or how many thugs are sent after him. Quenton plans to hire a hit man to take out his suspected adversary. Rumors are circulating on the street that a contract is out for the president of The Rond Group.

Colleen Simmons knows that the Rond Group initiated the takeover of Avery out of revenge (see The Rond Group). She also knows that Quenton is planning something against them. Colleen has been using Telepathy on all of the major players since the takeover, and has managed to use the information gained to her advantage. She hopes that by manipulating the others, she can obtain enough shares herself to control Avery! For additional information on Colleen Simmons see Mindlock (C4, pg. C19).

SCENARIO IDEA: A Count Savings store in the campaign city has been taken over by several gunmen (use 5 plus one additional gunman per hero). The gunmen are holding 20 hostages, including the employees, several unlucky shoppers and probably a DNPC or two. The gunmen are demanding $1 million and a safe exit in return for the hostages. There is also a journalists' convention being held at a nearby hotel so the event will be covered quite well by the media.

The gunmen have set up barricades in front of all of the store windows and exits, and they have pre-positioned lookouts in each of the buildings surrounding the store. There is one gunman is in the Manager's/Security office. The gunmen have orders to prolong the standoff as long as possible, and not to kill any hostages unless absolutely necessary. If any gunmen are captured, a successful PRE Attack or Interrogation skill roll will get them to turn on Mindlock (none of them know Mindlock's Secret ID).

Use Competent Normals for the gunmen. Each will have a gas mask, a walkie-talkie and a .44 magnum semi-automatics pistol (Note: the guns are really lasers, using the stats for .44 automags but are EKAs. There are no serial numbers or fingerprints on the guns). The leader also has a complete set of blueprints to the store. An explosive charge has been set up to create an escape route through the sewers, should it become necessary.

The entire event has been arranged by Colleen Simmons (as the villain, Mindlock) in an attempt to get either Quenton or The Rond Group to sell their interest in Avery Foods. She's hoping that each will blame the other, and that if enough negative publicity is generated one, or both, will sell. She has miscalculated, however; neither Quenton nor Rond will sell out. To further complicate things both may demand that the heroes take action to end the crisis.

BIO-INVESTIGATIONS LIMITED

ABBREVIATION: BioInv

PRIMARY OPERATIONS: Biological Research

PRIMARY COMPETITORS: ZenCorp; BioGen Research Labs

HQ LOCATION: Cambridge, England

HEAD: Dr. Shiela Radcliffe, CEO

WORTH: $27 Billion

HUNTED/WATCHED: 10 Pts (Less Pow, 11-) / 10 Pts (As Pow, NCI, 11-)

DESCRIPTION/BACKGROUND: Dr. Sebastian Radcliffe moved from his British home to America, in order to avoid military service during World War II. In America, Sebastian discovered that he possessed super powers. After extensive physical training and honing of his paranormal talents, he became the superhero Dr. America, and joined the Liberty League. Several years later, in the mid-fifties, one of his fellow team members, Billy Yank, was diagnosed with a rare form of brain cancer; he had only a short time to live. The rest of the team was stunned. Everyone felt helpless and all did what they could to keep his spirits up. One day Billy slipped into a coma. The doctors had done all that they could.

Frustration led Sebastian on a crusade to try to save his friend's life. After consulting every specialist in the U.S. and Europe, Sebastian decided that he would have to take matters into his own hands. He formed Bio-Investigations Limited, a not-for-profit corporation dedicated to researching Billy's condition. Sebastian managed to obtain several federal grants and hired a number of outstanding biochemists and neurologists to study Billy's problem. A cure wasn't discovered in time, however, and Billy Yank died in 1955.

In the 60's Bio-Investigations Ltd. was re-organized into a "for profit" venture. A new charter was drawn up, new articles of incorporation filed with the state and a million shares of public stock went on sale at the NYSE. The company has enjoyed great success since then.

Current projects include: Project: Merlin, a medical study of paranormals, headed by Dr. Helena Amory (see *Normals Unbound* pg. 60); Project: Knight, a licensed "Super Soldier" project headed by Dr. Bill Darwin; Project: Medusa, a program researching draining of super powers from metahumans, headed by Dr. David Burke; and the most recent program, Project: Doppleganger, which is designed to detect paranormal abilities in people (and interestingly enough, funded by several professional sports franchises), headed by Dr. Francine West. Information from all the projects are circulated between project heads so as to maximize research results and minimize doubling of efforts.

Past projects of note Project: Food of the Gods, a study of animal hormones and metabolic growth headed by Dr. Diana Whitmore. The good doctor was quite a practical joker and had planned to inject herself with a harmless saline solution while convincing her associates that it was an artificial — and very experimental — growth hormone. Ironically, she had gotten the syringes mixed up and injected herself with the wrong syringe, which endowed her with paranormal powers (see Shrinker, ***CHAMPIONS*** pg. C 23). (Note: The experiment was obviously a failure.) Another infamous program was Project: Book of Man, a study into the mapping of the human genetic code, headed by Dr. Timothy Blank. Blank was eventually fired for unscrupulous behavior and went on to become King Cobra (see *Champions Presents #2*, pg. 107).

Unbeknownst to Dr. Radcliffe, there are three spies among her staff. VIPER has an agent assigned to Project: Merlin, who reports back to a VIPER field officer through his company computer by way of a high-speed modem. Project: Knight has been infiltrated by an agent of COIL, who is assisting in development of an advanced serum. Lastly, Genocide has taken an interest in Project: Medusa and has managed to subvert one of the scientists on that project. (Note: Genocide's "mole" is Dr. Burke himself! Burke has perfected his Acting ability and doesn't hesitate when any of those mutant freaks offers to shake his hand)

So far, none of the spies has been able to acquire any truly damaging information from the company, thanks in large part to the complex electronic security systems it employs. The Security chief at Bio-Investigations Ltd., George Flemish, suspects all three of wrongdoing but has yet to produce any evidence of criminal behavior or policy violations. Ironically, none of the three spies knows of the other two.

The company employs the latest in high-tech defense systems. Every facility has seismic sensors, electric fences and high resolution security cameras (see "Security" in this book and "Sound the Alarm" in the Hero System Almanac 1). In addition to standard physical and electronic security measures, Bio-Investigations Ltd. is known to hire non-costumed paranormals for security. They favor supers with a high DEX and SPD, and those with especially useful powers (such as Entangle, Clairsentience and Mind Link).

All supers know that they can go to Bio-Investigations Ltd. for a "check-up" and medical treatment. Bio-Investigations Ltd. has been helping the super community for 50 years. They have amassed a huge amount of information on superpowers and put that information to good use, helping people overcome a variety of maladies (including some specific to paranormals). They donate millions of dollars every year to various charities, including the Paranormal Defense Fund.

While Bio-Investigations Ltd. remains the best known bio research organization in the world, its chief competitors continue to conduct similar research, sometimes achieving results before Bio-Investigations itself. Dr. Radcliffe's primary focus and concern for achieving quality results and the safety of her subjects and staff force Bio-Investigations to conduct more careful, thorough research. This has earned Dr. Radcliffe, and the company as a whole, the respect of the scientific community at large.

CAMPAIGN USE: Bio-Investigations Ltd. can be pivotal to any campaign. The company makes a good Contact (Base Cost + 3 pts.), as well as an excellent in for any character with a background in genetics. The company also works well in a super's origin (just ask Shrinker!).

If a super with an alien physiology becomes ill, Bio-Investigations Ltd. may be their last chance for a cure. Similarly, if a nefarious villain unleashes a deadly new virus on an unsuspecting (or even a suspecting) population, these are the people to call for help. If a reclusive billionaire wants superpowers, these people will try to give them to her (as long as she passes a psychological evaluation and signs the necessary waivers…).

A DNPC could easily get into trouble at Bio-Investigations Ltd. Suppose the DNPC is a new employee who has come under the scrutiny of Mr. Flemish. Suddenly the true spy frames the DNPC, causing her to lose her job and become a scapegoat for all of the company's problems and thefts over the months.

SLOGAN: Helping those who help the world

OPTIONAL: Dr. America has gone mad. He feels that paranormal powers destroyed the life he wanted to lead. Now, Dr. America's agenda is to destroy all paranormals. Billy Yank never died, he is in league with the doctor. In 1992, Dr. America killed all of the remaining members of the Liberty League, quietly and secretly, with a genetically engineered virus. He lets the world think that his company is benevolent, while his scientists work on horrific new diseases and biological constructs behind closed doors. He uses all of the information that Bio-Investigations Ltd. collects to increase his personal power.

For Dr. America's stats, use the Competent Normal write-up and add a 100 pt. Cosmic Power Pool.

SCENARIO IDEA: The PCs receive an anonymous phone call informing them that there will be a kidnapping attempt on Dr. Darwin, an employee of Bio-Investigations Ltd., and that there are two spies in the company as well.

The caller is Ben Rodgers, VIPER's assigned agent, who has discovered the other two infiltrators. Rodgers wants his competition eliminated. He has planted incriminating evidence of their espionage activities in their lockers (phone conversation recordings, security video footage, electronic mail, etc.) as well as in the lockers of any DNPCs that work for the company.

In addition, Rodgers will leak this information to the agents' respective organizations. As a result, Coil has severed all ties with its agent, and Genocide is preparing an assault against the company (to "do away with it once and for all"). Rodgers has arranged for a transfer of information to the local VIPER nest via a burst data transmission.

A short time after the PCs arrive to investigate Genocide will make its move, attacking the base and any obvious paranormals (including the PCs, of course). This is when Rodgers will try to send the transmission (allow PCs with Radio Hearing a PER Roll to detect this transmission).

B.L.A.D.E. INC.

PRIMARY OPERATION: Weapon and defense designs

PRIMARY COMPETITORS: Danco; Tauer Arms; Yoshida Corporation; SimCorp

WORTH: $76 Million

HQ LOCATION: Great Falls, MT

HEAD: Frank Westerson, President/CEO

HUNTED/WATCHED: 5 Pts (Less Pow, Mildly, 11-) / 5 Pts (As Pow, 11-)

BACKGROUND/DESCRIPTION: Frank always had a love of guns; any kind of guns. Frank grew up in a family of hunters and quickly learned gun safety and learned the basics of hunting. He became a life member of the NRA at the age of eighteen (a birthday present from his father) and joined the Marine Corps shortly thereafter. While in the military Frank became the company armorer; he was responsible for maintaining and repairing his unit's weapons. Frank later became a firearms instructor, teaching the craft of shooting. After two enlistments, Frank eventually grew bored with the Corps and mustered out.

Once out of the military, Frank opened a gun and ammo store in his home town of Great Falls, Montana. Violence was on the rise in the country and gun sales continued to rise. Frank was surprised at the quality of the guns he was seeing. While none were manufactured negligently, there wasn't that attention to detail and pride of craftsmanship he remembered being taught by his father. One of his regular customers suggested that Frank design his own gun. That was all it took.

Frank managed to collect enough investment money from friends and family members to start his own company, which he named Frank Westerson Guns. He designed and marketed several gun accessories, earning enough money to pay back his investors and establish the company. Frank designed a new rifle, as well as several models of shotguns. As word spread of Frank's superior workmanship and quality guns, sales began to increase. Soon Frank was driving a brand new Ford Ranger pickup and making deals on his cellular phone. Frank became a prominent businessman in the Great Falls area.

Although it remained a privately held corporation, Frank eventually took in a partner, David Killinger. David was willing to put in as much money as the company already had earned in order to be an equal partner. The new money was used to expand the company, developing advanced laser sights and kevlar ballistic vests. The company was renamed Ballistics, Lasers And Defensive Engineering, or B.L.A.D.E. Inc. In a short time, the company had over 100 employees and as many types of weapons and accessories in their inventory. Frank began pursuing defense contracts with his new M-3A1 assault rifle and various, newly-developed anti-personnel grenades, as well as plans for a new personal energy weapon.

B.L.A.D.E. Inc. has become a world-wide firm dealing in all forms of weapons and defensive systems. They are considered one of the leading players in armor research, coming up with the most impressive prototypes in both vehicle and personal armor. One of B.L.A.D.E.'s main competitors in the defensive materials field is Tran Defense Systems, a smaller armor-producing company based in Los Angeles.

Their weapon design capabilities are sometimes considered too unorthodox for conservative observers. One of Frank's more infamous creations was the "Gum Gun." Presented as a riot control system, the Gum Gun fired large chunks of expanding foam that hardened within minutes, rendering a large area impassable and anyone in the area immobile. Other unorthodox designs include one presented to the LAPD; a cannon-sized tazer to be mounted on the department's armored personnel carriers. Unfortunately for B.L.A.D.E., an unacceptable 4% fatality rate kept the design from ever being mass produced.

B.L.A.D.E. Inc. specializes in advanced technology weaponry and non-lethal weaponry, in an attempt to keep pace with the weapons research being conducted by the Pentagon. Among its chief competitors, Tauer Arms is the largest manufacturer of conventional small arms, while Danco currently leads in production of powered armor weapon system (although their sluggish sales would indicate otherwise). Yoshida Corp. and Lockley International continue to conduct research and development of their laser and gauss weapons systems, although they have not yet achieved a substantial market for these weapons. Still, their continued presence in the field of advanced weaponry constitute a significant concern on the part of B.L.A.D.E.'s Board of Directors.

CAMPAIGN USE: B.L.A.D.E., Inc. is a weapon-mongers dream come true. The company produces weapons of all kinds, from traditional firearms to the truly bizarre; no design is too crazy for consideration, according to Frank. That doesn't mean Frank will produce any outlandish design that is presented, but he has been known to manufacture items that other weapons designers wouldn't, as long as the price is right.

In addition, the company designs armor, for both vehicles and personal armor. The prices of such suits is usually quite high, however, keeping out of the hands of most save the wealthy, such as tycoons, corporations and governments.

SLOGAN: "Honed to a razor's edge."

OPTIONAL VERSION: Frank Westerson is working as hard as ever designing new weapons systems, but his latest models are geared more for the civilian market. While many of B.L.A.D.E. Inc.'s previous weapons were geared for military and paramilitary use, Frank has seen the increased demand for guns in the civilian sector. An astounding increase in the number of anti-crime bills and gun control legislation has helped increase demand for the firearms. Frank sees a perfect opportunity to realize a substantial profit from a relatively meager investment; all he has to do is refurbish his assembly lines for the civilian guns and break out the old molds.

Frank is a man driven by pure profit. He is also convinced that the end is near and he is determined to be one of the survivors. Frank's company contributes substantial sums to the NRA, pro-gun politicians, and to many right-wing survivalist organizations.

SCENARIO IDEA: B.L.A.D.E. Inc. has unveiled a brand new energy-based crowd disbursement weapon at a recent weapons show. The weapon discharges a mild electro-static shock over a large area, rendering anyone caught in it completely immobile for a short period of time. It is essentially a large stun gun (6d6 EB, NND, AE 6" Radius, OAF Gun, Bulky [½ DCV]).

Frank Westerson has arranged a demonstration of the weapon in a field near the convention site. At the demonstration, four men dressed as terrorists, in black coveralls and ski masks, will advance on Frank, who is wearing the weapon system, consisting of a large energy rifle and a power-pack worn on the back (the ensemble is rather bulky and looks like a flame thrower).

The four men are Yakuza, hired by Yoshida Corp. to steal the prototype weapon for the Yoshida technicians to study. The Yakuza agents are wearing insulated suits, which protects them from electrical attacks (treat as +4 PD/+8 ED Armor, with 75% Damage Reduction against electrical attacks, including the NND). The agents will grab the weapon and flee to a waiting van.

If they escape, they will drive to the center of the city, disassemble the gun and then split up, each taking a different part of the weapon. The agents have orders to meet a Yoshida rep at a Japanese restaurant near the local Yoshida Corp. corporate office. Alternatively, the GM can use Cy-Force agents in place of the Yakuza.

CARTER-MULLERING INDUSTRIES

ABBREVIATION: CarMul

PRIMARY OPERATION: Cybernetics research & development

PRIMARY COMPETITORS: CyberNet Research Ltd.; Yoshida Corporation; Future Scope, Inc.

WORTH: $185 Million

HQ LOCATION: Atlanta, GA

HEAD: Richard Carter, President

HUNTED/WATCHED: 10 Pts (Less Pow, NCI, Lim, 11-) / 10 Pts (As Pow, NCI, 11-)

BACKGROUND/DESCRIPTION: Cyrus Carter's love of science was strong. He was told during his boyhood years that a Scandinavian immigrant like himself could never be a famous scientist in America. Through strong desire and persistence, Cyrus proved them all wrong. He graduated from New York University with honors and eventually founded a research company with his long-time friend and college roommate, Karl Mullering.

As the years wore on, Cyrus turned more to his family. He had two boys, Devin and Richard. Each grew up with a gift for science, but Devin was somehow special. Devin earned multiple doctorates in various sciences, astounding everyone except Cyrus. Cyrus encouraged Devin's hunger for research, eventually offering Devin the position of Chief Researcher of CM Industries. Cyrus would later authorize the funds for Devin's pet project, the Cyberknights (see *Allies*). Richard became insanely jealous, barely managing to keep his feelings hidden from Devin, whom Richard saw as a naive and spoiled brat. Richard hated Devin and one day he would deal with him appropriately.

Richard began conspiring with Randall Montgomery, the head of one of his father's biggest rivals, the mega-conglomerate Montgomery International. Randall Montgomery, also the villain Master Control (see *High Tech Enemies*), saw a chance to do away with his brother's superhero team, the Cyberknights. Randall agreed to help Richard in return for Richard disbanding the team. The deal was made and Randall sent his S.T.R.I.K.E. agents to the Carter estate one evening to kill Cyrus. The attack was swift. Due to a miscalculation, however, the one witness, Richard's mother, was left alive. To this day she represses the memory and claims to know nothing about her husband's death.

Richard broke the news to Devin. Devin was hit especially hard by the sudden loss of his father. While Devin was still mourning his father's death, Richard enacted phase two of his evil plan and electronically transferred all of Devin's and his father's holdings in the company to himself. Before Devin realized what had happened, Richard had cut funding for the Cyberknights and Devin was fired as Chief Researcher. Devin left, dejected and is now believed dead (Richard knows the truth, however).

Richard continues to run the company, but owes favors to many less-than-scrupulous persons, including Randall Montgomery, the Duchess and Tahashi Yoshida, all of whom have helped Richard maintain control of CM Industries. In addition, the loss of Devin as Chief Researcher caused a steep decline in the value of CM Industries stock (the price fell to half its previous value in just one week). Richard is working hard to rebuild the company's reputation and CM Industries continues to be a major player in the area of cybernetics research. Without Devin as Chief Researcher, however, the company does not have the edge it once had. Designs are less revolutionary and advances in technology come more slowly now. Undaunted, Richard continues to keep up the image of a hard-working scientist.

The company is currently controlled by Richard Carter, who owns 76% of the stock. His mother owns another 10%, and the rest is divided up among private investors.

CM Industries remains, without a doubt, the leader in cybernetic research, due to its top notch research department. Yoshida Corp. maintains a powerful presence in the Pacific, accounting for nearly 65% of all cybernetic technologies currently used in Southeast Asia. CyberNet Research Ltd. and Future Scope, Inc. are CM Industries' only real competition in the North American market, however, with a combined share of approximately 57% of the domestic market. Future Scope Inc. is steadily gaining on CMI, however, thanks to their aggressive marketing strategies and expert research staff.

CAMPAIGN USE: CM Industries is responsible for many breakthroughs in advanced cybernetic research, including much of the gear used by the Cyberknights and other cybernetically-enhanced supers. Some of the early designs of Cyrus Carter were stolen and sold to the Soviets, eventually incorporated into the Scarlet Sentinel suit (a fact known to very few). CM Industries can be the source, or inspiration, of a hero's cybernetic gadgets.

CM Industries' main strength as a campaign company is its current leader, Richard Carter. Richard is a murdering, lying scum who has more than a few dark secrets kept tucked away. A man with so many things to hide certainly would go to great lengths to keep them hidden. After all, any man who would kill his own father to spite his brother is bound to commit more crimes! Anyone discovered stealing devices or data from CM Industries may well find themselves hunted down by Master Control or his S.T.R.I.K.E. agents.

SLOGAN: "When biology just isn't good enough."

OPTIONAL VERSION: Richard Carter could no longer live with the crimes he had committed against his family. He sought help and found it in the form of a kind priest, in Atlanta for a special religious conference. He literally bumped into the priest on the street and hit it off right away. The priest turned out to be the paranormal parishioner known as The Deacon (see *Classic Organizations*). The Deacon helped Richard see the error of his ways and turn from his evil path.

Richard has since sworn to do only good in his life. He donates company funds to the new Cyberknights, shares his company research with former rivals in the hopes of overcoming many birth defects and other human frailties, and he has forsaken his former evil associates (much to the chagrin of Master Control and Yoshida Corp.).

SCENARIO IDEA: CM Industries announces the design of a revolutionary new cybernetic hearing aid, one that will make all other hearing aids obsolete. The system is still in its experimental stage, however, and can only be tested on persons willing to sign the necessary waivers, etc., for secrecy and security.

In reality, some of the prosthetics actually contain a micro-receptor, which allows Richard to both send and receive signals to and from the device. The most obvious use is for the device to be used as a bug (for corporate meetings, etc.), but it can also be used to receive subliminal signals which are relayed to the subject's brain. These subliminal signals are undetectable by normal means (High-range Radio Hearing can detect them if within 3" of the subject) and act as a form of direct mind-control (treat as 6d6 Mind Control, IAF-Hearing aid, Only for emotions or basic commands [-½]).

Richard hopes to use the devices to regain his company's old edge. He will see that numerous eligible people get the cybernetic hearing aids, but only those people he wished to control will receive the actual "bug" models.

If using the optional version of CM Industries, then one of the company's researchers will be behind this plan (possibly with some help from Master Control to frame Richard, in the hopes of having him removed as President). Richard, following his new path of goodness, will know nothing about it.

CENTURION TRUCKS INC. U.S.A.

ABBREVIATION: CenT

PRIMARY OPERATION: Semi-tractor production

PRIMARY COMPETITORS: Panzerwagen; American Engine, Inc.; Spanov

WORTH: $63 Million

HQ LOCATION: Amarillo, TX

HEAD: Anthony Meiss, President

HUNTED/WATCHED: — / 10 Pts (As Pow, Lim, 11-)

BACKGROUND/DESCRIPTION: In 1968 Terry Wellers started a truck manufacturing company, called Terribuilt, in Beaumont, Texas. Things picked up quickly for the fledgling truck company, as the trucking industry boomed in the Seventies. Even with no real reputation to speak of, Terribuilt quickly carved itself a piece of the semi-tractor truck market. In a short time, their competitive rates and excellent workmanship earned them the respect of truckers and mechanics nationwide.

In 1973, the company went public. The stock value tripled in less than a year. Terribuilt continued to do well, and had nearly cornered the domestic market on large semi-tractors by the early eighties. Combined with their respectable overseas market, Terribuilt had established itself, without a doubt, as one of the country's leading truck manufacturers.

The wave they rode did not last. In 1981, Terribuilt fell victim to a hostile takeover by a German truck manufacturing company, Centurion Motors. The name of the new, merged company was changed to Centurion Trucks, Inc. The majority of the original employees were kept, but the new owners replaced the board of directors with their own people, and moved the corporate office to Amarillo, Texas. Terry Wellers, among others, left the company with a hefty severance pay check. Terry Wellers left Centurion a rich man and he couldn't be happier. He had always felt overworked, but now he can afford to relax and let someone else take the reins.

The new president, Anthony Meiss, is a successful corporate manager from Germany. His leadership style and natural charisma have taken Centurion from a profitable company to one of the country's greatest successes, a fact he is quick to credit to the company's first president, Terry Wellers.

Today Centurion Trucks manufactures all types of large trucks, from semi-tractors, to dump trucks, construction vehicles, and even armored cars. They accept contracts for custom vehicles, and they have provided armored vehicles for a few city law enforcement agencies, as well as Gauntlet Security Services. Their armored trucks are ranked among the toughest in the world, and a truck has yet to breached with any conventional weapon short of a TOW missile. Paranormal powers, that's another story. Centurion has a very active overseas market, most notably in Great Britain and the Middle East. Their biggest overseas competitor is Mercedes.

The company plans to expand further, building several new production facilities in the southwest and midwest under a program Meiss calls "Sharing Success." Several hundred Centurion personnel have transferred to the United States from Germany in the past year or so, a move which has surprised analysts but delighted politicians.

Centurion epitomizes quality American trucks. The company's reputation has endured several decades, and it clearly dominates the American truck market. Overseas is a different matter altogether. Centurion faces tough competition for the West European truck market from German truck production giant, Panzerwagen. Throughout Eastern Europe, the Russian-based Spanov (a state subsidized company) is a strong presence. While Centurion trucks can be found, their reputation as an American firm works against them here, thanks in large part to Communist propaganda. Where they are sold, they are usually extremely overpriced, again, helping to assure Spanov dominance in the Eastern Bloc countries.

CAMPAIGN USE: Centurion Trucks, Inc. provides armored cars to the world's leading banks, as well as to several police departments and security companies. A armored truck robbery is likely to involve a Centurion truck (or two), and the company's reputation will surely be on the line.

For a Centurion armored truck, use the stats for the GMC Panel Truck (*HERO System Rulesbook*, pg. 195) and add 5 STR and 12 DEF, giving the trucks a total of 45 STR and 16 DEF.

Centurion also manufactures construction vehicles, and regular semi-tractors for pulling trailers. Centurion trucks will find their way onto billboards, television shows and can be found at any truckstop on any American highway.

Because they also build custom-designed trucks, Centurion Trucks may receive a contract to build the heroes' team vehicle. They may also be contracted to build special vehicles for local police departments, or federal agencies such as PRIMUS.

SLOGAN: "Built for the long haul."

OPTIONAL VERSION: By the time he was fired by the new owners of the company, Terry had embezzled a personal fortune, hidden in numerous bank accounts across the country. He also managed to buy up a substantial portion of Centurion stock while he was president. In fact, Terry owns the largest single block of stock in the company to date, much to the chagrin of the new Centurion board of directors. Terry harbors much ill will toward the new owners of the company, and he intends to be the Centurion Trucks Inc. president once again, no matter what it takes.

Unfortunately for Terry, it may take much more than he thinks. Anthony Weiss is not only the president of the company, he is also a VIPER Nest Leader, transferred to the United States from the Bonn, Germany, Nest in a special test program sanctioned by the Supreme Serpent. In addition, Weiss has brought over a hundred of his top agents. Weiss' orders are to observe local Nest Leaders and rate them for efficiency and loyalty. Of course, the local Nest Leaders all fall short of perfection in Weiss' reports to his superior....

SCENARIO IDEA: Over the past few months Weiss has fostered an intense rivalry between several nearby VIPER Nests. This fact has not gone unnoticed by officials nor the media, as increased reports of battles between groups of VIPER agents circulate.

The characters should be quite curious about what's going on, and may do some investigating on their own to give them an idea of what's going on. What the heroes will receive is an anonymous tip leading them to a shipment of armored vehicles headed for a local VIPER Nest!

The shipment consists of four Centurion armored trucks being driven by VIPER Covert agents (see ***Champions*** or *VIPER*). When the heroes come upon the trucks, they will be en route to the VIPER Nest. They will drive through the city to the secret Nest hidden in two large warehouses on the pier, or located in a warehouse district if the city does not have a coastline (use the map on pg. ***5*** of ***Champions***). If the heroes attempt to intercept the shipment they will be attacked by a VIPER Force-1 (also from *VIPER*), who are safeguarding the delivery. (The GM may use another supervillain team in place of VIPER Force-1. Other suitable villain teams include The Ultimates (*Classic Enemies*) or The Destruction Company (*High Tech Enemies*).

Whether or not the heroes defeat VIPER Force-1, they may investigate the delivery of trucks. Appropriate role-playing and use of Deduction will reveal the fact that the Centurion trucks were ordered shipped to the warehouse by the company's Vice President, Roger Mueller. Mueller received verbal instructions from Weiss himself (a fact Weiss will vehemently deny). Even if the heroes can link Centurion to VIPER, Weiss has assured that Mueller will take the blame, and not Weiss.

DANCO

PRIMARY OPERATIONS: Weapon and armor manufacturer

PRIMARY COMPETITORS: B.L.A.D.E. Inc.; SimCorp

WORTH: $9 Billion

HQ LOCATION: Copenhagen, Denmark

HEAD: Leif Andersen

HUNTED/WATCHED: 10 Pts (As Pow, Lim, 11-)/ 5 Pts (As Pow, Lim, 11-)

BACKGROUND/DESCRIPTION: DanCo was founded by Bjorn Sorbye in the mid 1950s as a major manufacturer and supplier of arms and munitions for the Danish army after World War II. Although a privately held company, DanCo was backed by several influential international investors, including the multi-billionaire businessman Francois Decarte. With Decarte's backing, DanCo decided to try their hand at non-traditional designs. Bjorn went with his gut instincts and hired American weapons designer John Marker. John had been fired from several American weapons firms for his "unorthodox" weapons designs. All of Marker's concepts lacked the "practicality" required to be effective weapons (in truth, they were too exotic to guarantee sales). There were numerous arms manufacturers on the market, so DanCo needed to do something to stand out.

DanCo's first priority in their search for arms supremacy was to compete for Army contracts (including the Armies of foreign nations, such as the U.S. and Great Britain). In an attempt to impress military and government leaders, DanCo released the K-121 Battle Pod. The Battle Pod was a less-than-attractive turret designed to be added to an existing vehicle chassis (most commonly a tank). The Battle Pod's extra weight lowered the tanks' maximum speed, but added quite a bit more firepower. Unfortunately for DanCo, the Battle Pod was a failure. The only buyer of the Pod was the Kingdom of Awad. DanCo has sold two dozen units to the small Arab nation via Oman, but has since ceased production of the Pods. Several military commanders and government officials in Awad have reportedly complimented the Battle Pod.

With the overall failure of the Battle Pod, DanCo made a historic decision; rather than design large, vehicle-sized weapons, they would concentrate on equipping the individual soldier of the future, today. Thus, in 1960 DanCo released the DanCo Personal Defense Jacket Model 32, dubbed the PDJ-32. Overnight, the PDJ-32 became the body armor of choice for soldiers and mercenaries everywhere. DanCo continued to improve on the jacket's design and the DanCo PDJ-50 was released in 1972. The PDJ-50 was the lightest bulletproof jacket of its class on the market (use the stats for kevlar vest with the ¼ mass lim.).

In 1975, DanCo used its name to license the "ultimate" equipment package for a soldier — The "Ultimate Dogface" package. This "package" included the DanCo Heavy Personal Defense Jacket Model 42, The SimCorp Shiva Laser Rifle (with the Tiamat grenade launcher attached), six DanCo "Big Bang" flash grenades, a Grace Medical Supplies medkit, the McNeil T-1000 flight module, and Night-vision goggles. To demonstrate the effectiveness of the equipment to the U.S. Army brass, DanCo equipped ten members of the Army's elite 1st Ranger Battalion with the gear. The soldiers then assaulted division of regular Infantry soldiers in a demonstration field exercise. Using sound tactics and the superior gear, the Rangers were able to take the opposing side's Command Post and neutralize all of the opposing team while suffering only four "casualties" of their own. Sales skyrocketed after the results of the demonstration was leaked to the press.

Continuing their tradition of designing equipment for the troops, DanCo designers came up with the patented Positive Reflex Power Enhancers. The PRPEs were incorporated into the heaviest Personal Defense Suit yet created. After refining the product through testing, DanCo released their biggest selling item to date — Turtle Armor. In a marketing coup, DanCo hired professional soldiers (with the approval of the Pentagon, of course) to train the personnel who were designated to wear the armor. DanCo was surprised at the popularity of their armor; even corporations bought the armor for their security forces, as did several major police departments (though only for specialized units within the departments, such as SWAT teams). In addition to impressive sales in the domestic markets, DanCo sold varying numbers of suits to the governments of 30 different nations for their armed forces.

Today DanCo is run by Leif Andersen, the company's current President and majority shareholder. The company continues to enjoy brisk sales of its various products, including its highly acclaimed Turtle Armor. One project currently under development, however, that Leif is not aware of is Project: Tortoise. Project: Tortoise is the name of the weaponry and equipment secretly being developed for Genocide. Rick Miller (DanCo's Vice President in charge of European Sales) is heading Project: Tortoise. DanCo's R&D team has recently announced the completion of the "Snapping Turtle" combat armor (Genocide Rook Armor), which will soon be offered for sale by the company. At $1 million each they are expensive, but well worth the price. The armor has, of course, been in use for a short time by Genocide. (Note: Leif is aware of the Snapping Turtle armor itself, but knows nothing of his company's link to Genocide.)

Rick Martin, DanCo's European V.P., has ties to Genocide in the form of a Contact with Antoinette Devroue, Genocide's White Queen who oversees the organizations activities in Europe (see *The Mutant File* for additional information on Genocide).

DanCo has some of the best security measures around, relying mainly on guards in Turtle Armor. In addition, the company utilizes passwords, security fences, surveillance equipment, and so on. While far from impenetrable, no villains who have entered any of the company's facilities' grounds have escaped (not without injuries, anyway).

DanCo is above board, or as above board as a munitions and weapons company can be. In the soldier of fortune "industry," no one has as good a reputation for taking care of the "grunts'" needs. If it ever comes to light, however, that DanCo has been secretly selling equipment to Genocide, their good name will be lost forever and Leif will probably wind up in a Danish prison. DanCo is known as a name that individual fighting men (mercs and soldiers alike) can trust; "there ain't no shoddy workmanship in DanCo products."

OPTIONAL VERSION: DanCo's philosophy can be summed up as "Do it to the competition before they do it to you." DanCo is a big supplier on the black market, which accounts for more than 20% of the company's total profits. DanCo is also responsible for a significant percentage of Awad's military's firepower. Everything from advanced assault rifles to aircraft-mounted missile systems have been sold to Awad, always funneled through neutral Arab countries like Oman and Yemen.

From Central America to the Baltic States, if there is a civil war or border clash going on somewhere in the world you can bet DanCo will be field testing some new equipment. There have even been charges from world Human Rights organizations that DanCo has engineered armed conflicts simply to use as a testing ground for their new weapons. There is currently no evidence to support this theory, however.

Leif Andersen is not aware of Rick's close association with Devroue. If Leif were to ever find out, however, he would have Rick fired — or worse — and take over the project for himself.

Both B.L.A.D.E. Inc. and SimCorp invest millions of dollars in the research and development of advanced weapons systems. However, DanCo's persistence in "field testing" their equipment has kept their name at the forefront of the minds of many overseas buyers. Domestic sales, however, are much closer between the three weapons firms. SimCorp continues to produce weapons aimed at a civilian market, while B.L.A.D.E. Inc. has recently won several lucrative commercial and government contracts for prototype developments. DanCo's big seller in the U.S. is their patented Turtle Armor.

CAMPAIGN USE: DanCo is an excellent company for superhero origins and it gives a great reason for non-mutants to be hunted by Genocide. Villains can also get their start from DanCo, as Rick has no scruples about who he sells the suits to ("Of course I sold that idiot a Snapping Turtle. He had the money for it").

If a hero has powered armor, DanCo would love to get a look at it in order to evaluate it as a source of modifications to their existing designs ("Perhaps a deal could be arranged, Power Guy — unlimited use of our repair facilities in return for one small peek at your armor...up close"). Similarly, if some alien battle-suits come into the players hands, DanCo would be more than happy to study the and try to find out how they work (that task, if even possible, would likely take years to accomplish). If a hero wanted to increase his powers, DanCo might assist him in the upgrade, for a price.

SLOGAN: "DanCo..., We protect you!"

SCENARIO IDEA: Turtle Armor all over the city has gone crazy and the people inside the armor suits can't control them. The armor starts blasting indiscriminately, endangering innocents galore. DanCo immediately flies a representative out to investigate. The representative is an attractive blonde-haired woman named Michelle Parkinson. Michelle will try to contact a the PCs as soon as possible, as she has information regarding the incidents.

The incidents of randomly malfunctioning Turtle Armor have only occurred in the campaign city, and the incidents have occurred every five days. No other owners or operators of the suits have reported similar malfunctions. the next incident should occur in 2 days and the only suits in the city that haven't been deactivated are owned by Thomas Gripp, a wealthy commodities investor. Thomas owns five Turtle Armor suits which are worn by his security staff. Thomas has refused to deactivate the suits, contrary to the urging of Michelle. Gripp's estate is quite large and contains a private zoo with a number of exotic animals, including a dozen large tortoises.

As the time approaches, the heroes will see a van approach the estate's driveway entrance. A figure gets out, destroys the fence and approaches the house. The figure is dressed in power armor (a closer look reveals it to be Turtle Armor). As Gripp's Turtle guards try to apprehend the intruder they will start to move erratically, as if on strings. The figure exclaims "Fools, I am Galapogos, King of all turtles. You can do me no harm." He has a device giving him full control over the other armor suits and will use them to attack the heroes. All the while, the humans inside the guards will be pleading with the heroes not to hurt them. Galapogos will continue on towards the house. It's up to the heroes to stop him before he can reach Thomas Gripp.

The intruder is a maniacal lover of turtles who fancies himself their protector and savior. He discovered Gripp's private tortoise collection and has come to kill him for imprisoning the turtles, along with the lesser animals in his private zoo.

For Galapogos' stats use Turtle Armor (from ***CHAMPIONS***, page S43). The agents also have +5 to the listed DEX (No fig Stat), 8d6 AP EB, 5 points of Life Support, +10" swimming and +5 PD. Galapogos has the same, plus a special device (OIF) that gives him control over the Turtle suits and 75% Damage Reduction versus Physical and Energy attacks.

EYE-TECH IDENTIFICATION SYSTEMS

PRIMARY OPERATION: Security ID Systems

PRIMARY COMPETITORS: Yoshida Corporation; Impervious Security Technologies (IST)

WORTH: $47.5 Million

HQ LOCATION: Houston, TX

HEAD: Dharam Singh, Ph.D

HUNTED/WATCHED: 5 Pts (Less Pow, Lim, 11-)/ 10 Pts (As Pow, NCI, 11-)

BACKGROUND/DESCRIPTION: Years ago, while attending MIT, Dharam Singh met and befriended fellow students Victor Blackwell and Tricia Galloway. The trio were good friends through school. They delighting in discussing technical theories and debating their feasibility. Their friendship continued through their graduation from MIT. Dharam later learned that Victor had contracted a degenerative disease. Dharam tried to help, but Victor scorned Dharam's attention in favor of Tricia's.

It has been several years and the three have grown apart. Dharam and Victor were friends, and Dharam has never understood why Victor retreated from humanity. Dharam has since figured out Victor's secret and the two maintain infrequent correspondence. Because of Dharam's past friendship with Victor, Cy-Force has left Eye-Tech alone (for now...).

Dr. Dharam Singh went to work for a computer engineering firm in Miami after graduating from MIT. Work went well, but Dharam felt uneasy about having his family live in such a violent city as Miami. Things were much simpler before, although their standard of living was much improved after moving to Florida.

After several years Dr. Singh developed an interest in security systems. Each day he drove past the security guard at the company's front gate and wondered, "How can they keep unwanted persons off of the grounds?" Security and identification techniques became almost an obsession for Dr. Singh, until it began affecting his life at home.

At the urging of his wife, Dharam gave his notice at work, and started his own company. Dharam worked around the clock, sometimes taking meals in his home office. Using his vast knowledge and experience in computer design and programming Singh developed an advanced voice-recognition algorithm. The program was designed to recognize individuals by their voice signature, and was supposed to be foolproof.

Sales were slow, initially. Singh was a scientist, not a salesman. His few contracts provided just enough income to meet expenses and to continue developing other systems. Within two years Singh had developed several high-tech identification-recognition systems, including retinal scanners, photo-electric fingerprint ID systems, as well as his patented VORID System (short for Voice Recognition ID), an advancement over his earlier model. Sales rose dramatically as Singh began demonstrating his devices at various law enforcement and corporate trade shows. Rumor has it that Dr. Singh is currently working on a simplified, portable DNA recognition system.

Eye-Tech Identification Systems employs only a few dozen people, concentrating on product development rather than production. Several of his ideas have been sold to other companies in order to raise capital for his own research.

Eye-Tech is responsible for many wondrous identification devices, and continues to invest most of its profits in its research and development division. This has strengthened the company and has driven up the value of its stock to a level thrice that of its starting value. Eye-Tech is seen as a very lucrative investment. Unfortunately for the business world Eye-Tech remains a privately held corporation. Well over 60% of the company's shares are owned by Singh himself. The remaining shares are held by Eye-Tech's senior employees. Singh has seen that no single employee owns more than 5%, however.

Dr. Singh is always willing to discuss various scientific theories with interested persons and is a pleasant man to speak with. He is modest, given his achievements, and prefers to redirect compliments to his staff.

Eye-Tech Identification Systems, under the direction of Dr. Singh, has managed to stay ahead of his competitors through superior research and marketing. Yoshida Corporation maintains a poor percentage of U.S. sales of ID technologies, but excels in the Asian market. IST, on the other hand, remains Eye-Tech's biggest rival for domestic sales, with designs almost identical to those developed by Eye-Tech. Singh suspects IST of conducting corporate espionage against his company, but has yet to find any evidence of such.

CAMPAIGN USE: Eye-Tech provides numerous security devices, all of which are designed to identify the user. His products have less than a .05% failure rate, which has only helped to bolster his company's reputation for producing quality items.

Eye-Tech products can be found in many places where identification systems are in use, from laboratory doors to bank vaults. The company produces a variety of devices including devices capable of scanning a person's retina, fingerprint, voice or even blood for identification. Eye-Tech shares a reputation as one of the best companies in its field, alongside such state-of-the-art electronics companies such as Yoshida Corp. and Impervious Security Technologies (IST), a subsidiary of Montgomery International.

A superhero headquarters that has similar security systems installed may well have purchased them from Eye-Tech. A superhero team may contact Eye-Tech to install equipment, or to come out and service the equipment once it's installed.

Eye-Tech also has several contracts with government agencies including the Federal Court system and Stronghold. Rumors also exist that Eye-Tech has secured contracts to provide security systems for PRIMUS, but these rumors are unsubstantiated. If any such contracts exist they are highly classified. Many of Eye-Tech's biggest customers are other corporations, as the idea of increased corporate security increases in popularity. Dr. Singh also travels the country, on occasion, giving lectures at universities, technology conventions, etc.

SLOGAN: "We Never Forget A Face."

OPTIONAL VERSION: Although no longer close friends, Dr. Singh has kept track of his former friends, Victor and Tricia. Singh knows that Doc Digital is really Victor Blackwell, a fact that he has used to blackmail his rival. This fact alone has kept Doc Digital from destroying Eye-Tech outright. Dharam Singh remains bitter that Blackwell shut him out in favor of Tricia those many years ago and believes that it is he, not Blackwell, who should dominate the technological world.

Dr. Singh is now driven by a single goal — to thwart his long-time rival's plans at every opportunity. Singh has become obsessive in his work and increasingly demanding of his employees. This is causing him to become alienated from everyone close to him.

SCENARIO IDEA: Dr. Singh has sent a press release to every major television and cable network announcing the discovery of a new breakthrough cybernetic system. The prototype of this new system will be unveiled at a national press conference to be held at a large hotel in the campaign city.

Claiming to be concerned about security of the prototype, Singh will request that the heroes be present at the unveiling. The device is setup in the center of a large auditorium. A large crowd of scientists and company representatives fills the auditorium, making it very difficult to move the device by conventional means. True to form, the Cy-Force team shows up at the unveiling to attempt to steal the prototype. The heroes should intervene, trying to prevent the theft.

If using the main version of Eye-Tech, Singh is genuinely concerned about the prototype, which is a true technological breakthrough. The device, however, requires a rather bulky liquid helium coolant system, much like that used by the Henderson 2850 mainframe computer. Without the coolant system, the device will simply melt down as soon as it is activated. Neither Doc Digital nor Cy-tech know this. Singh will tell the heroes this at the first opportunity.

If using the optional version of Eye-Tech, the entire affair is an elaborate hoax designed by Singh to draw Cy-Tech into the open. Dr. Singh is counting on the heroes capturing the villains, thus striking a mighty blow against his old rival, Victor.

FIRST HERO'S BANK, INC.

ABBREVIATION: FHer

PRIMARY OPERATION: Banking

PRIMARY COMPETITORS: Olympia Bank; 1st National Heroes Savings & Loan

WORTH: $7.4 Billion

HQ LOCATION: New York City, NY

HEAD: Walter Drewerton, President

HUNTED/WATCHED: 10 Pts (Less Pow, NCI, Question, 11-) / 10 Pts (As Pow, NCI, 11-)

BACKGROUND/DESCRIPTION: First Hero's Bank was the brainchild of Walter Drewerton in the early 1980's. Several of Drewerton's friends were high-society figures and movie moguls. At one fateful cocktail party (which Walter is known to attend with relative frequency) the conversation turned to superheroes. While some of those in attendance found paranormals to be a terrible nuisance, there were those who found them utterly intriguing. One person in particular, a young movie-maker by the name of Ronald St. John (see Maverick Studios and *Normals Unbound*) brought up the idea of hiring paranormals for his movies. Ron quickly decided it was near impossible, however, unless an employer was willing to pay the heroes with cash. This was because so many heroes kept a secret identity and thus did not have bank accounts.

Months after that party Walter was still thinking about the comments Mr. St. John had made. Walter could hardly imagine a bank which allowed superheroes to open accounts without revealing their true names. The more Walter thought about it the more he convinced himself that there was indeed a market for just such a bank. The only problem facing Walter was how to identify these special "account-holders."

Then along came Eye-Tech, a high tech corporation specializing in the design of security and identification equipment. At a local corporate security trade show Walter examined Eye-Tech's wares for himself. They had every type of identification technology imaginable; retina scanners, fingerprint scanners, voice recognition devices, even thermal aura scanners, all with built in computer memory chips to hold employee data. This was exactly what Walter was looking for, and he wasted no time securing a contract with Eye-Tech for the delivery of several dozen of their best gadgets.

Soon after, with money from numerous capital investors, Walter Drewerton unveiled the first operational branch of the First Hero's Bank in New York City. Using equipment similar to the devices used to identify heroes in court without revealing their identities (refer to *Dark Champions*, pages 63-65, for more information), First Hero has set up a system in which heroes can open bank accounts in their heroic identities (the system is mainly used with sanctioned heroes, who are more easily identified and hence better risks). In addition to numerous branches now across the country, First Hero licensed and bonded employees will show up with their identification equipment wherever a hero has business to transact, thus providing a way for the hero to be identified. This system is not foolproof, but it is as good as such a system could get and still be practical (assume any use of Security Systems to be at a penalty of -3 or more). First Hero Bank of New York has branches in Los Angeles and Chicago and has recently inspired several imitators).

First Hero's Bank remains the first and best financial institution for paranormals. Their top of the line technology assures that customers will maintain their Secret Identity while still receiving first rate service. Several imitators have recently surface, a testimony to the success of FHB. Of the imitators, Olympia Bank (a Washington D.C. based company) and 1st National Heroes Savings & Loan (in New York City) have been the most successful, although FHB's assets outweigh those of the other two institutions combined. Of course, having such famous customers as Defender, Crossbow and Peacekeeper helps tremendously.

CAMPAIGN USE: Being the "Bank of the Superheroes" has generated a lot of business for First Hero's, since many people feel safe "banking where the superheroes bank." This confidence is well-placed: in addition to its state-of-the-art high-tech security systems (which were built and are constantly monitored by several of its hero clients), First Hero inserts a clause in its banking contracts which calls for the client hero to use his powers to defend First Hero banks against super-criminal attacks. Because of this, no robbery of a First Hero branch has ever been successful.

Since the hero also has a bank account in his hero identity with First Hero, a businessman can write a check made out to, for example, "Defender," with no problem. First Hero also makes loans; finances the building of bases, vehicles, and gadgets; arranges legal representation for superheroes; and so forth. However, there is a downside to this otherwise useful arrangement — a hero with a bank account and a means to be identified can be taxed. Defeating Dr. Destroyer is one thing — but not even a superhero can escape the IRS!

SLOGAN: "Bank of the Superheroes."

OPTIONAL VERSION: First Hero's Bank is the ultimate front for VIPER. The organization monitors the accounts of literally dozens of superheroes, watching their every financial move. Bought a house on the beach? They know. Just sold your car and deposited the money in the bank? They know. Got a loan to pay for that expansion to the base? They know. What better way to monitor, study or generally snoop on superheroes than from behind a one-way mirror?

VIPER is collecting data on a number of heroes for several reasons. First, the organization can use the information against the hero, if necessary, in blackmail schemes and so on. In addition, VIPER will investigate any other persons listed on the account (such as DNPCs) as well as any other accounts linked to the bank account. It would not take long for VIPER to uncover the hero's Secret ID unless the hero was exceptionally careful.

Second, VIPER can conduct secret surveillance and scientific studies on the heroes from special scanners designed to look like security cameras (-2 to PER Rolls to spot the difference). These gadgets may be designed to discover a hero's weaknesses (i.e., Susceptibility or Vulnerability) or to simply analyze their powers. This information can be spread among its field personnel and put to good use the nest time VIPER encounters that hero.

First Hero's Bank is also used quite extensively to launder money for the various VIPER Nests on the East Coast (at least those Nests that are not at war with one another). Walter Drewerton knows about the VIPER connection, but he knows very little about their actual day-to-day operations (ignorance is bliss, he feels). For instance, Walter knows that as many as half of all the Bank's employees (and board members) are somehow affiliated with or employed by VIPER, but he doesn't know which employees.

As an option, the GM can substitute any evil organization or nefarious master villain for VIPER. Examples of other groups or villains that work equally well are Master Control (from *High Tech Enemies*), the Master of Crime (*Dark Champions*) and Genocide (*Mutant File*).

NOTE: First Hero's Bank may not be suitable for a *Dark Champions* campaign, given the nature of its clientele. The GM should consider the likelihood of vigilantes being allowed to hold accounts as compared to their four-color counterparts. Ultimately, the decision the GM.

SCENARIO IDEA: While the PCs are in the bank taking care of business (or waiting on a friend who is), one of the tellers suddenly yells, "That's him! That's that super villain! Him!" She points at an unknown costumed wearing a utility belt, a backpack hooked up to bulky wrist-packs, and a poorly tailored costume. The "villain," appearing quite nervous, will insist that he is a hero by the name of Captain Courage and that he is only there to make a deposit.

If the PCs do not intervene at this point the teller will begin putting money on the counter and begging the confused "villain" not to harm her. If the PCs do intervene the costumed man will run (assuring the PCs of his guilt, of course).

The incident is simply a case of mistaken identity; the man turns out to be a self-proclaimed hero calling himself Captain Courage. He will insist that he is a hero, like the PCs, and will physically resist any attempts to subdue him.

CAPTAIN COURAGE

10 STR	12 DEX	12 CON	10 BODY	13 INT
12 EGO	10 PRE	10 COM	3+ PD	2+ ED
3 SPD	4 REC	24 END	21 STUN	

Powers: EC: Electro-mag powers (20 pts), OAF (Backpack), [8c], Jammed 14-; 3d6 EB NND (Def is Force Field/Wall), AE 4" Cone; 0 DEF/4d6 Body Entangle; 3d6 Flash (Normal sight), AP; Telekinesis 30 STR, Affects entire target (No squeeze/punch); Armor (+3 PD/+3 ED), OIF (Suit)

Skills: +2 Levels w/EC powers; PS: Dishwasher, 13-; Computer Programming, 12-; Contortionist, 11-; Cryptography, 12-; Inventor, 12-; Lip-reading, 11-; Lightning Calculator; Danger Sense, Immediate area, 11-

50+ Disadvantages: Wants to be a "real" superhero; Follows strict Superhero Code; Reputation (Well-liked local hero) 8-; Secret ID (Nathan Miles)

Alternatively, the costumed man can be an actual super villain disguised as a superhero in order to hold an account at the bank. If captured and questioned (or if bank records are checked) the PCs will discover that the villain has held an account as "Captain Courage" for several years, loading it with ill gotten money from various criminal acts.

FITZARTHUR PUBLISHING

ABBREVIATION: Fitza

PRIMARY OPERATION: Book Publishing

PRIMARY COMPETITORS: Tripleday Books; Fillerman & Lester Publishing; Connor Books

WORTH: $53 million

HQ LOCATION: New York City, NY

HEAD: Brian Malcolme, President

HUNTED/WATCHED: Varies / 10 Pts (As Pow, NCI, 11-)

BACKGROUND/DESCRIPTION: In the early 1920's Gerald Fitzarthur moved to New York City from Andover, Massachusetts, with dreams of publishing his own magazine. With his life savings Gerald purchased the equipment he needed and set up shop. Within a matter of weeks the first issue of "Tales Too Weird to Believe" was printed. The magazine, which published "weird fiction," was received with mixed reviews. Without increased readership, Gerald was afraid his dream would collapse.

It was then that Gerald received a letter from his old college roommate, a budding horror and mystery author by the name of Howard Pickman. It seemed that Howard was looking to sell a few short stories. Gerald was more than willing to publish Howard's work and soon a partnership was formed. Howard would supply original works of fiction, and Gerald would publish them. Sales of the magazine grew. Gerald eventually bought the publishing rights to Howard's stories and Fitzarthur Publishing was born.

By the mid-forties, Fitzarthur Publishing had become quite successful. The company acquired several smaller companies including Superzap Comics and Contemporary House magazine. With a solid financial base and a number of books on the Best Seller list, it seemed that Fitzarthur Publishing was destined for greatness.

In 1953 Gerald Fitzarthur and his entire family died of a mysterious ailment. Some suspected foul play, but nothing was ever proven. The Fitzarthurs were laid to rest in a quiet, unpublicized ceremony at East Lawn Memorial Cemetery. With the original ownership gone, shareholders lost their confidence in the company. With most shareholders trying to sell their shares and very few people buying, Fitzarthur stock plummeted in value.

Shortly after their deaths, a man named Brian Malcolme began buying all available shares of Fitzarthur stock. He acquired 60% of the shares before the word spread of mass buyout, after which the value of Fitzarthur stock skyrocketed. Everyone who hadn't already sold their stock was hanging on to what they had, confident that whatever Brian Malcolme's intentions were they would spell profits for Fitzarthur Publishing.

Their suspicions proved correct. Malcolme began liquidating Fitzarthur Publishing's assets, dissolving less successful subsidiaries and selling their successful comic line for a substantial profit. Brian Malcolme became the company's new President and CEO in 1958 and has maintained this position over three and a half decades. He directs the corporation in all matters financial. Fitzarthur Publishing no longer prints Howard Pickman's horror books. Although considered classics, Brian refuses to reprint Pickman's books for reasons known only to himself. Fitzarthur Publishing now publishes many self-help books, cookbooks and the like.

In reality, Gerald Fitzarthur and his family were killed as sacrifices for a dark, cult ritual. The ritual was intended to summon ancient beings known as the Forgotten gods. Even though he was too late to save the Fitzarthurs, Brian Malcolme managed to locate and stop the ritual. Brian had discovered that Pickman was somehow associated with the cult and resolved himself to stopping their nefarious plan.

Brian then decided to take over Fitzarthur Publishing to prevent Pickman's books from being published. Brian decided that this was the best way to protect the world from the evil incantations and magics that they contained. Some of the books describe real magic rituals which could be used to summon evil entities and generally wreak havoc upon an unsuspecting world. Brian Malcolme and his associates have located and destroyed nearly every copy of Pickman's original works and he continues his search for the remaining copies. Malcolme has gained a reputation in literary circles as an avid collector of Pickman's works. This is true, but not for reasons that they suspect.

Brian is also very concerned about the other 40% of Fitzarthur's stock, as he was unable to find out who really controls them. While he knows who the registered owners of those shares are, he can't yet determine who is controlling them. Brian believes that the criminal and supernatural organization DEMON may be involved, although he's not sure.

Brian has some supernatural powers himself, the result of many long years of research and fighting evil. (Use stats for Skilled Normal and add a 100 point Magic Power Pool, 10 pts of Mental Defense, 10 pts of Power Defense and the following skills: PS: Publisher 12-; PS: Occult Investigator 15-; KS: Magic 14-; Magic Skill 15-; KS: Occult 16-; KS: Mystic Artifacts 13-; Latin [Fluent].)

CAMPAIGN USE: Fitzarthur Publishing makes an excellent Watched for a character with a background in mysticism. Brian Malcolme is still looking out for the human race and wants to have tabs on possible allies (as well as enemies).

On another note FP is a great place for a job for that intrepid superhero; imagine a job as a freelance book writer. You have to meet deadlines, but you can write anywhere, thereby able to go anywhere for that adventure. In the optional version, of course, DEMON wants to keep tabs on all possible rivals and enemies. In fact, the optional version makes an excellent Hunted as well.

FP and Brian Malcolme also make great enemies. Malcolme, upon first learning of the PCs' involvement with an occult enemy, could assume them to be adversaries. As a Hunted, Fitzarthur Publishing itself is worth no points, although Brian Malcolme is worth 10 pts (8-) plus any additional points for a higher appearance modifier (Treat Brian Malcolme as being As Powerful, having NCI, and seeking to Mildly Punish the PCs). If using the optional version, Brian Malcolme is worth 15 pts as a hunted plus appearance (As Pow, NCI).

Fitzarthur Publishing's sales have fallen in recent years. In fact, the company's total sales are below those of all of its major competitors in the publishing field. This fact does not seem to bother Brian Malcolme in the least, nor has it had a significant impact on the value of Fitzarthur stock. This fact has some securities analysts puzzled, but no one has yet investigated to any extent.

SLOGAN: "Quality tomes"

OPTIONAL VERSION: Brian Malcolme is actually a Lesser Morbane of DEMON. He was also the true, evil force behind the cultists that gave the Fitzarthurs their ailment and eventually caused their deaths. Brian never did destroy all of Pickman's books. Indeed, Brian intends to keep the amassed occult knowledge of Pickman and Fitzarthur to himself (and DEMON, of course). DEMON does not want any rituals or spells to fall into the wrong hands (any hands but theirs).

Fitzarthur Publishing is maintained as a money laundering front for DEMON. While it continues to publish books of a mundane nature, Fitzarthur is no longer the publishing company it once was.

SCENARIO IDEA: The PCs are contacted by Lynda Crighton, the owner of a small occult bookstore called the Nightengale Bookery (see *Normals Unbound*, pg. 39). She explains to the PCs that she has discovered a rare Latin text in a collection she recently purchased from a widow. The text is an old, hand-written, 16th century spell book. While she is incurably curious about such matters, she has sensed incredible evil from the book and wants to be rid of it before dark forces come to take it from her. She asks the PCs to safeguard the book and find someone to give it to.

The book is protected my powerful magics and cannot be destroyed by the PCs. In addition, once one of the PCs takes physically the book from Lynda (even if only to examine it), they will be unable to part with it — literally. If they try to get rid of it by leaving it somewhere, it will show up in an unexpected place very shortly thereafter (such as in the PC's sock drawer, in a backpack, in the team's vehicle, and so on). Even transporting it to another dimension will not stop it from returning. The only way to get rid of the book is for another person (or entity) to willingly take the book.

While the PCs look for a way to get rid of the book, they will be watched (but not attacked) by DEMON. In addition, strange things will begin to befall the characters. Each PC will begin to get a little clumsier and suffer minor accidents and snafus (Treat this as each PC having gained 2d6 Unluck until they get rid of the book). This effect is purely psychosomatic, however; allow PCs with 10 pts or more of Mental or Power Defense to avoid these occurrences.

Mystical study will reveal that the powers mentioned above are the book's only real magic. There are no other magic abilities or spells contained within (which explains DEMON's unwillingness to fight over its possession). After a successful period of researching, whether by one of the PCs or a knowledgeable NPC, such as "Crystal" Claire Vosser or Blaise Morgan (*Normals Unbound*), the PCs will discover a way to destroy the book — by having someone accept the book who then dies while it is still in their possession.

To add a twist to the scenario, Stephen Pierce will hound the PCs for the book in an attempt to unlock the secrets and find a way out of his "contract" (see *Normals Unbound*).

FORDHAM CHEMTECH

ABBREVIATION: FordmCT

PRIMARY OPERATION: Chemicals, electronics, computers and computer software.

PRIMARY COMPETITORS: Dew Chemical Company; Micro Device Technologies; Yoshida Corporation

WORTH: $1.2 Billion

HQ LOCATION: Hudson City

HEAD: Jeffrey Claude Fordham III, President

HUNTED/WATCHED: 10 Pts (Less Pow, NCI, Mildly, 11-)/ 10 Pts (As Pow, NCI, 11-)

BACKGROUND/DESCRIPTION: Jeffrey Claude Fordham II had served the U.S. government as a chemical engineer during World War II and was quite familiar with many of the ongoing programs sponsored by the government. During that time, the U.S. government was secretly conducting extensive research in the area of chemical and biological weapons design. After leaving the employ of Uncle Sam, Jeffrey continued the research he had started years earlier for the government, and with the help of a few private investors he founded Fordham Chemicals. Fordham Chemicals won a lucrative, although highly secret, contract to produce chemicals for he U.S. government. The chemicals were to be used as part of a new type of nerve gas, which was intended to be used in Korea in the event of a massive Chinese invasion of South Korea. The invasion never came and the gas was never used. (Note: the gas is being held in a secret facility underneath the Rocky Mountains. This information is highly classified; not even Jeffrey Fordham II or his son know this. This data is held at the highest levels of government.)

Although the chemicals were never used in war, the incredible amount of capital the contracts generated for Fordham Chemicals put the company on square footing. Jeffrey now wanted to expand the company. Gaining several new investors, including Cherokee Bank & Trust and others, Jeffrey expanded the company; new plants and storage facilities were constructed and transport tankers purchased. Jeffrey also decided to branch out into new area of research and design, including the brand new microchip and computer fields. The company's name was changed to Fordham ChemTech to reflect its newfound diversity. Things were going well for Jeffrey; he was married, owned one of the most successful chemical companies in the country, and he was giving his son, Jeffrey Claude Fordham III, the best education money could buy. It was nearing the end of the '70s, and the next decade promised to be a boon for computer technology. Jeffrey was sure that Fordham ChemTech would prosper greatly in the '80s.

Suddenly, and tragically, Jeffrey's life was suddenly changed. While driving home from work late one rainy night, he became involved in a horrible automobile accident. The accident left Jeffrey paralyzed from the waist down and slightly brain damaged. He was jerked from the life of a successful businessman and sentenced to live out the remainder of his life in a wheelchair. Between his crippling injuries and his aging wife's increasing senility, Jeffrey was forced to pass control of the company to his only son, Jeffrey Claude Fordham III. Jeffrey Claude Fordham III was an honor student, and had graduated at the top of his class with a Master's Degree in business. The company would be in good hands — or so his father thought.

The decision to give the company to a bright, yet inexperienced college graduate did not sit well with the Board of Directors. They voiced their concerns, but to no avail. Jeffrey Fordham II still held the controlling shares of stock in the company; as long as he wanted his son to sit as the new President of Fordham ChemTech, the board had no choice but to tolerate him.

Although a genius in his own right, JCF III did not have his father's business savvy (at first). As a result, many of the company's private investors began losing confidence in the new young president. By the time young Jeffrey has brought the company around, true control of Fordham ChemTech had been usurped by the major shareholders. They have control over the board of directors, and the decisions that Jeffrey makes regarding the operation of the company have little bearing on the way the company is actually run. With the senior J. Fordham II essentially incapacitated, and his wife growing more senile by the day, the company is safely in the hands of the remaining shareholders; the controlling shares of stock are held by the elder Fordhams, who are in no condition to throw their weight around. Until their son, Fordham III, gains his parents shares of stock the company will continue to be run by the other board members under the direction of the remaining shareholders. This fact is kept from Jeffrey, who still believes that it is he who runs the company.

It should be noted that Jeffrey Fordham III is no fool. Quite the contrary is true; Jeffrey is an extremely intelligent young man and he has become quite the shrewd businessman.

Jeffrey is one of the youngest corporate leaders in America (age 29) and is one of the richest men in the world (his total personal worth has been estimated as high as $9 billion, although more conservative estimates put the figure closer to $4 billion).

Today, the primary focus of the company is microchip development and industrial chemical production. The company remains privately held, although the board has recently been considering putting Fordham ChemTech on the Hudson City Stock Exchange in order to raise additional capital to build several new plants in the western United States. The goals of Fordham ChemTech include maintaining its prized government contracts and excelling in computer microchip research (Fordham ChemTech currently holds roughly 7% of the world's microchip market). The company is also working on revolutionary new designs in flash memory technology, which allows data to be maintained in memory after the computer's power is turned off!

Fordham ChemTech's focus in the microchip field has put them in direct competition with both MDT and Yoshida Corp. The company specializes in producing clone microchips, patterned after the architecture of their rivals' chips, but with original micro-coding. Sales remain steady for their FC-36 computer microchip, a clone of the original MDT X86 chip. Several victories in Federal courts have allowed Fordham ChemTech to continue producing the clone ships, much to the chagrin of MDT.

CAMPAIGN USE: Fordham ChemTech is a prominent corporation in the U.S. in general, and in Hudson City in particular. It accounts for a significant portion of Hudson City's commercial income. The company's corporate offices are located in Hudson City, as well as two production facilities: a chemical production plant and a microchip production facility.

Fordham ChemTech is a large employer in Hudson City, as well. It employs over 2,000 people in it's two major plants, and 300 more in its corporate office. Fordham ChemTech employs all kinds of professions, including security guards, researchers, scientists and assembly line workers. The company can employ any of the PCs, especially those with scientific and research skills. It may also employ a DNPC or a follower.

SLOGAN: "Tomorrow's answers today."

OPTIONAL VERSION: Jeffrey is a dangerous man. Everything he becomes involved in has a habit of succeeding at the expense of others. When Jeffrey got involved in microchip research, for example, the company's staff reached a breakthrough in design but not before one researcher developed a rare form of cancer.

Jeffrey Fordham III has also been under investigation by both the SEC and the Department of Justice for some time; he is suspected of engaging in insider trading. While they have no hard evidence against Jeffrey, they continue to monitor his activities very closely and well as those with whom he associates (this includes anyone with Jeffrey a Contact, and anyone who Jeffrey owes a Favor to. Treat the SEC and DOJ as a single 10 point Watched, at 11-.)

There are some who believe that Jeffrey Fordham III owes his success to a subtle game of "seek and destroy," even going so far as suspecting him of arranging his own father's "accident" so that he could inherit the company. The truth is that several key investors (Cherokee Bank & Trust and Flag International) wanted Jeffrey Fordham II removed and his son installed as president of the company. It is they who had J. Fordham II's car sabotaged, causing the accident. All of this is unknown to J. Fordham III, who believes that he is simply the object of fate.

SCENARIO IDEA: Fordham ChemTech has developed a new type of spray-on, ultra-hard epoxy. Fordham claims that this new epoxy can be used to strengthen lighter materials, such as high-strength plastics, making light metals obsolete. The company plans to unveil this new chemical at an upcoming industrial trade show being held at the Hudson City Convention Center. The media has been playing up the announcement, as well as Fordham's intent to provide increased security at the convention in the event anyone attempts to steal the chemical.

The word on the street, however, is that someone is going to replace the chemical with a variant (and ineffective) chemical before the convention. The intent of the switch is to ruin Fordham's credibility with the public and lower confidence among Fordham's backers, ultimately causing the "liquid-epoxy" chemical program to be disbanded.

The PCs are hired (or simply asked) by Jeffrey Fordham III to safeguard the chemical until the trade show. Jeffrey will claim that he has received several threats to steal the chemical. The chemical prototype, along with its formula, is being held at a medium security facility outside of town. One night while at the facility, after the staff has all left for the day, a group of mercenaries will attempt to attack the PCs and steal the chemical and the formula disk amidst the confusion. They will also attempt to destroy any remaining copies of the disk, notes or other equipment that may hold the formula. For

the bad guys use Skilled Normals with appropriate weapons skills or any of the thugs from *Dark Champions* (page 139). Give each thug a weapon (pistol or sub-machine-gun), and possibly Armor (+7 PD/+7 ED), Act 11-, OIF (Kevlar vest). The thugs will attack either from a van or motorcycles.

Whether the PCs are successful in protecting the chemical or not, it will not perform as planned (it was already switched by Fordham himself). Jeffrey Fordham will accuse the PCs of tampering with the chemical and will press charges (anyone with Fordham as a Contact will not have charges filed against them). In reality, Fordham's researchers were close to discovering the formula, but would not discover it in time to unveil it at the trade show. Fordham, in a rush to make his investors happy, announced the breakthrough and the unveiling. By setting the PCs up, he has bought a little more time for his scientists to come up with the real formula before the investors back out.

FUTURE SCOPE, INC.

ABBREVIATION: FutScp

PRIMARY OPERATION: Robotics and cybernetics technology

PRIMARY COMPETITORS: CM Industries; CyberNet Research Ltd.; Yoshida Corporation

WORTH: $13 Million

HQ LOCATION: Atlanta, GA

HEAD: Michael Murphy Montgomery, President

HUNTED/WATCHED: 15 Pts (As Pow, 11-) / 5 Pts (Less Pow, 11-)

BACKGROUND/DESCRIPTION: Future Scope, Inc. was founded by Dr. Collin Montgomery (also the famed American superhero Stellar Paladin) in the mid '70s. The company was a privately funded and controlled research company which specialized in robotics and cybernetics, both Collin's favored fields of study. Collin divided his time between his roles as a hero and a scientist. As a result, he alienated his wife, Angela, and his two sons, Randall and Michael. When his wife was killed by Mechassassin in a failed retaliatory attack against Collin, he decided to hang up his costume and spend more time with his family. It was too late, however, as his older son, Randall, blamed his mother's death on Collin's cavalier "superhero" attitude and ran away from home (see Montgomery International). His other son, Michael, stayed with his father, however. They grieved together, and became very close.

Michael eventually became the superhero Crossbow, carrying on the Montgomery tradition. As Crossbow, Michael helped form, and ultimately reform, the hero team known as the Cyberknights (see CM Industries in this book, *Allies*, and *High Tech Enemies*).

Dr. Collin Montgomery, in the meantime, had achieved a breakthrough in cybernetic design and neural networks and Angel-3 was "born." Unfortunately, what was to be Collin's crowning achievement also turned out to be his downfall. Master Control, who had been monitoring Dr. Montgomery's work, learned of Angel-3's existence and sent his S.T.R.I.K.E. Units to recover the self-aware android. During the attempted abduction, Dr. Montgomery was unable to reach his Stellar Paladin armor. Angel-3 fought to protect her creator from the invaders. Nearly defeated, Angel-3 was rescued by the Cyberknights at the last minute. They were unable to save Dr. Montgomery or his lab, however.

Michael Montgomery has recovered slowly after the death of his father, and he still does not know that it was his brother, Randall, who was responsible. Michael has inherited his father's company, Future Scope, Inc., along with what money was left in his parents' estate. With it, Michael set out to rebuild Future Scope, Inc. from the ground up, in an attempt to carry on his father's dream.

Michael has enlisted the aid of his long time friend and teammate, Hardwire as one of the company's main design experts, although his association with Future Scope is not publicly known. Hardwire is trying to pursue Dr. Collin Montgomery's original designs and research on AIs. He is finally meeting with some moderate success, despite the lack of data from Angel-1, which was destroyed years ago in the attack that killed Collin. The company in general, and Hardwire specifically, are very anxious to convince Angel-3 to return and help them in their research, as Angel-3 holds the key to her own creation on that fateful day.

Last year, Michael offered public stock in the company, listing it on the local exchange. The revenue generated by the sale of Future Scope stock allowed the company to stay afloat during hard times over the last few months and contributed to recent projects which are expected to bring substantial capital to the company through sales.

Future Scope, Inc. is still a growing company. The company specializes in cutting edge technological advances, especially in the realms of robotics, cybernetics and artificial intelligence. Michael's' own expertise, as the superhero Crossbow, has brought the company more and more into weapons research. This has placed Michael in an ethical quandary. While the company is still struggling to rebuild and could desperately use the cash that weapons sales would generate, Michael doesn't want to become a major contributor to what is seen as a growing problem (namely gun violence). He is willing to negotiate sales with certain paramilitary groups and governments, however, and foreign governments are also prime customers. Michael is interested in primarily dealing with UNTIL, however; he sees their mission as an international extension of his own goals as a hero.

Michael has managed to maintain a separation between his private life as President of Future Scope, Inc. and his more "public" role as Crossbow. Michael runs his business as cleanly and honestly as possible, and is careful not to involve any of his employees in his hero activities. Michael does put his company's intelligence-gathering capability to good use, however, and is able to monitor the activities of several corporations that are known to associate with criminal elements, including Montgomery International, Yoshida Corp. and Duchess Industries.

When Michael Montgomery reformed the Cyberknights, he hoped to use the team to field test new equipment from time to time. In this way, Michael was able to convince the Board of Directors to help fund the Cyberknights. Richard Carter has used this recent development to his advantage. Richard, on behalf of CM Industries, has filed a lawsuit filed against Future Scope, Inc. for illegally using a team whose members' powers and names legally belong to CMI. Unbeknownst to anyone else, Richard Carter is simply using this tactic to disrupt his brother's team and to cause general annoyance. Richard is motivated by a hatred of his brother, who he knows to be the hero known as Hardwire. In addition, Richard knows that Future Scope's resources are limited, and he hopes to either win the lawsuit by default or to financially ruin Michael's company.

Future Scope remains a very viable contender in the cybernetics field, even though it ranks second to CM Industries in production and sales. Future Scope is quickly expanding its operations and research base, and the company's most recent quarterly earnings put it only slightly behind its biggest competitor, CM Industries. Many analysts expect Future Scope Inc. to surpass CMI as the industry leader in cybernetics research and production by the mid-1990s.

CAMPAIGN USE: Future Scope is a growing company, financially, but it is already a powerful player in the fields of cybernetic and robotics. The company is currently courting several defense contracts and a possible contract of major proportions with UNTIL. The company makes an excellent base for characters with a background in the appropriate sciences, or otherwise having an affiliation with Crossbow, Hardwire or the Cyberknights.

Future Scope's weapon technology is becoming a concern to several organizations, including SimCrop and VIPER; the former due to competition and the latter because of their desire for new gadgets and weapons.

It is possible that Master Control will one day seek to destroy his brother's company outright, but he is currently content to watch Michael squirm under the pressure brought to bear by his major international competitor's. Master Control maintains a close eye on Future Scope, Inc. and uses it to MI's advantage.

Future Scope is worth more points as a Hunted due to its ability to use the Cyberknights. In cases where Future Scope, Inc. itself is used as a Hunted, without intervention by the super team, simply deduct 5 Pts from the value (making the company Less Powerful).

SLOGAN: "We make it happen."

OPTIONAL VERSION: As it turns out, both Michael and Randall have a genetic condition which causes mild mania. Michael is slowly becoming mad, like his brother. Michael is continuing his father's work for one reason only. Michael knows that his father was not merely doing research on artificial intelligence, but on developing a method of actually recording imprints of brain activity, which included personalities, memories, and so on. Collin was developing a way to transfer the consciousness from one body to another — he was developing a way of achieving immortality!

Angel-3 was a fluke, Michael knew, but that fluke led Collin into a whole new direction in his research. Unknown to even Master Control, Collin managed to download his notes to another computer system via a coded transmitter. Michael has located that system and, with Hardwire's help, has continued research on his father's design.

He has managed to isolate a number of the properties necessary to effect the transfer of one mind to another body, but the process is not fool proof. Michael is continuing his efforts in hopes of finding a way of one day bringing his parents back to life. Michael also fears that Master Control may soon learn of his plan and again interfere.

SCENARIO IDEA: Master Control has designed an android made to look and act exactly like Angel-3. The android is not self-aware, however, and contains a large explosive. Master Control intends to send the android over to his brother, Michael, and detonate the explosive.

An employee of Montgomery International learns of the plan and contacts the PCs, who then rush to intercept the android. The employee can be a DNPC or Contact of one of the PCs, or simply a conscientious employee. In the latter case they will probably turn up dead once they are exposed as the source of the leak.

The PCs track down the android and confront her. Michael is expecting her and is in his hero ID, as Crossbow, looking for her. The PCs and Crossbow will arrive at the same time. Crossbow will defend the android (who he believes to be the real Angel-3) from the PCs, and call for assistance from his teammates if things turn violent. Unless the PCs can convince Michael of the truth, the PCs may well find themselves caught in a battle against the Cyberknights.

HENDERSON ELECTRONICS

ABBREVIATION: HendElc

PRIMARY OPERATION: Electronics

PRIMARY COMPETITORS: Yoshida Corporation; Micro Device Technologies; Yamomoto Electronics; Lockley International; Gable Soft

WORTH: $9.2 Billion

HQ LOCATION: New York City, NY

HEAD: George Wagner, President

HUNTED/WATCHED: 10 Pts (Less Pow, Mildly punish, NCI, 11-) / 10 Pts (As Pow, NCI, 11-)

BACKGROUND/DESCRIPTION: Donald Henderson, scion of the wealthy Henderson family, had always harbored an interest in electronics. Ever since he was a small child, Donald was fascinated by electricity and the devices that used that used it. As he grew older, he began studying electricity in earnest, eventually graduated from college with a degree in electronics. A short time later Donald began his own electronics company. In order to raise enough capital to get the company going the way he had envisioned, Donald invited his family to invest in it; he sold shares of his company's stock to his family. The privately held company known as Henderson Electronics made its debut in 1972.

Henderson Electronics spread into many different areas of electronics research and design, from computer microchips to electric motors, as well as metal detectors, TVs and radios. They have also produced complete computer systems, including the infamous HVAC. The early models of the HVAC project were wrought with faulty programming, earning them the nickname "havoc."

The Henderson Board of Supervisors, under the urging of Donald, agreed to put Henderson Electronics on the New York Stock Exchange in 1983. Scarcely a week later, Henderson Electronics was awarded a government contract to produce the mainframe computers for Stronghold. The news of the government contract stimulated the sales of Henderson Electronics stock, and all of the public offerings were gobbled up in record time. The result sent the value of the stock sky high, nearly quadrupling in just one week. The Henderson family, who still maintained the vast majority of shares (70%), made millions of dollars during that week. Most of the new issue was bought up by Yamomoto Electronics, with the rest going to various private investors.

1987 brought Donald Henderson's retirement. Donald sold his shares of company stock for a substantially higher amount than he had originally purchased them for, and 30% of the total shares of Henderson stock went on the market. Yamomoto sprang and came away with 10% more stock and the remainder was spread among various private investors. The new owners, however, voting as a block, decided to re-organize the company; everyone was fired except key personnel. The only original executive that was retained was Roger Hinkley, the company's Chief Financial Officer (CFO) and Yamamoto's "mole." Even the computer programmers were fired, with the sole exception of Brent Watley (a programmer with superhuman intelligence and an affinity for numbers). George Wagner was finally selected as a compromise president and elected to the position by the Board of Directors.

Henderson Electronics is still very much the leader in electronics. To everyone's surprise, Wagner does a great job and financial statements have never been higher. 6 years after the big shakeup, morale is again high. Still on the cutting edge of technology, Henderson Electronics was recently contracted by CommuNET to produce their "Netbook." Henderson Electronics' is well known for hiring open paranormals (as opposed to secret paranormals) for their security department. The company also utilizes electric fences, electronic locks, armed guards and surveillance cameras. Since 1987, nearly 10% of Henderson's total annual budget has gone to security.

Even without the Henderson family in control, Henderson Electronics is still one of the best electronics firms to work for. Although the shareholders voted the Hendersons out, Yamamoto can get none of their people in controlling positions in the company. Yamamoto is becoming dissatisfied. They will either sell their stock or try to buy the rest of it (using VIPER for fear tactics if necessary.

Henderson Electronics is a major player in the computer hardware market, along with several other companies. Henderson's strength relies on its numerous contracts with various government and local agencies. Henderson's long-standing relationship with the Stronghold facility reflects this. In commercial hardware and software development, however, Henderson is but one player in a huge field. Henderson develops equipment primarily for business applications, for which they maintain a respectable share of the market. Henderson Electronics is currently working on advanced mainframe computer systems in the hopes of luring long-time customers to upgrade their existing systems to Henderson's newest models.

OPTIONAL VERSION: Henderson was secretly taken over by Viper. Yamamoto Electronics has ties to Viper (see VIPER, page 11) and the majority of the remaining stock was bought by VIPER investors. The biggest project Viper has planned for Henderson Electronics is the invasion of Stronghold. VIPER plans to issue new software to Stronghold, with "back doors" written into the software so that with the proper passwords they can take over the computer systems. This is a long-term goal. Until it is complete, VIPER will be content to sell computer equipment.

CAMPAIGN USE: Henderson Electronics is very useful to the inventor PC; they can be hired in their Secret ID to work for Henderson's R&D division. Henderson Electronics could offer to buy a PC's invention, or attempt to sue the hero if they possessed a device similar to one developed by the company.

Conversely, if the heroes need a special piece of equipment, Henderson Electronics would be happy to help out (as long as they get good publicity or a healthy fee, of course). If the heroes happen across an alien spaceship (and we all know how often that can happen), they might ask Henderson Electronics to examine any electronics or electrical components inside of it. Henderson would jump at the chance to see and examine an extraterrestrial computer design.

Jobs for DNPCs anyone? Henderson Electronics makes a great employer for a DNPC (or even a PC for that matter). Perhaps the DNPC will start to figure out some things that he or she shouldn't have. If the DNPC gets the hero involved, it would almost certainly lead to an adventure.

LOGO: A computer screen with the letters "H" and "E" superimposed on the front.

SCENARIO IDEA: Freddie "the fink" Furghetti contacts one of the PCs (preferably one who with Streetwise) and offers him some important, time-sensitive information for ten bucks. If the hero pays him, Freddie will tell the hero about a break-in at a nearby Henderson Electronics plant, which is scheduled to "go down" at 5 p.m. tonight. The criminals will be entering via a stolen DrayCo freight truck. Freddy doesn't know anything else and will refuse to reveal the source of his information (he secretly overheard two men discussing it at a restaurant).

As it turns out, the truck was scheduled to arrive at the Henderson Electronics plant at 5 p.m. to pick up a shipment of circuit boards. The driver, a DrayCo employee, is still in the back of the truck, tied and gagged). There are 30 bad guys dressed in urban camouflage fatigues (with a black, gray and white pattern), armed with FN-FAL rifles (treat the criminals as Competent Normals). Once they arrive, they will blow open the delivery bay door with explosive charges (no subtlety here, folks), then enter the building. They will disarm and bind the security guards that cooperate, killing any that resist.

The objective of the mission is to steal as much experimental software as possible in the shortest amount of time. The thieves will attempt to leave by stealing cars from the parking lot, 5 to a car, leaving the truck behind to implicate DrayCo in the theft.

The thieves are actually mercenaries hired by Yoshida Corp. to set Henderson's software program back a few months (just long enough to develop their own, comparable software using the stolen data).

HYPE PRESS, INC.

ABBREVIATION: HypePrs

PRIMARY OPERATION: Magazine publishing

PRIMARY COMPETITORS: Main Publishing; International Press

WORTH: $386,000

HQ LOCATION: San Carlos, CA

HEAD: James Boyden, President/CEO

HUNTED/WATCHED: 10 Pts (As Pow, Question, 11-) / 10 Pts (More Pow, 11-)

BACKGROUND/DESCRIPTION: Jim had always been fascinated by daredevils and risk-takers: stuntmen, cops, barnstormer pilots, Navy SEALs — anyone who risked life and limb in the course of their job — earned Jim's respect and admiration. Jim graduated from high school and went straight into college. Well into his first semester, Jim got the idea to publish his own newsletter; one dedicated to the very people he so much admired. Working out of a spare bedroom in his parents' house, Jim put out the first issue of his new publication, called Danger International. The newsletter was a mild success on campus, and picked up a few dozen subscribers from classified ads in adventure magazines.

After two years of publishing D.I., however, James had learned quite a bit about the publishing business. He decided that he would try publishing a full fledged magazine, complete with glossy pages, a color cover — the works. He didn't feel that his topic of choice would support the magazine, however. If people wouldn't spend a few dollars for his newsletter, why would they spend five times as much for a magazine about daredevils?

One day they came, in all shapes and sizes, with varying abilities and powers. The paranormal and metahuman superheroes captured the hearts and imaginations of the entire country. Whether they loved them or hated them, almost everyone was talking about them. Supers began appearing in the news, then on talk shows. NBS had even begun dedicating a nightly segment to the happenings of various superheroes. James was among the fans, scanning up and down the list of cable channels, watching news footage of his favorite costumed vigilantes. Then it hit him. Why not produce a magazine about superheroes? It was a natural progression, James thought.

James took out a personal loan to finance the project and within two months he published the first issue of SuperHype magazine, complete with a full color cover. The magazine was an instant hit with superhero fans of all ages. While James could scarcely afford advertising, word of the publication spread by word of mouth. What began with 1,000 copies, created in James' bedroom, soon became a national sensation. Years later, SuperHype now boasts a circulation of over 200,000. It is available in a few stores, but the majority of the magazine's sales are from direct subscriptions. James has also incorporated the publishing company and hired a small staff to help him put out the magazine.

SuperHype is totally dedicated to stories about superheroes. No detail is too small, no fact too trivial, as long as it concerns one of America's beloved superheroes. James will publish articles about vigilantes, but these are generally expose-type stories or editorial commentaries about the subject's tactics or methods of crime-fighting (James respects what vigilantes are trying to do, but he feels they are going about it the wrong way).

Some typical topics covered in the magazine include superhero romances (which superhero is dating which superheroine), fights between superheroes and supervillains and the latest in paranormal legislation. While SuperHype takes a relatively neutral stand on paranormal legal issues, the magazine will cover in earnest efforts to pass any kind of legislation concerning supers. The magazine also has a letters section, listings of superheroes across the country who maintain Public IDs (with each hero's home address, telephone number and vital statistics, like birth date, favorite color, etc.). Much to James' chagrin, SuperHype has become known as the "National Inquisitor" of the superhero world. While a few stories are embellished, James will not publish any story without at least one credible source. Of course, a source can be anonymous and still be credible, can't they?

The staff of SuperHype consists of James, who also doubles as Editor-in-Chief, Karen Symke, who does layouts and typesetting, and Alex Brown, the Art Director. James also employs two full-time field reporters, Terry Wahler and Bob Goedrich. (the GM should feel free to replace these two with his own NPCs.) The magazine also prints a large number of articles from freelance writers. Hype Press pays an average of $250 for each article that is printed, and pays as much as $1,000 for breaking stories.

Not many companies publish periodicals dedicated to superhero (or supervillain) fans, but there are a few. Main Publishing (a subsidiary of Main Communications) is responsible for Hero Talk, having recently bought out that publication, and International Press has incorporated a superhero column in its weekly tabloid. Neither publication boasts the following of SuperHype, however, who's near cult-like following continues to astound professional publishers (especially those who declined James' investment offers some time back).

CAMPAIGN USE: Any PC with a Public ID runs the risk of picking up Hype Press as a Hunted, although they will only be hunting the PC to ask numerous personal questions. While this may actually lead to a physical altercation (especially if the PC is short tempered), the journalist will not be seeking a fight. SuperHype reporters tend to be rather persistent, although they are not suicidal, and show up in some of the strangest places (in restrooms, the back seats of heroes' cars, in restaurants dressed as waiters, and so on. (This is the GM's opportunity to have some real fun at the PC's expense; time to make the PC earn those Public ID points!).

Characters with a background in journalism may also work for Hype Press, either as a field reporter or indirectly as a freelance writer. Both options allow the character to be aware of details involving the topic of their assigned story (which may actually be the PC's alter ego), and gives them the perfect excuse for showing up at every encounter.

Hype Press reporters tend to push the First Amendment issue a bit far, and rely on journalistic freedoms extensively to get into situations and areas they really have no business being in. In short, they can be quite obnoxious.

SLOGAN: "Pure Hype!"

OPTIONAL VERSION: As a youth, James once was playing on a bridge and slipped, barely managing to cling to the edge. He spotted a passing superhero and yelled for help. To James' shock, the hero kept flying and never came to his aid. James is convinced that the hero heard James yelling and simply refused to help.

Years later, James Boyden still clings to that bitter memory. James secretly hates all superheroes because of that incident. As a result, James has dedicated his energies to revealing superheroes as the frauds they really are. He sends his reporters out to cover stories that are likely to cause damage to a hero's reputation or private life. Heroes with a Public IDs are easy prey, and James delights in publishing stories detailing the very personal aspects of the heroes' lives.

Note: The GM may use one of the PCs in the group as the object of James' hatred. That hero will be the subject of regular articles which are damaging to his reputation or otherwise interferes in his life in some way. Some suggestions include publishing a story about the PCs alleged romance with a supervillain, a brush with the law, the PC's flagrant use of profanity around young children, and so on. All of these articles may be real of made up, but James will print them just the same.

The GM may allow the PC to take Hype Press as a Hunted at the start of the campaign, although it can be much more fun letting the hero discover their Hunted over the course of several adventures.

SCENARIO IDEA: James Boyden and one of the PCs (one with a Secret ID) are contacted by an anonymous caller. The caller tells the PC that he knows his Secret ID and he wants $50,000 in order to keep quiet, otherwise the caller says he will go to the media with the information. The caller really does know the hero's Secret ID, having obtained it with some crafty detective work and Deduction. The hero, fearing putting his loved ones at risk, should somehow agree to meet with this person. The caller will meet the PC in a public park and will ask the hero to come in his Secret ID, so as not to attract unnecessary attention.

If the hero refuses to comply with the caller's demand for money, he will then contact James Boyden and reveal the hero's Secret ID, which James will be all too happy to print. If the hero complies with the caller's request, he will contact Boyden anyway and arrange for field reporters to be in the park, with cameras equipped with telephoto lenses. The PC will be photographed during his "liaison," and any visible display of powers will be recorded and subsequently published in SuperHype magazine.

The anonymous caller turns out to be a man in his mid-twenties, paralyzed from the waist down and bound to a wheelchair. He was struck by a stray blast during a recent battle between supervillains and the PC's group (the GM can fill in the details here). This is the man's revenge.

IRONBRIDGE INDUSTRIES, PLC

ABBREVIATION: Irnbrdg

PRIMARY OPERATION: Electrical engineering

PRIMARY COMPETITORS: LKT; Montgomery International

WORTH: 87 Million

HQ LOCATION: Midlands, U.K.

HEAD: Herbert Marston, President/CEO

HUNTED/WATCHED: 20 Pts (As Pow, NCI, 11-)/ 10 Pts (As Pow, NCI, 11-)

BACKGROUND/DESCRIPTION: Herbert Marston was born to relatively poor parents in 1937. It was the tail end of the great depression and its effects were felt as far away as England. From an early age, Herbert combined intense ambition with a talent for management. After a limited, technically-oriented education and brief military service with the RAF, he worked his way up to management level in industry by the time he was 30. Shortly thereafter, with funds he managed to squirrel away for years, Herbert Marston started his own company, Ironbridge Industries Ltd.

Over the next ten years, Marston built his company into a significant power in the engineering business from virtually nothing. Ironbridge became a well-known British company, earning numerous contracts with construction and manufacturing firms throughout the United Kingdom. Eventually, he filed the appropriate papers with the British Commerce departments and turned Ironbridge into a Public Limited Company (PLC). Marston kept his company off of the public stock exchanges, however, preferring to maintain control over the direction of his company.

Ironbridge weathered the recession of the late '70s, primarily through restructuring the company. Ironbridge branched out into several new areas, including microelectronics research, bio-electrical integration, cybernetics, hydroelectric power production and good old fashioned electronics manufacturing (radios, televisions and calculators).

Each area is run by a different subsidiary of Ironbridge Industries. In fact, because Ironbridge is so diversified now and because most of the companies remain privately held (i.e., off of the stock market), very few people realize just how varied Marten's empire truly is. Ironbridge is huge, but it is influential; Marston has utilized Ironbridge funds to good ends, such as supporting various British Conservative Party campaigns and even allocating funds to Britain's elite Special Tactics Operational Personnel (STOP). Despite his political contributions, however, Marston quietly holds politicians in deep contempt.

Ironbridge continues to hold a strong share of the electronics market in Britain, and it has contracts with both the BBC and British Rail to supply electronics components. The strength of Ironbridge Industries comes from its sales to overseas firms, however, especially those in the Middle East such as Saudi Arabia, Kuwait, Bahrain and Awad. All of the Middle Eastern countries employ large numbers of western construction firms in the development of their cities and industries.

Herbert Marston is a well-respected businessman in Europe. He has many friends and contacts within the economic community and in certain political circles as well. There are rumors that he may also have connections with a European action of VIPER. It cannot be denied that Marston is an influential man. Marten's influence and power go much deeper than Ironbridge Industries, however.

In his quest for "real" power, Herbert Marston has created a cellular organization he called Project: Armor. The organization consists of various project cells, each with its own specific duties. These cells include: the Special Munitions and Investigation Technical Hierarchy (SMITH), tasked with developing operational standards for the other cells; the Cellular Unified Intrusion Recovery and Assault Special Squads (CUIRASS), which operated in the field with trained agents; and the Major Actions Cadre and Executive (MACE), the supervillain arm of the organization. (Note: see *Kingdom of Champions* for additional information concerning Project: Armor and MACE)

Marston continues to secretly use Ironbridge resources to support Project: Armor, and likewise uses Project: Armor to advance his company. The arrangement has proven very profitable for Marston, but he still craves true power over people; he is dissatisfied with the shallow power that wealth brings.

Ironbridge Industries has flourished, putting it on par with other major electronics manufacturing and electrical engineering companies of the world. Chief among its competitors are LKT and Montgomery International. MI has recently begun and advertising campaign against Ironbridge Industries in an attempt to rest control of the company's meager European market share. This action is as much a game to Randall Montgomery as it is a precursor to further hostile actions.

CAMPAIGN USE: Ironbridge Industries PLC is a privately held company run by a megalomaniac. While Marston himself is not very dangerous, per se, he has vast resources at his disposal (not the least of which is his personal villain team, MACE).

Ironbridge Industries has seen much of its growth as a result of diversification. It is possible that Marston may wish to acquire additional companies, perhaps in the United States, as a way of branching out his "organization" even further; it would be quite convenient to have an American company from which to launch attacks against his colonial adversaries.

SLOGAN: "Building a bridge to advanced electronics."

OPTIONAL VERSION: Marston has become increasingly twisted in his perceptions of the world around him, so much so that control of the company is now in the hands of Tina Robertson, Senior Engineer at Ironbridge Industries (also the villainess Battleaxe). After years of coaxing Herbert Marston and feeding his ego, Tina has worked herself into a position of power within the company. She has even managed to acquire a broad power of attorney from Marston so that she may make administrative decisions in his place. Eventually she plans to get rid of Marston once and for all, but she has not decided when that time will be.

For the time being, Battleaxe is running Ironbridge Industries as Marston would so as not to raise too much suspicion. None of her teammates know about this switch of power yet. Tina wants to keep them ignorant for as long as possible, figuring that unrest in MACE would be its greatest threat at this point.

SCENARIO IDEA: Ironbridge Industries PLC has finally made its move against an American company — Powertronics, a small electronics engineering firm located in California. The company has filed a bid for the company with the SEC. The offer is sitting well with the shareholders and a hostile takeover seems imminent. Doing some quick research on Ironbridge, Powertronics Board of Directors discovers a link between Ironbridge Industries and the villain team MACE. The board decides that the best way to stave off the takeover is to bring the facts to the shareholders and let them vote on the issue. The board members are confident that the shareholders won't sell out to a company with ties to a paranormal terrorist group, and they are confident that this information will cause the SEC to delay the takeover pending an investigation. Such a delay and subsequent investigation should be enough to get Ironbridge to drop its takeover attempt.

The board, however, fears for their safety at the upcoming board meeting and has asked the heroes to attend. The heroes may either be in costume or plain clothes, and they may position themselves wherever they think is appropriate: on the stage with the board members (this is the board's preference), in the audience among the shareholders, or anywhere else they decide upon.

A short time into the meeting, MACE will make its move. Several members will try to cause a distraction (probably Charmer and Grenadier), while the others attempt to kidnap the President of Powertronics. The heroes were expected and MACE should be played accordingly. If MACE cannot achieve their objective of kidnapping the President, they will try to capture any one of the board members and then flee.

LKT

PRIMARY OPERATION: Electronic and mechanical engineering

PRIMARY COMPETITORS: Montgomery International; McNeil Aviation; Thermodynamics, Inc.; Outflight Systems

WORTH: $386 Million (equivalent)

HQ LOCATION: Toronto, Canada

HEAD: Maximillian Lanier, Walther Keuler and Annabella Torrelli; Presidents

HUNTED/WATCHED: 10 Pts (Less Pow, NCI, Mildly, 11-) / 10 Pts (As Pow, NCI, 11-)

BACKGROUND/DESCRIPTION: There was an incredible amount of technological expansion and growth in the international markets during the '70s. Three firms in particular prospered immensely: Lanier Robotics, an electronics and robotics firm in Canada; WKT, a German avionics and flight systems production company; and Torelli Motors, an automotive engine and transmission production company. The three companies continued to grow through the '70s and into the even more prosperous '80s. Each of the three companies began expanding their production and involvement into other areas. Soon the three corporations were competing almost toe to toe across the board in several world markets. WKT began developing and manufacturing automobile drive trains, Torelli Motors manufactured robotic motivators and servos, and Lanier Robotics produced aircraft landing gear systems.

Then European attitudes began to change; there was talk of forging a common market, even of creating a common currency. The three former competitors and industry rivals sat down together and talked business. The Presidents of all three companies sat together in a conference room in a London hotel and began negotiating a truce; an alliance. No, it was much more. They were discussing a merger. With the three companies merging into one international conglomerate, they could bring their remaining competitors to their knees and dominate their markets on an international level. Only the few American firms, protected and yet restrained by their own ridiculous Antitrust Laws, would pose any serious competition for the international giant.

After three straight weeks of negotiations an agreement was reached. In a move unprecedented in the business community, three corporate Presidents, representing their respective agreeable Boards of Directors, signed into a contract to merge their companies. Maximillian Lanier (Lanier Robotics), Walther Kueler (WKT) and Annabella Torelli (Torelli Motors) became the first ever, corporate joint Presidents, with equal status and power to be shared by all three. The new company was named, quite simply and to avoid argument, LKT, after the "founders."

Arrangements were made to replace all existing shares of stock in their old companies with equivalent values of stock in the new corporation. The personnel and staff levels of the new company were streamlined; thousands were laid off, and many more faced pay cuts, initially. Once LKT was through its restructuring and all of the company's books were brought up to speed, however, most employees' salaries were brought back up (evening the pay scales for the employees of all three countries) and many of those who had been laid off were rehired.

LKT now dominates the international scene when it comes to technical design, engineering and production. The company specializes in electronic and mechanical drive and motivator design and manufacturing. Their work covers everything from aircraft and ground craft drive trains to robotic arms and artificial musculatures for prosthetics, as well as "lift-loaders." The company has done designing of more exotic equipment as well, such as exo-skeletons and deep pressure suits, both designed for commercial, non-military uses.

The company maintains three separate and equal Presidents, as well as three separate Boards of Directors who all have equal weight. The three Boards have come to be known in the European business community as the Triad. For matters requiring a combined decision, the three boards meet twice a year, each time at a different member's national headquarters. Each board member receives a vote at these meetings. General Board meetings are held by the individual national Board of Directors monthly.

LKT has a broad base of production, covering everything from aircraft parts to car engines. Because of this LKT has numerous competitors. While LKT does not dominate any one field of production individually, its diversity assures its success as a company. As long as LKT can remain competitive in each of its production areas, the company will continue to see profits and remain a viable force in the mechanical engineering arena.

CAMPAIGN USE: LKT is a huge international conglomerate. The company is responsible for developing a large number of components for civilian and military vehicles, including aircraft, hovercraft and various ground vehicles. The company has offices in major cities in a number of countries including the United States, England, Switzerland, Austria, France, Brazil and a new corporate office in Russia.

Any hero or hero team which utilizes robotic equipment or an exotic vehicle is an excellent candidate for LKT products. The company is recognized as a leader in its specialty fields, and a number of domestic companies which produce vehicles or robots purchase some of the smaller component parts from LKT.

SLOGAN: "Three times the experience — three times the quality."

OPTIONAL VERSION: The three Presidents are, in fact, clones of the originals developed by a madman named Dr. Schrumm. Schrumm grew the clones and implanted restructured memories in the aims of controlling the three companies. His plan has worked, thus far. No one knows the truth behind the strange and unexpected merger.

Dr. Schrumm uses the vast resources of the three companies to further his own megalomaniacal plans, which include the complete destruction of the PCs and every other goody-two-shoes hero (of course). His long-term plans include the complete subjugation of the nations of the world, but he is content to subjugate the U.S. first.

Schrumm often utilizes LKT equipment to carry out his plans. He usually hires citizens of the country in which an operation is conducted, and occasionally uses foreign mercenaries. Schrumm himself is a genius, but he is quite deranged. He suffers from asthma and is bound to a wheelchair due to a disease he contracted as a boy. (Treat Dr. Schrumm as a Skilled Normal with 50 pts of Science skills and a 50 pt Gadget Pool, changeable only in a lab.)

SCENARIO IDEA: Robots at several production and assembly plants in the area have begun malfunctioning. They are assembling items backwards, throwing parts across the room, and attacking employees and technicians. The problem is narrowed down to a part manufactured by LKT. The company denies any negligence or wrongdoing and agrees to cooperate in any investigation. The heroes are invited out to the LKT manufacturing plant in a nearby U.S. city, where they find everything in order. The only clue is that the robots at each of the plants was recently refitted with these new parts from LKT. The PCs will be asked to ride along with the next shipment.

The recent shipments of LKT robotic parts are being hijacked by the Corporate Raiders and replaced with substandard parts, thus leading to the malfunctions. The Corporate Raiders have been hired by a rival company to hijack and replace three shipments. The Raiders have one shipment left to go. Their routine is to stop the truck with a diversion, hit the driver with a stasis field, and replace the parts using Pulse's teleport ability.

LOCKLEY INTERNATIONAL

ABBREVIATION: Lockley

PRIMARY OPERATION: Multinational conglomerate

PRIMARY COMPETITORS: Yoshida Corporation; Montgomery International; LKT

WORTH: $119 Billion

HQ LOCATION: White Plains, N.Y.

HEAD: Jacob "Jake" Lockley, President

HUNTED/WATCHED: 20 Pts (As Pow, NCI, 11-) / 10 Pts (More Pow, 11-)

BACKGROUND/DESCRIPTION: "What do you mean you don't know where he is? He's got the Maynowitz account! Find him. Find him and then fire him! I don't need this kind of aggravation, this kind of incompetence, in my life. What's that? Too harsh on him? Who asked you? You're fired!"

"Jake" Lockley has always hated his given name, though he refuses to change it (for reasons known only to him). To Jake, business was more than a way to make money — it was his life. He worked his way through community college and eventually went on to a university on a scholarship, where he graduated with a degree in business administration. Jake shifted from one executive position to another, but he was constantly passed over for promotion for one reason or another. Jake claims prejudice (why else wouldn't they promote someone as bright as himself?), although the real reason was Jake's attitude; he had a poor one and it showed.

Eventually he became fed up with the way other people mismanaged their companies and Lockley began planning his own company. With an expert business plan and the backing of some very wealthy and influential persons, Jake took the position of company President of a successful engineering firm — Lockley Enterprises. His cutthroat business tactics and somewhat cold personality (the same traits which kept him from being promoted) have given him a reputation as the Scrooge of the corporate world. Lockley is also extremely intelligent, however, having a "sixth sense" of sorts when it comes to business dealings (this is not an actual power, but rather a reflection of his business skills).

Lockley Ent. has grown steadily since its founding in 1974. The bulk of its growth came from numerous civilian vehicle parts production and engineering design contracts and government defense contracts. Lockley Ent. also earned a substantial income from its sales of machine parts to other companies such as TDI and McNeil Aviation in the U.S. and Ironbridge Industries of England. The name of the company was changed to Lockley International when the company acquired a number of small to mid-sized foreign corporations. Some of the foreign companies now owned by Lockley Int. include Nohei Beverage Corporation of Japan, Gîeret Engines Ltd. of Germany and Wingo's of Australia.

Lockley International's holdings run the gamut of production categories, including engine and power plant production, publishing, mechanical and structural engineering, oil drilling and refining, construction and real estate, professional sports franchises, mining and ship construction. In short, Lockley Int. owns a little bit of every major commercial market. Unfortunately, this also means that both Lockley and his company are closely monitored by the SEC.

Lockley International, including all of its many subsidiaries, currently has an annual income exceeding the gross national product of many industrialized nations. Jake Lockley himself has managed to hang on to a substantial portion of the company's stock (he owns 28%), making him the company's largest single shareholder. His control over the company (i.e., over the Board of Directors) is not absolute, but he has yet to have a single decision of his overruled by the Board. It has also been rumored that Jake Lockley is, in fact, also the armored superhero, Powerlocke. Jake has emphatically denied any such allegations, he does openly support the hero, as well as many others whose goals are to fight crime and rid the world of "human predators."

Jake Lockley is an old salt in the business world, even though he is a few years shy of his 40th birthday. He is well known in public circles and attends many high society functions. He is single and has never married, nor does he have any children (which he calls a "little liabilities"). Jake Lockley has a very dry sense of humor and thinks business almost 24 hours a day. He schedules meetings of all kinds through his office. With what little spare time he has, Jake can often be found at either the racquetball court or the upper-class nightclubs having a martini.

Lockley is one of the "big five," with total sales in the billions annually. Only the largest companies can compete on a scale close to, or exceeding, Lockley International. Corporate espionage is commonplace, and Lockley has instituted increased internal security measures as a deterrent. This

has slowed the competition, but has not stopped them. Lockley denies allegations of counter-espionage on the part of his corporation, but the truth is that Lockley is too stubborn to sit back and suffer hits from his rivals without inflicting a few of his own. This is exactly what Yoshida and Montgomery expect, and so the corporate war continues....

CAMPAIGN USE: Lockley International is the company with its hands in everything. Its holdings include numerous other corporations, including foreign companies in nearly every major industrial country in the free world. The President, Jake Lockley, is a man obsessed with business and with making money. He cares little about the feelings or desires of others, unless it will help him better his company's (or his own) position. Once, Lockley even applied for membership for his company into the European Community (a joke whose humor was lost on the chairman of the EC).

Lockley can be a complete jerk, but he is not without his good points... well, good point. While he cares most about making money, Jake Lockley acknowledges the important role that superheroes play in the world and he is always willing to help a known superhero (or hero team) in order to make the world a little safer for everyone — especially for Lockley International.

SLOGAN: "Doing it right."

OPTIONAL VERSION: Jake Lockley is not only a miser and cutthroat businessman, he is power hungry as well. Several foes oppose him in his quest for power, however, including several VIPER nests. They know of Lockley's association with the hero Blastaar and they do not want Lockley in the Oval Office!

Lockley will use the PCs to further his own goals, even if it means sacrificing them so that he may continue in his mad bid for national, and ultimately world, domination. Eventually, however, the PCs will begin to see Lockley for his true intentions, at which time he will enlist the services of a mercenary supervillain team to engage the heroes while Lockley escapes out of the country.

SCENARIO IDEA: The local VIPER nests have declared war on Lockley and his company in order to help "persuade" Powerlocke to call off his campaign against VIPER. Lockley enlists the aid of the PCs to help counter any VIPER attacks.

NOTE: It is up to the GM to decide if Lockley is, indeed, the hero Powerlocke. Alternatively, the GM can substitute one of the PCs in place of Powerlocke, giving the PC an instant connection with Lockley International.

MCNEIL AVIATION

ABBREVIATION: McNlAv

PRIMARY OPERATION: Aeronautic engineering and manufacturing

PRIMARY COMPETITORS: Drummond Engineering; Pegasus inc.; Outflight Systems

WORTH: $8 Billion

HQ LOCATION: New York City, NY

HEAD: Laura McNeil

HUNTED/WATCHED: 10 Pts (Less Pow, Mildly, NCI, 11-) / 10 Pts (As Pow, NCI, 11-)

BACKGROUND/DESCRIPTION: Ian McNeil felt good! He was on a tramp steamer, bound for America. WWII was over, and an ex-RAF fighter pilot was on his way to the land of opportunity. He had a Ph.D. in Engineering, a love of flying and determination. However, in 1949, that was all it took. Ian started a company that took chances. In a conservative business environment, he was the risk-taker. Things didn't always work out, but enough did to keep the business afloat. As the years went on, lots of changes took place in Ian's life. He got married, had a son, his business flourished and, ultimately, he retired. John McNeil, Ian's son, took over the family business in 1975, and continued the risk-taking environment. It paid off! In 1980, McNeil Aviation went public (with the McNeil family retaining 75% of the shares).

Things were looking good, McNeil even landed a lucrative UNTIL contract to build a flying suit (Project: Screech). Then disaster struck. Lisa Avalon, a junior engineer on the project, found out that some unscrupulous managers in McNeil had made a deal with the Medellin drug cartel. The winged armor was slated to be used to tip the balance of power in the war on drugs. Lisa went to the police, but they wouldn't believe her. Only one person took Lisa's accusations seriously — her supervisor (and John McNeil's daughter) Laura. The Medellin cartel would kill to get the armor, and had the resources to do it. So, in a fit of desperation, Lisa and Laura started a fire in the lab, destroying the prototype, and all the plans. McNeil stock plummeted. In 1989, Laura McNeil took over the company, because of her father's stress-related illnesses and failing health. Since that time, Laura has rebuilt McNeil. Even Project: Screech was completed, although nine years after it's inception. McNeil has just completed its new contract with the military to produce inexpensive one-man combat helicopters (called the "Mosquito Hawk").

Laura McNeil is a bit overbearing. She really wants McNeil Aviation to excel, under her care. Laura is trying to prove herself, to her father and grandfather. She has fired all of the crooked managers, that had ties to the crime cartel, and is still in the process of rebuilding McNeil. The somewhat delayed completion of Project: Screech, however, has helped put McNeil on its feet.

For stats for the UNTIL Screech agents, use the stats for Competent Normals (***CHAMPIONS***, pg. 134), add Bluejay's powers, with the following modifications: switch +12 PD/ +12 ED Armor for the listed PD and ED, and reduce the Multipower to 40 active points and 8 Charges on each slot.

McNeil has ridden the coat tails of their reputation for about as long as they can. Sales are beginning to decline, and Laura McNeil is beginning to get worried. Against aviation industry giants like Drummond Engineering (developers of several military aircraft) and Outflight Systems (manufacturer of commercial jet engines), McNeil is going to have to change its strategies soon or fail. Laura has been hesitant to institute any significant change, and the subject has not yet been broached at the Board meetings, but she knows well that times are changing. McNeil is going to have to change to survive.

CAMPAIGN USE: McNeil can be used in a variety of ways. If a PC flies, it might be that McNeil wants to examine them to see if their mode of locomotion can be replicated. If a hero uses a focus for flight, then McNeil might have made it or want it. PCs can be watched or hunted by McNeil (Especially

nasty if McNeil has screech agents at their disposal). A contact or favor with McNeil Aviation or Laura McNeil can be just the thing needed, when trying to gain information on that UFO you've just captured.

For good PR's sake, McNeil might sponsor a hero team or create a hero team. A brand new superhero, might want to buy a plane, helicopter or jet pack. McNeil is just the company to go to for cheap rates, especially if your superhero identity endorses their product. If the optional version is being used, then Laura McNeil makes an ideal hunted. Imagine the hero, alone. He hears a low hum and looks around, just in time to see a lone assailant strafing him on a one-man helicopter!

SLOGAN: "Conquering the skies"

OPTIONAL VERSION: Laura McNeil is power-hungry. She wants to make McNeil the most powerful corporation on the planet, with herself as its Queen! She has been buying out her father and grandfather, so that soon she will be sole ruler of McNeil. McNeil has a cadre of it's own screech agents, to deal with spies and to do clandestine raids. Also, Bluejay (***Champions***, pg. C20) is occasionally in Laura's employ.

SCENARIO IDEA: The Medellin Cartel has had a grudge against McNeil Aviation, since 1980. They now feel the time is ripe to get revenge (and the plans to the reconstructed Screech armor). PCs can get involved by walking past McNeil as the crime takes place. The PCs can get a call from the police, McNeil, or a DNPC working late at McNeil, or a player character might work for McNeil.

Another avenue for adventure, is to have the heroes contacted by "the mysterious Mr. Crime." The newest crime czar in the city, Mr. Crime gives tips on other criminals' activities. This could lead to an ongoing campaign to learn the identity of Mr. Crime (he is in fact the deputy DA Harvey Noble). The bad guys are Competent normals (***Champions***, p. 134) with AK-47s. There should be two agents per hero and one additional agent for each McNeil security guard present. (Note: if you have not run the scenario Mob Rules from ***Champions***, this can be a great intro adventure.)

MONTGOMERY INTERNATIONAL

ABBREVIATION: Montgy

PRIMARY OPERATION: Megaconglomerate

PRIMARY COMPETITORS: Lockley International; LKT; Ergon Oil & Power

WORTH: $460 Billion (estimated)

MAIN HQ: London, England

HEAD: Randall Montgomery, President

HUNTED/WATCHED: 25 Pts (Mo Pow, NCI, 11-) / 13 Pts (Mo Pow, NCI, 11-)

BACKGROUND/DESCRIPTION: Randall Montgomery learned to hate his father. When he was young it was because he never really had a chance to know him. Dr. Collin Montgomery was always either running about as the American hero Stellar Paladin or buried in his scientific research. Later, Randall grew to hate his father. Randall blamed his reckless "hero" attitude for his mother's death, who died at the hands of a vengeful Mechassassin. Randall could stand no more and ran away from home. He had left his family for the shores of his native homeland, England, determined to rebuild his life. They were fools.

In the years that he was in hiding Randall had amassed a small fortune in both cash and criminal contacts, gained through odd jobs and minor crimes. He used his newfound resources to buy out a small research company located in London. The company quickly expanded as patents and breakthrough engineering designs earned Randall both fame and fortune. Still, he would not accept calls from his father, who was eager to renew their relationship. They were fools.

In a few short years, Randall's company had grown remarkably, encompassing dozens of companies throughout the world. Randall had learned quickly the value of cold, calculated planning. His cut-throat business practices and amazing business sense earned him a reputation as a formidable force in the corporate sector. Randall was also known and highly respected for his knowledge and accomplishments, however, particularly in the fields of scientific research and electronic and cybernetic engineering.

Montgomery International has become an international conglomerate in every sense of the word. Its holdings stretch to every corner of the globe. Indeed, no one person knows the exact makeup of its holdings. Subsidiaries own subsidiaries, which control stock in other firms... There is no industry that is untouched by the influence of Montgomery International; Randall has seen to that. Entire national economies respond to shifts and changes within the corporations. Montgomery International is the epitome of megacorp.

Randall runs Montgomery with an iron hand. His business and management tactics have earned him the respect of his subordinates. In actuality, they fear him. Randall is ruthless to the point of being almost sociopathic; he does not tolerate failure well, and he rules MI more like a feudal nation than a corporation. MI is the harbinger of the all-powerful corporations predicted for the future, the kinds of companies that people become enmeshed in such that they can never leave. Randall also leads a double life, as the master supervillain known as Master Control (see *High Tech Enemies*). Originally intended as a way of instilling fear in his competitors, Randall has parlayed his activities as Master Control, as well as those of his subordinates, into effective intelligence and espionage efforts to further his company's success. Though he rarely engages in face-to-face confrontations with other paranormals, he is one of the most formidable psionicists on the planet, and his battlesuit gives him extraordinary power in confrontations. However, Randall much prefers to simply pull the strings and let others do his dirty work for him. Only his three personal bodyguards, the S.T.R.I.K.E. Units, know that Randall Montgomery is actually Master Control. Every one else believes the cover story, that Master Control secretly works for Randall.

As Master Control, Randall uses information garnered in his business dealings to good effect. He manages to keep his two lives separate, however, making appearances as the powerful corporate President without referencing his activities as Master Control. He denies all connections with Master Control and his agents, and in fact Randall has staged some raids against his own holdings to maintain the public perception that he is just another victim of the powerful crime lord's activities.

CAMPAIGN USE: Montgomery International is one of the largest conglomerates in the world. While not the richest corporation in existence, it is surely among the top ten and its diversity makes up for what little it lacks in capital resources. Montgomery is the classic megacorp, lending itself well to any modern or dark future campaign, such as *Dark Champions* or *Cyber Hero*. With its innumerable subsidiaries, a character is likely to work for a company owned by Montgomery and not even realize it.

While Master Control and Randall Montgomery are one and the same, no one knows this but his closest loyal followers. It is widely known in criminal and business circles that Master Control actually works for Randall Montgomery, although no one can prove that either. Randall relies on the belief that he and Master Control are allied to intimidate many of his associates in crime and business, between which the line is often blurred.

Montgomery International has grown to such an immense size that they have competitors in nearly every major area of production. Its largest rivals, however, remain steadfast in their pursuit of global economic superiority. Lockley International is MI's primary competitor, having bought out numerous small companies in its road to becoming a conglomerate, but LKT and Ergon Oil & Power are still corporations causing real concern to MI's Board of Directors. Their persistence in overseas markets is an obstacle that MI has yet to find a legal solution for. Randall Montgomery is beginning to look at other alternatives, however....

SLOGAN: "Controlling the future."

OPTIONAL VERSION: Randall Montgomery is beginning to fall apart. His intense hatred for his father is a front, designed to cover up his guilt over not staying to protect his mother from Mechassassin like his brother, Michael had, and the guilt he feels for causing his father's death. Randall wants desperately to reach out his brother, Michael, but has embroiled himself so deeply into the world he has created as Master Control that he cannot escape it. He becomes enraged when facing defeat not because he desires to win, but because he is afraid of being exposed as a complete and utter failure. Randall Montgomery is a living tragedy.

SCENARIO IDEA: Montgomery International has become the subject of an expose by Inside Affair, a documentary-style television news program on NBS. The program has alleged a connection between Randall Montgomery and Master Control deeper than anyone suspects (namely that Randall and Master Control are one and the same). Randall is in a quandary. he doesn't want the program to go unpunished, and yet direct intervention could substantiate its claims.

Randall Montgomery schedules an interview with a reporter from Inside Affair, which the PCs will learn of (either through a DNPC who works at the studio or via an NBS press release). While being interviewed, Randall and the reporter will be attacked by a large number of Black Guard agents as well as an android wearing armor made to look exactly like Master Control's. Randall will stay in the area just long enough to be photographed with the decoy Master Control, then he will flee.

The PCs will undoubtedly intervene to save the reporter (and perhaps Randall). If the PCs capture the decoy, the network will broadcast an Inside Affair exclusive revealing Master Control to be, in reality, an artificially intelligent android. If the decoy escapes, then the program states that Master Control's true identity cannot possibly be Randall Montgomery and remains a mystery. Either way, Randall will make good his escape, satisfied that his Secret Identity is safe.

For the decoy's stats, use the write-up for Master Control, but divide the Multipower and all associated slots in half (thus making it a 45 pt. Multipower with a 4 ½ d6 Ego Blast, 9d6 Mind Control, and so on).

EDITOR'S NOTE: The description of Randall Montgomery is revised somewhat from that presented in *High Tech Enemies*. The CHAMPIONS Universe is undergoing some continuity changes that will be detailed in a later product, and this revision is a reflection of those changes.

PARAGON EMS, INC.

ABBREVIATION: Pargn

PRIMARY OPERATION: Paramedic services

PRIMARY COMPETITORS: LifeTech, Inc.; Superior Ambulance Company; Gold Cross EMS

WORTH: $12 Million

HQ LOCATION: New York, NY

HEAD: Calvin Roberson, President/CEO

HUNTED/WATCHED: — / 3 Pts (Less Pow, Lim, 11-)

BACKGROUND/DESCRIPTION: Calvin was like most other teenagers in some regards; he was rambunctious, energetic and felt invulnerable. Unlike most kids his age, however, Calvin had a strong love of science and biology. Although unsure about what profession he wanted to pursue, he was sure it would have something to do with science.

One fateful afternoon, while walking home from school, Calvin was nearly struck by a speeding truck. He had been walking with his headphones on (a practice his mother was constantly nagging him about) and hadn't heard the truck roaring up behind him. A local superhero happened by moments before the truck would have hit poor Calvin. With just seconds to spare, the hero managed to divert the truck from hitting Calvin, but causing it to hit a wall.

After determining that the driver was not seriously injured, the hero lectured Calvin about the dangers of wearing headphones on or near a busy roadway. Calvin felt horrible and asked what, if anything, he could do to repay the hero. "Study," he said, "and someday perhaps you can save me or someone else." With that the hero flew away. Calvin thought for a moment as the ambulance arrived to tend to the truck driver, then suddenly it hit him; he new what he would do with his life — he would become a paramedic, specializing in treating paranormals.

Calvin finished school and entered into an Emergency Medical Technician training course with the help of a community scholarship. He announced his plans to treat paranormals at his graduation. The announcement was met with surprise and caused excitement in the media. Calvin was an instant media celebrity and his name was broadcast on every local station. The story eventually went national, on Worldview News. This attracted the attention of several influential (and extremely wealthy) persons and organizations. They contacted Calvin and offered to fund a new medical service company with Calvin at the reins. A short time later Paragon EMS was formed.

Calvin has taken the money from his investors and built a high-tech emergency medical service specializing in treating paranormals of all kinds. Paragon always purchases the latest in medical equipment, thus staying on the cutting edge of medical technology. In addition, Paragon donates money to research centers who develop specialized equipment for treating paranormals. Such centers include Henderson Electronics and Yoshida Corp.'s Bio-medical Technologies Division. Some of Paragon's equipment is unique, built specifically for Paragon to their specifications.

Some of Paragon's equipment includes special energy draining devices to lower those persistent force fields (treat as a Suppress), hyper-sharp syringes to penetrate thick hide and light armor (treat as ½d6 KA, Penetrating), multi-phasic defibrillators for reviving patients through thick armor or who are immaterial (2d6 Aid Body, Indirect, Affects Desolid), and other gadgets. Paragon has built a reputation for being able to handle any kind of medical emergency...any kind.

Paragon personnel typically wait for a battle to end before attempting to treat a patient, unless it is reasonably safe to do so (such as when the battle has moved and the wounded person is left behind). One exception is when immediate action is needed to save a life. Of course, it's ultimately the EMT's decision whether or not to enter a battle area to treat a patient; the courts have held that a paramedic who cannot treat a patient due to extreme risk to himself (such as in the middle of a fight between the Champions and Dr. Destroyer) is not liable for the worsening condition of that patient, even if the patient dies before the EMTs reach him.

Paragon treats paranormals almost exclusively, largely because many others either won't or can't, either due to insurance limitations or prejudice. Of course Paragon will treat normals, as well, if there are no other medical personnel available or close enough to respond to a call. Paragon EMS, Inc. receives some funding from billing those supers who are able (and willing) to pay. The majority of their funding comes from various sponsors, including the Peacekeeper Foundation, Grace Medical Supplies, CM Industries (strictly for PR purposes) and several independent, anonymous sources in high society. (Note: The GM may designate one or more wealthy NPCs — or PCs — as being among the anonymous donors to Paragon EMS, Inc.)

Paragon is the only true "super" EMS service, maintaining all of the latest in exotic life-saving equipment. Other services have acquired similar equipment in an attempt to remain viable in the expanding field of paranormal rescue and life-saving. Superior Ambulance will respond to calls involving paranormals more so for the notoriety and media exposure, earning them a reputation as the "film at eleven" ambulance company. LifeTech and Gold Cross EMS are investing large sums of money in modernized equipment. Both companies have recently begun offering special accounts to paranormals, similar to those offered by Paragon. Paragon remains the premier meta-human rescue company and still beats out the others in public opinion and name recognition polls.

CAMPAIGN USE: Paragon EMS, Inc. is the medical service for supers. They will respond to calls for aid by heroes and villains alike; this is required by law, but Calvin has made it clear to his employees that he will not tolerate any discrimination whatsoever. The most seriously injured gets treated first, period. The result is that heroes and villains alike receive care and treatment by these dedicated professionals (much to the annoyance of some vigilantes and ultra-conservative groups). PCs that are severely wounded or close to death may find themselves looking up at Paragon EMTs, called in by one of the hero's teammates or a concerned citizen.

Paragon maintains several ambulance vans in each city. In addition, those areas with a high number of emergency calls often have an air vehicle available (this can be a helicopter that is owned by Paragon, one leased by a local hospital or even a grav-jet donated by a super team or government agency).

SLOGAN: "That metahumans may live."

OPTIONAL VERSION: Calvin is driven to help others because he is terminally ill. While undergoing a routine examination, Calvin discovered he had a rare neurological disorder. The doctors ran dozens of tests and determined that Calvin had eighteen months to live; two years at the most.

Calvin has kept this information to himself. He is unmarried with no living relatives and doesn't want to worry his staff. He also does not want Paragon to have to endure a hostile takeover bid from some megacorp sniffing an easy kill. So Calvin has been keeping his illness a secret. Over time he will begin to deteriorate, however. He will slowly lose his coordination (assume he loses 1d6 Active Points of Dexterity each month) until he no longer has control over his motor functions (i.e., reaches a DEX of -30), when he will die a month later. Note: If using Calvin Roberson as a recurring NPC, use the rules for Negative attributes in *Hero System Almanac I* (pg. 14). In addition, give the PCs a base PER Roll each month to notice Calvin's decline in coordination (allow Paramedic or PS: Physician as complimentary skill rolls).

SCENARIO IDEA: Paragon EMS, Inc. has gained in popularity and numerous heroes and hero teams, especially those that are sanctioned by local or state governments, are buying contracts with Paragon for medical service. All of these developments are very discomforting to certain villains in the city. The villains feel that the heroes are being unfairly favored simply because they are paying for the services (this is not entirely true). Therefore the villains have decided to extract revenge on the company, and any heroes who interfere, to make an example of them.

One of the PCs will hear a radio call to Paragon for help, indicating that a paranormal (who is not identified) is injured in a downtown alley. In reality the villains plan to ambush the EMTs, wounding them and destroying their vehicle and equipment. The first time this happens the heroes will arrive just after the villains depart and will be unable to catch them.

The following night a similar call is put out to Paragon EMS. This time the PCs will arrive just in time to see the emergency crew arrive and be attacked by the villains. The villains will attack and attempt to disable the vehicle and destroy all the equipment inside. When the heroes intervene the villains focus their attack on them. If the villains suffer 25% casualties they will attempt to flee.

As an alternative, the villains could be hired by a rival medical or ambulance service who wants to eliminate their competition. In this case the heroes will have heard of several of these attacks, each on a different medical company. The time the heroes encounter the villains will be when the Paragon crew responds to the bogus call.

PEGASUS, INC.

ABBREVIATION: Pegas

PRIMARY OPERATION: Aeronautical engineering

PRIMARY COMPETITORS: Outflight Systems; McNeil Aviation

WORTH: $47 Million

HQ LOCATION: Chattanooga, TN

HEAD: Bethany Johnson, President/CEO

HUNTED/WATCHED: 5 Pts (Less Pow, Question, 11-) / 5 Pts (Less Pow, 11-)

BACKGROUND/DESCRIPTION: Bethany Johnson gained fame as one of America's first female astronauts. Her contributions to various space shuttle missions earned her a reputation as a hard working and dedicated engineer among the aviation and space exploration community. Later she became even better known as the first female test pilot to exceed Mach 4 in an aircraft. Her other achievements are well documented in *The Journal of Modern Aviation*, by Fitzarthur Publishing.

Several years back, Bethany retired from the space program and pursued her first love, the study of flight. With her pension to live on, Bethany poured her life savings into the creation of a brand new company, which she named Pegasus, Inc. after her favorite flying horse from ancient mythology. Bethany hired the best available flight engineers and researchers in the aviation field, including a few former employees of McNeil Aviation.

With dozens of combined years of experience between them, the design team developed a design for a one-person, jet-powered flying wing suit. The design would allow a person to fly without the aid of a bulky aircraft. The design was finalized and a prototype developed. After several unsuccessful tests and numerous design modifications, a working unit was produced. The suit, code-named Pegasus One, was able to travel at speeds of up to 125 mph. The design revolutionized personal air travel and Pegasus, Inc. quickly became the hottest name in aviation circles. Numerous companies were making offers to buy out the company, interview programs wanted to book the female executive, and the Department of Defense wanted to talk contracts.

Pegasus became a stable competitor in the aeronautical business, due in large part to that first design. Since then, their designs in miniaturized flight and propulsion systems have come to set the standard in the industry. Utilizing miniaturized phasic battery packs produced by Thermodynamics Inc., Bethany's company has managed to develop a number of flight suits which can be used alone, or incorporated with powered armor suits (such as those used by Master Control's S.T.R.I.K.E. Units). While other companies have produced equipment similar to those made by Pegasus, none have been able to equal their quality.

Bethany is now in her late forties (young for a person with her background) and is quite attractive. She is also a quick study and a tough experienced businesswoman. Bethany constantly seeks to keep Pegasus, Inc. true to the ethic and goals she has established. Her main fear is that some major conglomerate will find a way to buy out her company and force her out as its leader. If nothing else, Bethany is an idealist who wants to run a strong, respectable company.

Pegasus Inc. was the first company to produce a powered flying suit, but that exclusive status was soon lost as other companies developed similar (in some cases stolen) technology. Pegasus has focused their Research and Development on developing personal flight systems, where their main competitors have remained more diversified, spreading their resources to cover personal as well as commercial aircraft flight systems.

CAMPAIGN USE: Pegasus, Inc. designs many different types of aviation equipment. Her company's designs have appeared on the costumes of more than a few superheroes (and villains), and she has served as technical consultant on Ron St. John's hit television series, Capes of Wrath (see Maverick Studios).

PCs with flying harnesses or similar mechanical wing foci may have purchased them directly from Pegasus, Inc. Characters may also have based their designs on one of Pegasus, Inc.'s models, or vice versa. Particularly crafty persons could have stolen the plans directly, downloading them from the Pegasus, Inc. mainframe computer.

Bethany is more than willing to assist heroes who are trying to design flight equipment. She may also volunteer one of her staff to aid a hero team in need of their expertise. The company is always eager to examine exotic flight equipment as well; they are always looking for ways to improve their existing products.

SLOGAN: "The sky is not the limit."

OPTIONAL VERSION: On a previous space shuttle mission, Bethany was exposed to freak radiation. All of her crew mates from that mission are now either dead or have developed some type of paranormal powers. Bethany, however, has developed a degenerative disease which is destroying the neural cells of her spine. Within five years she will be completely unable to walk. At present, she walks with a slight limp and the use of a wooden cane.

Because of her condition, Bethany has allocated a significant portion of her company's resources to researching new ways to stimulate muscle growth and use. One of the company's earlier designs was a bulky harness-like suit, which was connected to the subject's brain and various muscles by means of electrodes inserted through the skin. The electrodes carried signals from the subject's brain directly to the muscles, allowing the signals to bypass any damaged neural cells (such as those in Bethany's spine).

The suit is now obsolete, having led to more advanced models. While still difficult to conceal, the current model looks like a diving suit with circuitry running over its surface.

Bethany hopes that her research will eventually lead to a cure for many diseases that affect the muscles of its victim, such as polio, muscular dystrophy and multiple sclerosis. Her company's achievements, thus far, have attracted the attention (and funding) of several groups, including Future Scope, Inc.

SCENARIO IDEA: Ten advanced flight units are stolen from a Pegasus warehouse. Fearing the suits will be used in crimes, Bethany contacts the PCs for help. She will offer as much assistance to the PCs as they need, to the point of providing diagrams and schematics for the stolen gadgets.

The suits were, in fact, stolen by Cy Force agents under the direction of Doc Digital. Doc Digital intends to discredit the Pegasus products. To do this, Doc Digital hires ten agents to attack an armored car. (Note: The agents are hired and paid through a third party, so they don not know exactly who they are working for.) Doc Digital equips the agents with appropriate weapons, light armor and flight gear made to look exactly like the units that were stolen from Pegasus.

The PCs will hear about the attack on the armored car. Upon arriving, the PCs will confront the agents in the stolen flight gear (or so they believe). The units worn by the agents will malfunction in various ways, such as by exploding (3d6 KA, Explosion), spinning out of control, suddenly losing power in mid-flight, and so on (treat this as a 14- Activation roll, with a failure indicating a malfunction).

Any knowledgeable PCs (meaning those with Electronics, KS: Aeronautics or SC: Aeronautical Engineering) will notice that the flight units are defective. If allowed to examine them, Bethany will confirm that the units worn by the agents are not those stolen from the warehouse.

An investigation can lead the PCs to Doc Digital and the real flight units. This may also culminate in a fight between the PCs and Cy-Force (see High Tech Enemies).

QUICKCORP

ABBREVIATION: QckCrp

PRIMARY OPERATION: Franchise retail corporation

PRIMARY COMPETITORS: Northland Corporation

WORTH: $16 Million

HQ LOCATION: Rutherford, NJ

HEAD: Cheryl Carlisle, President

HUNTED/WATCHED: — / 5 Pts (Less Pow, 11-)

BACKGROUND/DESCRIPTION: QuickCorp began as a chain of convenience stores on the east coast. The chain of stores, called QuickCorner, grew in popularity and in sales until there were thousands of QuickCorner convenience stores (called QuickMart in some portions of the midwest) across the country. The stores sell everything from milk and bread to tire gauges and window cleaner — everything you would expect to find in a corner convenience market. QuickCorner stores can now be found in every major city. They are open 24 hours a day (with the exception of a few stores in very crime-ridden areas, which are closed from 12 a.m. until 5 a.m.).

The corporate executives know the potential for robberies in the stores and have established employee safety training programs designed to raise awareness and promote safe practices. Cheryl Carlisle, herself, has been the victim of a robbery when she was a store clerk years ago. This memory has not faded for her, and Cheryl puts the safety of her employees above all else. Unfortunately, not all of her staff underneath her feel the same way. Still, Cheryl has seen that funds are allocated to increasing security among all of the stores in the chain; video cameras are being installed in all of the stores (treat as Clairsentience, OAF Camera, Activation 14- [due to scanning]), along with silent alarm triggers (in the cash registers) and cash drop safes.

QuickCorner stores became nationally famous both for their 68 ounce "Big Slurp" sodas, as well as the pitched super battle between the Champions and Eurostar, which utterly destroyed a city block with the exception of a lone QuickCorner store. QuickCorp pays media figures (primarily sports figures and superheroes) to act as sponsors for the stores, sometimes putting their likenesses on the "Big Slurp" cups.

With the success of the QuickCorner chain, QuickCorp has begun expanding in recent years, adding new retail services such as their QuickPress dry-cleaning shops, QuickPhoto one-hour film developing shops and QuickOil car tune-up and oil-change shops. These newer shops can be found primarily in larger cities which are often used as test centers for the company's new ventures and promotions. While they can be found scattered throughout the country, these latter specialty shops are far less common than the company's original chain, the QuickCorner convenience marts.

QuickCorp is expanding throughout the midwest and even Canada, having established itself as a main player in the rest of the U.S. (QuickCorner is one of the largest franchise convenience store chains, collectively known as the "big four.") QuickCorp, guided by Cheryl's business savvy and experience, has recently completed the purchase of a small chain of convenience stores in Illinois (the Big Boy Jim's chain). The company is also currently negotiating a deal with Nikoshima Foods of Osaka, Japan, to open a joint-owned and run chain of convenience stores in Japan.

The goal of QuickCorp is to provide expedient, yet efficient, services at a reasonable price to consumers. Of course, to most people, a reasonable price is somewhat higher when the service includes a large does of convenience. The corporation is quite stable, thanks to the success of its convenience store chains, and sales are on the rise from its newer specialty shops. QuickCorp also runs an aggressive advertising campaign year-round, with new television and radio commercials appearing each month. Very few people in a given town don't know the snappy QuickCorner jingle, "Get what you need at QuickCorner..."

QuickCorp's strongest competitor is the Northland Corporation, which owns the Circle 7 convenient store chain. QuickCorp's sales are second only to this national giant, which maintains a respectable lead in sales. The main toll used to increase sales are television ads, typically depicting enthusiastic young adults buying copious amounts of liquid beverages and then piling into a convertible.

CAMPAIGN USE: QuickCorp is the parent company of a variety of "convenience" businesses, all of which are standard fare for any campaign city. The shops can serve as dressing for a scene involving the heroes or NPCs. One of the local QuickCorner stores can be the scene of an encounter. For example, robberies, shoplifting, fights and gas drive-offs are all common occurrences at the various QuickCorp facilities.

A character's DNPC or Follower may also work in one of the businesses, running a register, changing oil in cars or developing film. Such a position could put the employee in contact with many of the city's more interesting people. It's amazing what can be learned from working at a QuickCorner store.

SLOGAN: "Get what you need at QuickCorner."

OPTIONAL VERSION: QuickCorp is becoming a very lucrative business, especially for Cheryl Carlisle. Cheryl runs a fairly straight-forward company, but is known to be rather susceptible to bribes. Several employee strikes have been averted by timely "donations" to the appropriate labor union's Board of Directors. Cheryl sees everyone as merely bribes in varying amounts. She is intelligent, but not at all caring of people — only money matters to Cheryl.

After several employees were killed in robberies at the company's QuickCorner convenience stores, Cheryl engaged in official posturing and made plenty of noise to the press about the sanctity of life and the need for increased security. To date, however, Cheryl has only seen that token measures are taken at her stores. "Not cost efficient," she says.

To anyone she does not know or trust (which accounts for almost everyone) Cheryl is quite charming, relying on her good looks and acting ability to convince inquiring minds of her sincerity. Behind closed doors, however, Cheryl can be an absolute witch. She has been known to fire employees for so much as whispering during board meetings.

SCENARIO IDEA: QuickCorner has been the target of a very bizarre prank. It seems that kids who have been buying bubble gum from these stores are coming down with some very strange conditions, such as purple skin, incessant belching and dizziness. While none of the victims have displayed more serious effects, the authorities are becoming concerned. Curiously, none of the same brand of gum bought at stores other than QuickCorner have caused these effects. Nonetheless, all of the gum has been pulled from every store, just in case.

The culprit is, in fact, Foxbat (see *Classic Enemies*). He has concocted a chemical formula which reacts with the saliva of those who eat it, causing one of the effects mentioned above (determined randomly). The Idiot King's intent is simply to cause disruption among the city's stores and to distract the heroes while he goes about his true plan...to kidnap the Governor's pet cat, Boots!

SIMCORP

ABBREVIATION: SimCrp

PRIMARY OPERATIONS: Weapons manufacturing

PRIMARY COMPETITORS: B.L.A.D.E. Inc.; Tauer Arms; DanCo

HQ LOCATION: Buffalo, NY

WORTH: $64 Billion

HEAD: Colleen Simmons, President

HUNTED/WATCHED: 10 Pts (As Pow, Lim, 11-) / 5 Pts (As Pow, Lim, 11-)

BACKGROUND/DESCRIPTION: When he started Simmons' Guns in 1858, John Adams Simmons didn't know that he was starting something that would last over a hundred years. The .45 caliber Simmons Peacemonger was one of the most popular handguns in the late 1800s. The gun earned Simmons a reputation for accuracy, that still survives today. In the early 1900s, under the guidance of Abraham Simmons, Simmons' Guns expanded their production to include dynamite and other assorted munitions, including ammunition for their extensive line of guns. In 1922, the company was re-named and Simmons Ordinance was born.

The Simmons family started a family tradition of giving each Simmons child 1,000 shares of the company. In 1939, realizing that war was inevitable, Jacob Simmons decided to take the company public, issuing 10,000 shares of Simmons Ordinance at $100 each share. The money generated went into research and development. SO decided accuracy and advanced engineering were the way to go. Simmons Ordinance came out of WW2 as a multimillion dollar company.

Jacob died in 1948 and Joanna Simmons inherited control of the company. Joanna was of gypsy heritage and gifted with second sight (a form of Precognition). Joanna used her second sight ruthlessly. She got the inside scoop on every board member, and used that information to blackmail them into accepting her as head of the company. Under Joanna's iron handed rule, SO expanded and bought out many lesser companies. Joanna's son, Robert, took over in the '60s. One of his first acts as the new President was to push for the adoption of a new company name — SimCorp. Robert married soon after and had 5 children; 3 girls and 2 boys.

In 1988, Robert died in a plane crash while on vacation with his family. There were only a few survivors that day. Colleen Simmons was one of them. Colleen inherited everything, and now owns 54% of the stocks of SimCorp. Colleen inherited more than the stocks from her family, she also inherited her grandmother's mental powers (see Mindlock; ***Champions***, pg. C19).

SimCorp has one of the most elaborate security setups as possible. Barbed electric wire fences, Retina scans, encrypted passwords, and so on. All security guards use SimCorp Light Battle Armor (use Turtle Armor stats). Curtis West is the security chief at SimCorp. He is also the only employee that knows of Colleen's double life. Curtis is fanatically loyal to Colleen. As soon as someone of importance gets hired at SimCorp, Colleen has a "talk" with them, during which she searches their mind to uncover their true loyalties. Since Colleen took over SimCorp, there has never been a successful infiltration of SimCorp.

For the most part, Colleen keeps her activities as Mindlock separate from her duties as the President of SimCorp. SimCorp has one of the better rates of pay, in the weapons industry. Colleen has used a lot of management techniques taught by the Japanese in order to try to improve morale and increase productivity. Colleen is beginning to fall in love with Curtis (and she knows he feels the same for her), but she is still hiding her true feelings from him. As time goes on, SimCorp will start playing more by the rules than in the past, relying less and less on unscrupulous business tactics.

Today, SimCorp concentrates on research and design of advanced individual weapons, such as handguns and rifles (for the civilian markets), and more complex weapons for the military markets (either domestic or foreign). SimCorp invests millions of dollars in special designs of new weapons, such as the new 7.5mm caseless rifle and the 74mm Medium Anti-tank Weapon (MAW), both of which are in military field testing by the U.S. Department of Defense. SimCorp also develops energy projection weapons, although the company spends but a fraction of its resources on such items. Most of SimCorp's energy weapons are relatively inexpensive — and often substandard — replicas of existing weapons.

The weapons market is getting more and more difficult to compete in, no thanks to new anti-gun legislation. SimCorp has remained undaunted in the face of mounting government pressure to stop production of their so-called "assault weapons," which include most of SimCorp's semi-automatic firearms. Tauer Arms remains their main rival in the gun market. Tauer Arms manufactures handguns popular with law enforcement agencies, including the Tauer Arms .40 caliber semi-automatic. SimCorp has responded by producing a new line of semi-automatics in a variety of calibers, at almost 15% below the retail price of the Tauer guns.

CAMPAIGN USE: SimCorp is one of the best companies to purchase high-tech weapons from. SimCorp is your one stop weapon headquarters. Heroes can contact SimCorp to round out their equipment inventory. Want a blaster? No problem. They'll even design it to your specifications, though they always keep a copy of custom designs for themselves.

Did your heroes find a high-tech relic from an ancient civilization? Let SimCorp look it over; they'll be happy to, especially if the device shows potential as a weapon. SimCorp is a great place for an eccentric DNPC (or PCs, for that matter) "inventor" to have a job. SimCorp may also try to acquire a character's secret weapon to study it. Does Captain Maser have a new, more efficient blast gun? You can bet that SimCorp will want to get their collective hands on it.

SLOGAN: "Reliability — SimCorp"

OPTIONAL VERSION: SimCorp is trying to dominate the weapons market. They will use any means possible. For some reason, Colleen seems to have the best information available. Rival business quake with fear when they hear that SimCorp is interested in them. SimCorp has a reputation of playing dirty to get what they want.

SCENARIO IDEA: Someone has stolen a large shipment of prototype SimCorp weapons and ammunition. What's worse, the weapons and ammo are being sold to the street gangs. While the company makes press releases and official statements to the media, the bodies are piling up. The authorities call in the PCs to stop the madness.

The weapons are the new 7.5mm caseless rifles, and were intended to be shipped to the Army for field testing (use the stats for the M16A1 but lower the STR Minimum to 12). Unfortunately the Army canceled the testing at the last minute and were returning the rifles to SimCorp. A total of 24 of the rifles were been stolen, along with 10,000 rounds of the special caseless ammo (the rifle can fire only the special caseless ammo produced by SimCorp).

As the PCs investigate, they learn that only members of the Kay Deuces (a medium-sized black street gang known for running drugs and weapons) are being killed. Furthermore, the suspects in the shootings are always described as Hispanic males. The PCs eventually uncover a gang war being waged between the Kay Deuces and the Varrio Pueblo Boys (a Hispanic gang known for violent turf wars).

The mastermind behind the gang war is Curtis West, Colleen's chief of security and love interest. Once Curtis heard that the military had canceled the testing, Curtis arranged for the Varrio Pueblo Boys to "acquire" the shipment of rifles for $50,000. Curtis cover was that the rifles were stolen. He still pockets the money however, and best of all — the weapons are still field tested (albeit on the city streets), thus assuring SimCorp of future sales to other buyers. Colleen does not yet know of his plan, but will fire him and contact the PCs if she discovers it.

TRAN DEFENSE SYSTEMS, INC.

PRIMARY OPERATION: Ballistic materials and body armor

PRIMARY COMPETITORS: Advanced Body Armor; Second Life Vests

WORTH: $11.6 million

HQ LOCATION: Los Angeles, California

HEAD: Duc Van Tran

HUNTED/WATCHED: — / 5 Pts (As Pow, Lim, 11-)

BACKGROUND/DESCRIPTION: In 1975 two Vietnamese brothers, Duc and Thuan Tran, fled their country in the hopes that they could make their way to the United States. They suffered through several long weeks in squalid conditions aboard a merchant ship, until they finally arrived at Miami, Florida. Duc and Thuan quickly contacted relatives in Los Angeles, an aunt and uncle who had fled Vietnam several years earlier. Their aunt and uncle arranged for them to come to California, and were instrumental in helping them obtain their U.S. citizenships. Duc and Thuan grew up in L.A., and quickly became absorbed in their new culture, but each in a very different way.

Duc worked in his uncle's grocery store, learning how to run the business and earning money for college. Thuan, meanwhile, fell into the clutches of an Asian street gang. One fateful summer day, Thuan was gunned down in front of his Uncle's store as Duc looked on. Holding his dying brother in his arms, Duc swore to try to bring his brother's killers to justice. With a strong desire to protect innocent lives, Duc applied for the police academy. He was accepted but did not graduate because of an injury he suffered during training.

During the academy, Duc had become fascinated by guns and ballistic science. Soon after, and with the help of his Uncle, Duc started a small company, Tran Defense Systems Incorporated. Using his knowledge from college and the police academy, he began designing body armor and anti-ballistic materials.

His products quickly received notice and acclaim from the right people, and Duc's company grew. Tran Defense Systems now employs over four dozen people. It has gained several prestigious contracts from area state and local law enforcement agencies, including the very police department that Duc had attempted to join several years earlier. Their product line includes standard kevlar vests and helmets, custom-designed concealed kevlar clothing, anti-ballistic Plexiglas, and exotic items (such as bulletproof seat covers).

Tran Defense Systems now enjoys notoriety and a reputation as one of the country's leading producers of anti-ballistic materials. Their customers include celebrities, politicians (past and present), foreign governments, the U.S. government, and even certain paranormal groups, including Executive Sanction!

Duc is so confident that his armor products will save a life, that he has put up $50,000 of his own money to be paid to the estate of anyone who is killed as a result of a flaw or failing of Tran's armor. Only one person has ever died while wearing a Tran vest (a police officer who was struck by a stray shot from a Viper cannon during a battle in Houston) and Duc paid the promised $50,000 to the man's family. TDS Inc. also established the Captain Star Memorial Scholarship Fund, named after the Washington D.C. hero slain in the 1990 "Night of Villainy" battle against "Villainy International."

Tran Defense Systems produces some of the best quality body armor in the world. The company's production, however, is lower than more conventional body armor manufacturers, such as Advanced Body Armor (of Yuba City, California) and Second Life Vests (currently the largest producer of body armor). Tran has relied on his products' reputation to maintain market share, which remains around 24%. Eventually, Duc plans to expand his production facilities and compete on a much larger scale.

CAMPAIGN USE: Although they do not produce powered armor suits, Tran Defense Systems is a leader in ballistic materials and personal body armor. They are an excellent source of kevlar vests or other high-tech "ballistic cloth" material, so common in many of the costumes worn by paranormals today.

Tran Defense Systems will go to great lengths to maintain their reputation, and often uses news footage of battles between supers who are known to use Tran's patented material in their costumes as testimony to the durability of their products.

Tran Defense Systems plays equally well in either a four-color campaign or in a gritty, street-level campaign like *Dark Champions*. The lack of references to "super powers" and the material the company produces makes it an excellent choice for either universe.

SLOGAN: "Nothing Gets Through Tran"

OPTIONAL VERSION: Duc Tran is completely consumed by greed, and could care less if his products stop a fly, let alone high velocity projectiles. The company makes many outrageous claims that cannot be substantiated and dodges investigations whenever possible. Duc, himself, has been convicted of fraud several times in the past, but this information is not common knowledge. Duc maintains papers allowing him to return to Vietnam at any time, and would flee at the first sign that his attorneys could not stave off a serious law suit. While his products are adequate, they are far from being "top of the line."

SCENARIO IDEA: After a brief encounter with several VIPER agents, the heroes discover that the agents are wearing body armor manufactured by Tran Defense Systems Inc. When they investigate, Duc Tran will deny any knowledge of the vests until pressed.

The truth is that the local VIPER Nest Leader is holding Duc's aunt, Loc, hostage and is forcing Duc to manufacture the vests for the Nest. Duc will do anything to help the heroes, so long as it does not endanger his aunt.

The Tran body armor is equal to 10 PD/6 ED Armor, OIF — Helmet and Suit; a marked improvement over the standard VIPER armor, with the exception that the armor does not work well against heat (only 3 ED vs. heat, microwaves or flame). Tran will point this flaw out to the heroes at the earliest opportunity.

If using Tran Defense Systems with *Dark Champions*, simply replace VIPER with a suitable criminal organization, such as the Yakuza, Mafia or one of the Chinese Tongs.

YOSHIDA CORPORATION

ABBREVIATION: Yosh

PRIMARY OPERATION: Micro-electronics & circuitry production

PRIMARY COMPETITORS: Micro Device Technologies; Yamomoto Electronics; Lockley International; Henderson Electronics

WORTH: $18 Billion

HQ LOCATION: Tokyo, Japan

HEAD: Tahashi Yoshida, President/CEO

HUNTED/WATCHED: 25 Pts (More Pow, NCI, 11-) / 10 Pts (As Pow, NCI, 11-)

BACKGROUND/DESCRIPTION: In the late 1970's Jiro Korando founded Korando Electronics. Jiro had recently left a high-level position with a major electronics firm after disagreeing with the company's President over a business matter. Jiro sought to transfer his experience and knowledge to his own company, which he hoped would one day dominate the world electronics market.

With tremendous effort, discipline, and a little luck, Jiro's company grew. By 1980, Kirando Electronics had acquired several small companies, along with all of their assets. With its initial success, and the personal computer explosion of the 1980s, Kirando Electronics flourished both in Japan and in the growing European and American markets.

In a bold move to put his company closer to the top of the electronics market, Jiro merged his own company with his biggest rival, Santori Inc., in a friendly takeover. The new company would be headed by Jiro as Chief Executive Officer and President. Santori's boss, Tahashi Yoshida, became the Senior Vice President. The new company's name was Korando Incorporated. The new, larger, company landed several lucrative contracts with the Japanese Defense Force, and quickly established itself as a major economic force in Southeast Asia, if not the world. Korando Inc. became a leading supplier of micro-electronics for military equipment.

On August 5, 1986, Jiro Korando was found dead in his home in Tokyo. The official coroner's report listed the cause of death as a drug overdose. A brief investigation by the local authorities confirmed that the death was a suicide. Jiro Korando was actually assassinated by Ronin, on the orders of Tahashi Yoshida, and the murder made to look like an accident. Yoshida's contacts in the local police department kept the investigation "brief." (Note: The exact motive for the killing is up to the GM, but it may include simple power lust or even revenge for a long past family dishonor against Yoshida.)

Three days after Jiro's death, Tahashi Yoshida, a 43 year old business man from Nagasaki, was unanimously elected the new CEO by the board of directors, and the name of the company was changed to the Yoshida Corporation. Yoshida-san remains the company's CEO and President to this day. He runs Yoshida Corp. with a strict leadership, reminiscent of the feudal Japanese system of discipline and respect. His employees are expected to obey unquestioningly.

Yoshida Corp. owns several subsidiary companies including Kiko Video Game Company (which produces licensed superhero arcade and home video games), Kensato (audio tape manufacturer) and several others. Yoshida Corp. has several executive offices throughout the world, including Manhattan, San Francisco, London and Bonn, Germany (and quite possibly the GM's campaign city).

Mr. Yoshida is a ruthless leader, and an equally ruthless business man. He punishes dishonorable acts, including failure, with swiftness. Several employees have simply "disappeared" over the years, usually while on business trips abroad (i.e., outside of Japanese jurisdiction). Yoshida Corp. will often provide financial backing to supervillain teams, in an attempt to curb the development of its competitors through acts of violence and sabotage. Mr. Yoshida is careful to disallow any direct connection between himself and the villains, however.

Since he is hated (and feared) by so many, Mr. Yoshida has a personal bodyguard — Ronin. Ronin is an extremely dangerous paranormal who will protect Yoshida at any cost. Ronin often undertakes overseas "missions" for the Company. These missions include VIP protection, sabotage and assassination.

Among the electronics and microelectronics companies, Yoshida is by far the largest and most diverse, with entire divisions and facilities dedicated to microcircuitry research and design. Yoshida even maintains a secret division, called Project: Buddha, which is dedicated to obtaining and analyzing alien technology. It is rumored that the division headquarters, somewhere in the Japanese mountains, houses quite a collection of alien technologies. Its competitors in microchip production are gaining larger portions of the market, and much faster than Yoshida expected. The company is currently trying to develop a new chip using a mix of Earth and alien technology.

CAMPAIGN USE: Yoshida Corp. can become the employer for any computer or electronics oriented character, especially those with engineering skills or related Sciences. Yoshida is also known for their extensive research and development facilities. It is quite possible that Yoshida could be following a PC with electrical powers — or any energy powers, for that matter — in order to reproduce that technology for the military markets.

Yoshida Corp. is a powerful Japanese conglomerate, enough so that they are considered to have "Non Combat Influence" if used as a character's Hunted or Watched. Yoshida may act as a sponsor for a hero or hero team, even if only on a limited basis. The board of directors could also elect to hire a team (or an individual) outright, either temporarily or permanently. Any paranormals hired by Yoshida Corp. would likely find themselves safeguarding Yoshida Corp. equipment, high ranking personnel and other valuable assets.

In *Dark Champions* campaigns, Yoshida Corp. quickly becomes a major source of high tech-equipment for the PCs. A Contact or Favor with Yoshida Corp. can be the justification for many wondrous gadgets. It is recommended that Mr. Tahashi Yoshida, himself, be treated as more of an enigmatic force (i.e., no Contacts or Favors with him directly).

SLOGAN: "Honor, Quality — Yoshida"

OPTIONAL VERSION: Tahashi Yoshida holds honor above all else. He is sympathetic to the problems caused by all those paranormals running around unrestrained. Mr. Yoshida makes regular contributions to international charities, and publicly denounces supervillains and terrorists. Not a few of his contributions to the U.S. government have ended up in Stronghold.

Yoshida Corp. is very active in the electronics and microcircuitry fields. They are helping to close the gap between Japanese and American microchip manufacturers. With offices located throughout the world, they can plant corporate spies to ferret out its competition's latest technologies and other valuable trade secrets.

SCENARIO IDEA: The PCs encounter several groups of gang members armed with high-tech weapons (energy weapons, if the GM so desires). This is a good opportunity to involve a DNPC as a gunshot victim or as a witness to a gang hit using these weapons. The PCs eventually discover that the weapons are manufactured by Yoshida Corp., and have been smuggled into the U.S. by the Japanese Yakuza. The heroes must go to Tokyo to stop the guns at the source. Yoshida Corp. will resent the Americans snooping around, and will offer little assistance in their investigation. As it turns out, Yoshida Corp. has been the target of several thefts, including the weapons in question.

The scenario will likely culminate in a confrontation between the PCs and rogue, gun-running Yakuza members in the land of the rising sun. Japanese authorities will not look kindly at undisciplined American supers slinging energy blasts around Tokyo and may call out their own state-sponsored heroes to deal with the PCs!

Some possible alternatives to use as the weapons smugglers are Eurostar, Terror Incorporated, or even Doctor Destroyer. For a *Dark Champions* campaign the smugglers could be part of an extensive operation run by the Master of Crime.

Background/History: Ozeki Honda's earliest memories were of growing up in an orphanage in Nagasaki. His father, he was told, was a Tokyo businessman and his mother a Nagasaki club dancer. Ozeki's conception was less than planned and his mother abandoned him as an infant.

Years later Ozeki witnessed one of the marvels of modern science firsthand; the explosion of an atomic bomb over Nagasaki. Thousands of people died, and Ozeki, barely a year old, became very ill. He was moved to one of the neighboring cities with other survivors, however, and quickly recovered, much to the surprise of the medical staff watching over him.

Ozeki was later adopted by a kind and gentle couple from Osaka, Mariko and Tahashi Yoshida. Ozeki lived with them for many years. His adopted father, a WWII veteran and Japanese traditionalist, taught Ozeki kendo, the honored Japanese art of swordsmanship. Ozeki's adopted father insisted that his new son would someday become a powerful

RONIN

Val	Char	Cost
20	STR	10
26	DEX	48
25	CON	30
14	BODY	8
18	INT	8
20	EGO	20
30	PRE	20
10	COM	0
8+	PD	4
5+	ED	3
6	SPD	28
8	REC	2
50	END	0
68	STUN	31

Combat Stats

OCV: 9
DCV: 9
ECV: 7
Phases: 2, 4, 6, 8, 10, 12

Costs

Char:	212	Base:	100
	+		+
Powers:	254	Disad:	387
	=		=
Totals:	466		466

Cost	Powers	END
37	2d6 HKA (2 ½ w/STR), AP, Penetrating, 0 END, OAF (Katana)	0+
21	Danger Sense, Usable out of combat, IIF (Katana)	
15	1d6 HKA (1 ½d6 w/STR), Penetrating, 0 END, OAF (Wakazashi)	0+
10	Martial Arts (usable with swords)	

Maneuver	OCV	DCV	Notes
Martial Block	+2	+2	Block, Abort
Martial Throw	+0	+1	4d6 + v/5
Martial Disarm	-1	+1	30 STR

Use Art with Dai-sho (Katana-Wakazashi)

Cost	Powers	END
40	Armor (+24 PD/+16 ED), Act 15-, OIF (Samurai armor)	
24	Missile Deflection (vs. all attacks), +2 to Roll	
4	+2" Running (8" Total)	1/5"
5	Instant Change	

Cost	Skills
2	Fringe Benefit: Wakashira for Dai Nippon Sho-kai (Yakuza gang)
3	Ambidexterity
3, 3	Combat Sense, 13-, Tactics, 13-
3	Riding (horse), 14-
3, 3	AK: Japan, 13-, AK: Tokyo, 14-
2	KS: Japanese History, 13-
3	Weaponsmith (swords), 11-
1	Language: English (Japanese is native)
12	+4 Levels w/ Swords
20	Base (Honda Castle, Japan)
40	Followers (32 Bushi; 100 pts each)

100+	Disadvantages
20	Enraged if dishonored, 14-, 11-
10	Enraged if Japan is insulted, 11-, 11-
20	Follows Samurai code of Bushido (Com, Total)
20	Sworn loyalty to Tahashi Honda (Com, Total)
10	Wants to return Japan to "traditional" values
10	Dependence: 2d6 after 1 minute if not in reach of sword.
10	DF: Samurai armor (Concealable)
15	Reputation: deadly Japanese mercenary (extreme), 11-
10	Watched by Honda, 14-
10	Hunted by UNTIL, 11-
5	1d6 Unluck
15	Secret ID (Ozeki Honda)
211	Villain's Bonus

warrior and fight for the lost honor of Japan. His father went on to tell Ozeki that one day he would inherit the family's sacred dai-sho, the two swords worn by samurai. The dai-sho had been in their family for more than 10 generations. More than that, it was enchanted, blessed by the great Kami Susano-Wo, the very Spirit of warrior courage and impetuosity and guardian of Yomi, the Shinto Hell. Ozeki was enthralled by the stories his father told him, but he believed the swords to be just that — stories.

Tragedy struck again when Ozeki was 20 years old; his mother had become sick and died. After a period of mourning, Ozeki's father took Ozeki to the a secret part of the house and uncovered a pair of swords well-hidden among ancient garments and scrolls. He handed the swords to Ozeki. "These are yours," he said. Ozeki bowed and gracefully took the swords. He unsheathed the katana from its beautiful black lacquered scabbard and stared in awe. The blade was the sharpest, most finely crafted and ornately decorated he had ever seen. Suddenly a misty figure appeared. It wore ancient Samurai armor and motioned to Ozeki. Ozeki jumped to his feet and held the sword out in front of him. The figure smiled, bowed and disappeared. Suddenly Ozeki's body began to change. Years of latent mutant abilities, dormant since the atomic explosion, began to surface. His father stared in awe as Ozeki grew larger, stronger — more powerful.

That was 28 years ago. Ozeki now works as an executive bodyguard for his adopted father, Tahashi Yoshida. He dons the armor of his ancestors and becomes the paranormal Ronin for critical missions. When not working as Ronin, Ozeki still wields impressive power as both Yoshida Corp.'s premier security man and as the Wakashira for the powerful Dai Nippon Sho-kai Yakuza organization (see *Dark Champions* for detailed descriptions of the Yakuza organizations).

Personality/Motivation: Ozeki is completely loyal to his adopted father. He maintains his birth name, however, to avoid embarrassing (and thus dishonoring) his father should the connection between Ozeki and Ronin ever be revealed. To this day, no one but Ozeki and Yoshida himself know of their true relationship.

Ozeki is a fierce traditionalist, and believes that the ways of feudal Japan are best. He seeks to return Japan to the traditions of the past. Ozeki himself follows the code of Bushido at all times, and only Yoshida can override Ozeki's will once his mind has been made up.

Ozeki serves his father with undying loyalty; he would commit seppeku for his father without hesitation if asked. He serves Yoshida in the hopes that one day Yoshida will become the ultimate Oyabun in Japan, and thereby pressure the government into bringing Japan back into the traditional ways set forth by the Kami. If Yoshida were to die, Ronin would avenge his death and then begin an all out war against every non-traditional element of modern day Japan and her allies (including the United States).

Quote: "It is only my duty to honor that spared your life before. Dishonor me again and I will kill you...."

Powers/Tactics: There is little doubt that Ronin's primary attacks are his swords. He will use only one at a time unless fighting multiple opponents. As a matter of honor, he will not use his swords to wound people unless he is so ordered (by Yoshida) or unless they attack him with a Killing Attack first. Otherwise Ronin will simply use his Martial Arts maneuvers or attack foci with the swords.

Ronin also has 32 followers; they are all members of the Dai Nippon Sho-kai Yakuza organization (treat each as Skilled Normals with 5 SPD, light armor, Katana, a Martial Arts package and Loyalty to Ronin).

Appearance: Ronin wears a black and red suit of high-tech armor (secretly manufactured by Yoshida Corp. based on plans stolen from DanCo), which is indistinguishable from real thing. The armor plates and helmet are black with red trim, and all cloth portions are red. The Yoshida crest (in red) is emblazoned across the chest plate. Ronin wears a full ceremonial face mask (to protect his Secret ID). In his Ronin armor, he stands a full 6 ½ feet tall.

When not in his Ronin form, Ozeki appears to be a well-built Japanese man with carefully groomed jet black hair. He is clean shaven, wears dark, one-color suits and sunglasses.

CORPORATIONS: AN OVERVIEW

WHAT IS A CORPORATION?

In order to understand what a corporation is and how it differs from other types of businesses, it is important to review each type of business "entity. "What follows is a brief description of each type of business, based on its ownership, as well as a summary of the legal responsibilities and liabilities of each.

DEFINITION

SOLE PROPRIETORSHIP

The simplest form of business is the sole proprietorship. The sole proprietorship is a business owned by one person or, in the cases of states with community property laws, a married couple. The owner is legally and financially liable for everything his company does. All the profits of the company belong to the owner and are claimed as personal income when filing tax returns. The owner is also responsible for all debts the company amasses. In short, the owner "is" the business. Most home-based businesses and many smaller neighborhood stores are sole proprietorships.

PARTNERSHIP

A partnership is an association by two or more persons who own a business jointly. It arises from an agreement between partners who carry on a business for profit. The partners share the responsibilities and liabilities of the business, both legal and financial. Partners are also agents of each other, and may bind the entire partnership in agreements.

A partnership can be run by one partner with other partner(s) simply providing financial backing. In this case the partner controlling the business is called the general partner. Partners who provide financial backing without exercising any true control over the business are called limited partners (also called investment partners or silent partners). Limited partners agree to take the financial risks associated with the business without having any direct influence on the operation of the company. Limited partners may not make decisions concerning the company's day-to-day operations. They essentially become investors and may make or lose money based on the company's success or failure. Their liability, however, is limited to their investment in the partnership.

CORPORATION

Unlike the sole proprietorship and partnership, a corporation is an entity unto itself. It is recognized as a separate legal entity, distinct from the people it employs. Businesses, foundations, churches and cities may all be corporations. Each establishes a charter, elects a governing body and keeps its assets separate from those people that make up the organization.

In terms of size, influence and visibility the corporation has clearly become the dominant business form in the Western world and in most other free-market economies. In 1909, only one manufacturing corporation had assets exceeding $1 billion. By 1991, 377 billion-dollar corporations held 71% of total manufacturing assets. With each passing year more of the industrial, financial and distribution sectors of the economy are run by large corporations.

NOT FOR PROFIT CORPORATION

A corporation can become a not-for-profit corporation, commonly referred to as "non-profit corporation." To become a non-profit corporation simply involves meeting local and state requirements, applying for non-profit corporation status with the Internal Revenue Service and paying associated permit and filing fees. The non-profit corporation enjoys certain advantages over other businesses.

The chief benefits of being a non-profit corporation are the major tax breaks allowed by the IRS (this is often a major consideration for a corporation becoming non-profit). Becoming a non-profit corporation does not mean that the company cannot make money. Non-profit corporations are allowed to allocate funds for administrative expenses, payroll, research and other business-related expenses. What a non-profit corporation pays its staff will vary, depending on the goals and size of the company. Some non-profit corporation CEO's make a very good living.

Examples of non-profit corporations include churches, charitable organizations (such as the Salvation Army and the Muscular Dystrophy Foundation), research organizations and some social aid groups. Hero groups may decide to incorporate as non-profit corporations, as well.

A SHORT HISTORY

We can trace the origins of corporations to the towns, universities and monastic orders of the Middle Ages. Each held assets separate from the individuals or members that made them up. Universities, for example, often collected impressive libraries of tomes and reference books with which the students and professors could study. These libraries belonged to the university, not to the individual staff members. Simple marketing activities began with the development of inter-regional trade, including caravan and maritime commerce. Merchant guilds became the precursor to today's modern commercial corporations. In ancient Rome, the rights of ownership could only be vested in what were called "legal persons. " This term would today include human beings, legally established associations of persons, foundations and corporations.

Corporations were better defined by the English courts during the 15th century with the legal principle of "limited liability." Limited liability means that whatever is owed to the corporation is not owed to the people that make up the corporation, nor is the corporation's debt the debt of the people that make up the corporation. In the United States this feature was further expanded in 1886. In the case of Santa Clara County vs. Southern Pacific Railroad, the courts ruled that a corporation is to be regarded as a person, thus clearing the way for complete separate, legal ownership of assets by corporations, which were now recognized as legal entities.

WHY INCORPORATE?

Incorporating involves extensive filing of applications, the payment of fees. It can take weeks or even months to receive final approval. So why would anyone bother going to the trouble of incorporating?

Corporations enjoy a unique legal status. They are considered legal "persons" that exist for economic or social purposes. Corporations themselves are not owned as property. Corporations may own the same kinds of property as an individual. This can include real estate, buildings, vehicles, mechanical equipment, patents, copyrights, bank and credit accounts and stock in other corporations. This is an important aspect of corporations, which sets it apart from all other forms of business ownership.

Through incorporation much of the risk and liability associated with conducting business is transferred to the corporation. If the corporation issued, for whatever reason, the employees of that corporation needn't worry about losing their personal assets. Any judgments handed down will be the responsibility of the corporation to bear; any fines or attorneys fees will be paid out of the corporate accounts.

It is important to remember that even though corporations are subject to litigation, individual employees can still be held criminally and civilly liable for their own actions. Simply working for a corporation does not mean that that corporation is going to take responsibility for an employee's actions, especially if those actions are illegal. In addition, an individual may also beheld partially liable for any actions that result in the corporation being sued.

Example: *A data entry employee decides to withhold payments from another company for supplies that have already been received. The corporation can still be sued civilly and held responsible for the payments, even though the action was caused by a single employee. The employee will also likely find himself unemployed and could be sued in civil court for damages, or charged with fraud.*

ANATOMY OF A CORPORATION

Running a small business is difficult. Running a corporation can be a nightmare. With so many different functions to monitor, executives from one division often have no idea what executives from another division are doing. Sometimes this is by design. Other times it is simply a product of the corporation's immense size and reach.

Example: *The Chief Financial Officer of a corporation hates one of the PCs. The CFO does everything in his power to harass the PC, including spending company funds on hiring villains to attack the hero. He then doctors the company's financial records to cover up the embezzlement. Unless someone intentionally investigates and thoroughly examines the company's financial records, no other employee in the company will know what the CFO is doing.*

Regardless of size, all corporations share several common features. Some of these features are required as a condition of corporate status while others are optional. All of them help the corporation to operate in the most efficient method possible — at least, that's what they are intended for.

CHARTER

The Charter is an official document which outlines the basic principles, rules and bylaws of the corporation. Every corporation must have one. Often quite lengthy, charters detail the procedures used to hold board meetings and elect board officers. A charter can be written by anyone, but is usually written by corporate law attorneys. This is to ensure that it is written in such a way as to safeguard the corporation from any future legal challenges to the charter.

The charter must be filed with the state in which the company incorporates and is a matter of public record. As undesirable as it may be, there is nothing to prevent any private investigator, or supervillain for that matter, from obtaining a copy of a company's charter, along with the names of the corporation's primary officers: the President, Secretary and Treasurer. Incorporated hero teams whose members are also on the Board of Directors had probably all have either a Public ID or at the very least a private life, rather than a Secret ID — their identities wouldn't stay secret for very long.

OFFICERS

By law, every corporation must have three primary officers; President, Secretary and Treasurer. Each holds an important position, overseeing a specific aspect of the company.

PRESIDENT

The President heads the Board of Directors. His duties may include chairing board meetings, signing into effect corporate policies, and other executive functions. His role is different from that of the Chief Executive Officer because the President deals with the corporation on a larger scale than the CEO. The president handles transactions between companies and acts as a liaison between the owners of the company (the shareholders) and the managers.

In some companies the positions of President and CEO may be held by one person. This is a common practice, especially among smaller companies with few employees. For stats for a generic corporate President or CEO, use the High-powered Executive or CEO from the Corporate NPCs section.

SECRETARY

The corporate Secretary is responsible for all of the administrative and record keeping functions of the corporation. Often, in larger companies, the Secretary will act as a supervisor to an administrative staff. In such instances the Secretary will have designated mid-level managers who work directly with the employees, while the Secretary concerns himself primarily with functions on the Board of Directors. For an average Secretary use the High-powered Executive write-up, but substitute PS: Corporate Executive with PS: Corporate Secretary.

TREASURER

The Treasurer is in charge of financial management. All fiscal matters fall under the auspices of the company Treasurer. Some of the functions of the Treasurer include handling the employee payroll and signing checks, authorizing large expenditures, and performing internal audits of financial records, either for individual divisions or the entire company.

Companies with a large number of employees often are divided into separate divisions, each maintaining its own financial records. In these cases, Assistant Treasurers would handle the records on the division level. The Treasurer would merely oversee the Assistant Treasurers, concerning himself with the "big picture. " For a generic company Treasurer use the stats for the High-powered Executive, substituting KS: Accounting, 12- for High Society.

ADDITIONAL OFFICERS

The top three mentioned above need not be the only officers in a corporation. Officers can be created to perform any one of numerous positions. Examples of other positions include Vice President and Assistant Secretary. These other officers may or may not be on the Board of Directors.

MANAGERS

From section heads to line supervisors, managers supervise the employees in various areas. Whereas the officers on the Board of Directors oversee the corporation as a whole and answer to the shareholders, managers supervise the actual operation of the company and answer to the Board of Directors.

Managerial positions can be created (as well as eliminated) as the need arises. Positions may be filled by persons appointed by the Board of Directors, or they may be elected into the position via a shareholder election. Some of the more common manager positions are listed below.

CHIEF EXECUTIVE OFFICER

The CEO is the top manager for the company. He oversees all of the company's personnel and responsible for the day to day operation of the company. He oversees every function of the company and directs the employees to carry out the instructions and policies handed down by the Board of Directors. The CEO is responsible for the day to day operations of the company itself. The CEO is a manager, seeing to the inner workings of the corporation.

The CEO is often the first person to receive credit for a corporation's success, and is almost always the first to receive blame for its failures. The position of CEO is one of high public exposure and usually requires a very charismatic person to fill the position. At the very least it is advantageous to have a charismatic CEO because he represents the corporation both at business meetings and to the public, via the media. One of the best known CEOs in America is Lee Iacoca, the CEO for the Chrysler Corporation in the 1980s. He was credited with turning the failing Chrysler Corporation around and making it a strong competitor in the auto industry.

In larger companies the CEO often delegates his authority to other managers who, in turn, report to the CEO. This frees the CEO to concentrate on more important and more urgent matters which demand his personal attention. For the stats of a generic CEO, use those provided in the Corporate NPCs section.

CHIEF MARKETING DIRECTOR

The ultimate aim of marketing is to acquire, retain and satisfy customers. The Chief Marketing Director is responsible for developing and maintaining company policies that will achieve those goals. He also oversees the various personnel who carry out those policies.

Marketing encompasses a wide variety of functions including advertising, mail-order sales, public relations, retailing and merchandising, sales, transportation, wholesaling, marketing research and pricing of goods. In larger companies each of those functions is more likely to have its own director. Titles for such positions range from Chief, Director, to Vice President in Charge. While the title for these directors may vary from company to company, their function is simply to manage their division. Some common management positions in marketing include the Advertising Director and the Public Relations Director.

Example: *Dyna-Mech Incorporated has a large Marketing division made up of many sub-divisions. Each subdivision deals with a specific aspect of marketing, such as advertising, public relations, etc. Each sub-division also has its own Section Chief.*

CHIEF ADVERTISING DIRECTOR

The Advertising Director is responsible for developing new advertising slogans, commercials, display advertisements and so on. In addition, the advertising department, in conjunction with the other marketing departments, may conduct consumer surveys in order to better gauge the public's reaction to a given product or service. Everything from a product's name, packaging and distribution method are scrutinized by the advertising executives. Some appropriate skills for an Advertising Director include Oratory, Trading, KS: Marketing and Advertising and of course PS: Advertising Director.

This much responsibility is often more than one person is able to handle, so there is often a staff of marketing personnel dedicated to the task, all under the direction of the Chief. In some cases, companies hire outside agencies to perform these functions. Advertising is big business and Advertising Agencies often command huge sums of money to develop ad campaigns for their clients. The U. S. Postal Service, for example, recently paid a New York firm $100, 000 to develop its new logo.

PUBLIC RELATIONS DIRECTOR

The Public Relations Chief is responsible for maintaining a positive image for the company and acting as a liaison between the company and the public. The Public Relations department may monitor the media for stories or reports concerning the corporation. The Public Relations Chief also prepares information to be released to the media and act as spokesperson for the corporation. Some duties of P. R. personnel include reading prepared statements at press

conferences, being interviewed by individual reporters and appearing on talk shows. In each case, the representative is acting as an official representative of the company. Public Relations personnel must have excellent communication skills. Some suggested skills include Acting, Oratory and Persuasion.

CHIEF COUNSEL

The Chief Counsel is the head lawyer for a company. He advises the Board of Directors in matters involving legal disputes over contracts, sales and insurance. In addition, the counsel represents the company in legal proceedings, such as lawsuits and other various courtroom hearings. While it is impossible to be an expert in all areas of law, he is well versed in all facets of Business Law. (For additional information concerning use of the skill KS: Law, see "Taking Care of Business: Law") Any corporate attorney working for a large or powerful corporation will be an expert legal researcher and litigator(assume he has KS: Business Law 12- as a minimum as well as Oratory and a high PRE; some legendary attorneys may have a KS: Business Law score of 16-, or even higher!).

The Chief Counsel may also have a staff of attorneys working under him. Large companies dealing with controversial products or procedures will almost always have a staff of lawyers on its payroll. The importance of the counsel cannot be overstated — at times it is the corporate attorney, alone, who keeps a company from ruin.

WEARING MANY HATS

In some smaller corporations it is common for one person to hold several positions. For example, one person could be the President, CEO, and Public Relations Manager all in one. The type, and amount, of work that each person does will depend on the size of the company in question.

In very small companies, such positions as CEO and Public Relations Manager may not even exist. The number of employees in a company is the biggest factor used to determine whether or not additional positions are needed. Obviously a small corporation with only ten employees does not need a separate President and CEO. One person could easily handle the functions of both positions. The same holds true for other positions within the company, such as Vice President and Marketing Chief, Treasurer and Chief Financial Officer and so on.

BOARD OF DIRECTORS

The Board of Directors consists of a number of elected or appointed persons who exercise control over the companies managers and make policies for the company. While the individual members of the board may also work for the company, the board itself is a detached organization, overseeing the corporation as a whole. They are not involved with the day to day operations of the company. The Board of Directors are elected by the shareholders of the company in annual meetings. In the case of a private corporation, new board members may be chosen by the current members of the board.

The Board of Directors must, by law, include the three highest officers(sometimes called the "top three"): the President, Secretary, and Treasurer. The board may include others as well, depending on the size and structure of the company in question. Other persons who might serve on the Board of Directors are major stockholders (if the corporation is publicly held), other appointed officers and even relatives of board members.

Board meetings are held at least once every year. Emergency meetings may also be called to discuss urgent issues or crises. Such crises may include a no-notice hostile takeover attempt, an act of sabotage or violence at a corporate facility, an unexpected court ruling which affects the immediate operations of the company or any number of other circumstances.

SHAREHOLDERS

Stock represents ownership in a company. Stock is purchased in units called "shares, " which represent a portion of ownership of the corporation; each shareholder literally owns a fraction of the company. If a company has declared itself a public company and filed the necessary paperwork with the Securities and Exchange Commission, then private parties may purchase stock in that company. About 10, 000 U. S. companies currently sell stock to the public, tapping an enormous (and relatively cheap) source of capital. Shareholders receive quarterly financial reports from the corporation, along with any profits passed on by the company, called dividends.

A company may opt to remain privately held. In private corporations, only a select group of people may own stock in the company; the company's stock is not offered for public sale. Ordinarily, the originators of a company are the ones who purchase the stock, which represents their investment in the company. Private companies aren't held accountable to government regulators or to public shareholders. Some of the largest private companies include Cargill, a Minneapolis-based agricultural products marketer, with revenues of $47 billion in 1993.

VOTING

Share-holders may attend annual shareholders' meetings, and vote in any general elections held by the Board of Directors. This is the shareholder's right as a part owner of the corporation. Each shareholder is sent an information packet from the corporation containing a notice of the upcoming meeting, the agenda for that meeting, a notice of any elections to be held and a proxy ballet (explained below).

Each share of stock entitles the owner to one vote. Thus, a person who owns 200 shares of stock in a company has 200 votes. It is obvious that whichever side of an issue has the most votes (i. e. , the most shares) on their side will win. Most matters that are taken to a vote require only a simple majority (50% plus one vote) to pass, unless the corporate charter, or its amendments, indicates otherwise.

Owning stocks in a company could be considered a Perk (1 point Fringe Benefit), especially if the company is especially powerful or is controlled by a villain or nemesis of the PC. Having a character who is a shareholder in a major company could also justify spending a few of those experience points the player has been saving up on a higher level of the Money Perk.

PROXY VOTES

A person must be present in order to vote in a shareholder's meeting. It isn't always practical, however, for shareholders to attend annual corporate meetings, whether due to geographical distance, medical complications, or any other factor which would inhibit a shareholder's ability to travel to the meeting site.

To solve this problem the proxy vote was created. A proxy vote is the transference of votes from one shareholder to another, or to the Board of Directors. The shareholder gives power of attorney to another person who may then vote that person's shares at the meeting.

Example: *Lockley Enterprises holds its annual shareholders meetings in Chicago. Margaret Taylor, who lives in Sacramento, owns 200 shares of Lockley stock, but she cannot attend the shareholders' meeting to vote. Margaret contacts her friend Julie, also a shareholder, who lives near Chicago and plans to attend the meeting. Margaret offers to allow Julie to vote Margaret's shares by proxy at the upcoming meeting. Julie accepts and Margaret fills out the proxy ballot, indicating Julie as the recipient of Margaret's proxy votes, and mails it back to the corporation.*

It is important to realize that allowing someone to vote their shares doesn't guarantee that they will vote those proxy votes the way the other shareholder wishes. It is quite possible for a person to convince a shareholder to relinquish voting rights for one election, only to vote against the wishes of that person. This can be avoided, however, by drawing up a contract requiring the proxy vote to be cast in accordance with the wishes of the shareholder.

A common tactic is for each side to try to "buy" the proxy votes from various shareholders in order to secure a majority vote in the election. Everything from simple promises of a better future to large sums of money (or even threats of violence) may be used to convince a shareholder to allow someone to vote their shares by proxy.

NON-VOTING SHARES

There is a special type of shareholder that is not allowed a vote in any corporate elections, called a non-voting shareholder. Much like the limited partner, the non-voting stock holder invests money in the company's stock but has no direct say on how the company will operate. A company may issue "non-voter" stock when it needs money, but does not wish to increase its number of voting shareholders. In this way control of the corporation does not shift and it lessens the likelihood of a takeover attempt.

The main reason for buying non-voting shares is to collect dividends. Companies will often offer a higher return (read: larger dividends) on non-voting shares to make up for the lack of voting power. A character who owns shares of non-voting stock in a company should not have to buy it as a Fringe Benefit, because they receive no other benefit from owning the stock other than receiving dividends (which can be better reflected by purchasing increased levels of Money, if the dividends are substantial).

TAKING CARE OF BUSINESS

Corporations are, by nature, active players in the world of economics (and just as often in the world of politics). Regardless of the company's primary focus — whether it be manufacturing, consulting or investing — every company has one common purpose: to make money.

Companies compete with each other to develop bigger and better mousetraps, and may resort to less-than-scrupulous methods to ensure their own success. Companies may attempt to undermine their competitors efforts, sway politicians to enact strict regulations to stifle the competition, steal the competition's secrets or simply buy them out. None of these things are as easy as they sound, but all are very real possibilities in the corporate world. Rare is the company that relies completely on the honesty and integrity of rival companies. Playing fair is a relative term in business. Billions of dollars are at stake and no one is in the game to lose.

TAKEOVERS

A takeover is an attempt to buy a majority of stock shares in a specific company. A majority is defined as 50% of the total voting stock in the company plus one share (remember, non-voting stock has no controlling influence on the company).

Example: *Yoshida Corp. has a total of 2,000,000 shares of public stock held by various stock holders. A majority would be 1,000,001 shares. If any one interest (a person, business, or group) owned this many shares of Yoshida stock, they would effectively control the company. They could then elect a new board of directors, fire company personnel and replace them with their own. Their actions would go virtually unopposed because they could not be voted out of any decision.*

It is not necessary to actually own the majority of shares to control a company. Simply controlling those shares (such as by proxy) is enough. Takeovers are generally categorized as either friendly or hostile, depending on the motives of the buyer and the willingness of the company being bought.

Example: *Lockley International buys a 30% share of stock in Kernogg's. Lockley International owns several subsidiaries that together own an additional 21% of the stock in Kernogg's. Lockley has direct control over its subsidiaries, so it now has effective control over Kernogg's.*

FRIENDLY TAKEOVERS

If a company wants to be bought out and the decision to cooperate with the buyer has been reached by the board of directors (or the shareholders via a shareholders' meeting), the transaction is considered a friendly takeover. Friendly takeovers are more commonly known as mergers. Friendly takeovers can occur for a variety of reasons, ranging from a financial bail-out to simply merging with a larger company in order to take advantage of the buyer's financial strength. Friendly takeovers seldom effect the employees of the purchased company in any significant way.

Example: *Terribuilt Trucks has suffered tremendous losses and their net worth is going through the floor. Without the finances to expand or recover, Terribuilt will surely go out of business. Offering more public stock for sale will not solve the problem because nobody is going to buy stock in a failing business. Along comes Centurion Trucks, Inc. who offers to buy Terribuilt. Terribuilt's board of directors votes to go along with the sale in order to save the company. Centurion purchases Terribuilt, which then becomes a subsidiary of Centurion.*

HOSTILE TAKEOVER

A hostile takeover occurs when a party purchases controlling shares of stock in a company against the wishes of that company's board of directors or shareholders. Hostile takeovers can be prevented in a number of ways. The idea is to make the potential purchase undesirable, which usually means making the takeover attempt too expensive to pursue. One method involves the target company buying additional shares of its own stock in order to maintain a controlling number of shares. The company attempting the takeover would need to buy many more shares in order to acquire the amount needed for a takeover.

Another option is to raise the value of the stock of the target company so that the controlling shares needed to effect the takeover are simply too expensive to purchase. This can be accomplished by increasing demand for the stock through any of a number of means, including simply leaking news of the takeover attempt to the media. Once the public gets wind of the attempted takeover, buyers will be scrambling to buy shares of the company being attacked. Why? Because the hostile company is trying to buy as many shares as it can, thus increasing demand; increased demand of a stock sends its value up.

Example: *Yoshida Corp. attempts to buy out Centurion Trucks Inc. The Centurion Trucks Inc. board of directors gets wind of this and decides to dump as much of the company's liquid capital into buying shares of its own stock, thereby preventing Yoshida from obtaining them. After several days of fierce trading on the exchange, Yoshida obtains 37% of the Centurion stock, Centurion itself acquires a total of 34% and other various shareholders acquire 29%. Very few shares trade hands after that because they know the value of the shares will rise;*

and it does. Knowing they cannot obtain the 50%+ required to control the company, Yoshida sells all of its shares of Centurion stock to eager buyers for a large profit. In response to Yoshida dumping its shares, the price drops again and eventually levels out. The end result: Centurion Trucks Inc. is still intact (as are the directors' jobs) and although the takeover bid failed, Yoshida Corp. has made a huge profit.

If the company generates the capital necessary to drive through the takeover attempt, then financial manipulation of the stock ceases to be effective. The target company does have a third alternative, however, which is to obtain a court order barring the hostile company from buying any more shares of stock. If all attempts to block the action are unsuccessful, however, the target company becomes another asset of the company conducting the takeover.

Hostile takeovers can be a serious threat to PCs who are either employed by a corporation or own one. A takeover by a rival company can spell the end of a young executives career as he is laid off and replaced. The best defense against such a fate is for individuals to have a Contact in either the purchasing company or in another company. This way, even if they lose their job, the executive can get another lucrative position elsewhere.

A DONE DEAL

Once a company has been bought by another company it becomes the property of the purchasing company. The bought-out company itself becomes an asset. What exactly happens at that point is up to the purchasing company. There are three basic options: the purchased company may be retained as a subsidiary, it may be completely absorbed, or it may be liquidated.

If a company is retained as a subsidiary it continues to operate as a separate corporation, with its own board of directors, managers, employees and so on. The difference is that the company is now owned by the purchasing company via a controlling number (i.e., majority) of shares of stock. While the subsidiary will earn its own profits, the "parent" company may dictate policies to the subsidiary; this includes determining how those profits will be spent. The only way out of this situation is for controlling shares of the subsidiary's stock to be bought by another party.

The company may also be absorbed, with all of the company's assets transferred to the new owner. A name change usually accompanies such a move. Personnel changes are also common, especially in management and higher positions. The logic is that it is better to have personnel loyal to the "parent" company in those positions, so as to secure the new owner's interests.

Liquidation refers to the total disbanding of the acquired company: all assets are sold off, personnel fired and the company completely dissolved. Any money remaining after settling the old company's debts becomes profit for the parent company. This option is used when the purchasing company sees value in the company's assets, but does not feel that continued operation of the company will be profitable.

POLITICS

Politics play a large role in business, primarily because the government sets the rules by which the corporations must play. Below is a brief overview of some ways that politics effect business.

POLITICAL ACTION COMMITTEES

Regardless of their line of business, corporate officers and managers all know the power of the government. Corporate boards also realize that the people who author and pass these laws are only human, and therefore susceptible to the same influences and temptations as any other person. Especially susceptible are those who rely on substantial donations to re-election campaign funds.

Corporations will often allocate a certain amount of money toward Political Action Committees (or PACs). The PAC's function is to lobby legislators to pass laws and regulations beneficial to the corporation or to prevent the passing of laws that would have a detrimental effect on the company. This essentially places the corporation headlong into the political arena, making contacts with various state and federal lawmakers. PACs may consist of a professional lobbyist or donations to a certain politician's campaign fund. Both are designed to sway the opinion of the politician in the company's favor. The bottom line is that money talks and politicians listen!

A character could, conceivably, work as a lobbyists for a corporation or corporate interest rather than being employed by the corporation as an executive or manager. Lobbyists will have several important skills, including Bureaucratics, Conversation, High Society, KS: Legislators, Oratory and Persuasion (the last two often being the most crucial).

EDWARD BORMAN, LOBBYIST

9 STR	10 DEX	11 CON	10 BODY	12 INT
11 EGO	13 PRE	12 COM	2 PD	2 ED
2 SPD	4 REC	20 END	20 STUN	

Skills: Bureaucratics 12-; Conversation 12-; Hobby: Debating 11-; KS: Legislators 11-; KS: Lobby Topic 14-; Persuasion 13-; PS: Lobbyist 12-

25+ Disadvantages: Physical Limitation: Smoker (Infrequent, slightly limiting)

Notes: Edward spent much of his time in school arguing with his teachers. It didn't matter that he was usually wrong, he simply enjoyed the spirited debate that always followed his disagreement. He eventually graduated and eventually became a lobbyist. Edward can debate an issue into the ground, whether he knows anything about the subject or not! He has recently been hired to do just that, as the legislators in the capitol begin hearings on a new bill that was recently introduced.

Edward can be used to represent the interests of nearly any corporation or special interest group in the campaign. He can lobby for or against paranormal registration, homeless programs, foreign policy, and so on. Likewise he can lobby the local city hall, the state capitol or even Congress — wherever the GM has a need for his services, Edward will be there.

PAYOFFS

While there are federal and state regulations dictating limits on campaign contributions, corporations may opt to provide "less formal donations" to political figures. These can include expense-paid vacations to company-owned resorts, use of corporate jets or stock options. In an attempt to get around campaign contribution limits, corporations may contribute funds to various PACs and special interest groups who in turn give the money to the politician's campaign fund. This kind of financial shell game is technically illegal, but it is also very difficult to detect and even more difficult to prove. Bribery is the obvious skill of choice for characters involved with PACs.

The legality and ethical value of such "gifts" are often in question. Both corporations and politicians can be very subtle, however, when the need arises — neither party benefits from a public inquiry (or grand jury investigation). Both companies and the politicians will go to great lengths to keep these dealings secret. Everything from hecklers in an audience to blackmail and prearranged accidents can be used to keep secrets from reaching a curious public. These lengths may, themselves, lead to adventures.

Example: *Ergon Oil & Power indirectly contributes several million dollars to the campaign fund of a particular Congressional candidate. This fact is discovered by an overzealous Jimmy Dugan. The Congressional candidate has based his campaign on fighting big corporations and protecting the environment, so news of his "secret supporter" will not sit well with the voting public. The candidate then hires a supervillain team to "silence" Dugan. The heroes get word of this and move to protect Dugan, and may even investigate these allegations themselves. As it turns out, Jimmy Dugan plans to confront the candidate at an upcoming campaign speech, which will also be attended by the villains. Things could get real interesting in a hurry!*

Keep in mind that not all politicians are corrupt. The effectiveness of PACs or payoffs are strictly up to the GM. It is the responsibility of the GM to set the tone of the campaign and to fill in the details of the campaign world. If the GM does not want corporate and political corruption to play a part in his campaign, then they won't. It's as easy as that.

LABOR UNIONS

Unions are private bodies made up of employee-elected representatives, which act as a liaison between the corporation and the employees. Unions typically have their own board of directors, much like a corporation, which consists of both member-elected and union board-appointed officers. Member-elected representatives are often employees, themselves. They are chosen for their leadership ability and familiarity with the employees' problems and viewpoints on various issues. Union representatives will commonly have the following skills: Bureaucratics, KS: Employer Policies (referring to the Union's member's employer), KS: Labor Laws and PS: Union Representative.

Unions also raise grievances with a company, negotiate employee contracts and file lawsuits all on behalf of their members. The union is often the bane of corporations, due to their active role as a legal watchdog.

Like corporations, unions will often have their own PACs with which they lobby legislators for laws beneficial to their members. Less scrupulous unions seek the passage of laws that benefit themselves; they care little, if at all, about the members they represent. Union PACs often carry as much weight as the company PACs, if not more. It is not uncommon for politicians to receive contributions from both a company and an employee union.

LABOR AND MANAGEMENT

Some companies enjoy good working relationships with the unions who represent their employees, while others are in a constant struggle. Class action lawsuits, threats of organized strikes (euphemistically called "job actions") and general boycotts are all extremely effective tools used by unions to bring companies to the bargaining table.

Most companies do not tolerate such power struggles. Corporate executives generally see aggressive unions as much more than a simple nuisance — they represent a serious threat to the stability of the company as a whole. Massive strikes have been known to cripple a company, bringing operations to a screeching halt and costing millions of dollars in lost profits. Some companies take drastic (and sometimes illegal) actions to prevent such disruptions. These actions can involve arranging negative publicity for the union, taking administrative action against the workers (such as layoffs or demotions) and even outright violence against the workers.

Example: *The working conditions at Blacklocke Mining Co. are very poor. So poor, in fact, that the miners have gone out on strike. The strike is arranged by their union, the Allied Mine Workers. Blacklocke is losing millions of dollars each day that the strike continues, so it threatens to fire all of the workers if they do not return to work. This doesn't work, so the board of directors decides to hire some supervillains to rough up the workers. The board doesn't want anyone hurt or killed, but wants the workers to return to work. The superheroes will likely be called in to rescue the workers from the supervillains — or vice versa (miners can be a nasty bunch!).*

SCENARIO TIE-INS

Adventures can spring up from a variety of union organized activities: an organized strike may tie up traffic on a major freeway or bridge, striking workers may sabotage a company's building or equipment and fights could break out between the workers and thugs (or villains) hired by the management. Some prime targets for sabotage include pier docks (where imported supplies and other goods are received by a company), production facilities, laboratories, shipping lanes (for trucks, trains, jets or boats), administrative offices holding the company's files, as well as research and development (R&D) centers. Disruption of any of these facilities will likely cause an extensive delay in the operations of the company, possibly resulting in lost profits, pulled contracts, diving stock values, wavering consumer confidence and a faltering credit rating for the company.

While not all real unions engage in illegal activities, such activities are more common in adventure fiction and in the superhero genre. These tactics are therefore presented in an attempt to address the role of labor unions in the adventurous world of paranormals and their potential effect on the superhero campaign as a whole.

DARRYL PHILLIPS, UNION REPRESENTATIVE

12 STR	10 DEX	9 CON	12 BODY	10 INT
12 EGO	14 PRE	8 COM	4 PD	2 ED
2 SPD	4 REC	18 END	23 STUN	

Skills: PS: Union Representative 13-; Bureaucratics 12-; KS: Labor Laws 13-; Oratory 14-; Persuasion 13-; Hobby: Model trains 11- Perks: Contact: Civil Attorney 11-

25+ Disadvantages: Watched by private detective 11-; Distrusts corporate representatives

Notes: Darryl is a man who inspires the hundreds of employees whom he represents. His sheer presence and confident voice have carried the union members through many hard times, from strikes to layoffs and back again. Darryl himself is a paid full-time union representative, drawing his paycheck from the dues paid by the general membership. While he has been approached to run for president of the union, he is happy to remain a representative. Darryl feels uncomfortable in positions of authority and prefers to simply mingle among his former co-workers whom he now represents. Darryl's beer belly and five o'clock shadow belie his true personality; that of a concerned union brother, willing to go the extra mile to help one of his members.

ESPIONAGE

As each company strives to reach the top of their particular market, their rivals are doing the same. Companies jealously guard their technological developments and trade secrets, so as to keep the competition from duplicating their efforts and eroding any edge they currently enjoy in the market. A company will seldom share its methods or formulas with anyone unless they are already so commonplace that they have become public domain.

Companies will often keep their valuable data under lock and key, controlling access to this data even among their own employees. Just as actively as corporations guard their secrets, there are likely to be others who want to steal them. Some corporations even employ professional spies to obtain secrets from rival companies. For an example of a typical corporate spy see the NPC write-up in the NPC section of this book.

Another consideration are powerful employee unions, who may use espionage or sabotage to undermine a company's operations in an attempt to force them to negotiate on the union's terms. In order to strengthen their own position, and to keep track of executive decisions regarding union/company relations, a union may conduct their own version of corporate espionage (see the section detailing Unions, above).

Regardless who is conducting the espionage, having a person on the inside can be extremely helpful. Anyone who is part of an organization, such as a company, but who is secretly working for someone else is called a "mole." Moles conduct themselves as regular members of the target organization, all the while secretly transferring important information to their "real" employer. A mole includes anyone who is covertly conducting surveillance from "within" the target organization. Applicable skills for a mole include Acting, Concealment and Disguise. Undercover law enforcement agents, journalists doing an expose story and foreign agents posing as tourists are all examples of moles.

This ongoing game of "hide and seek" is a fact of corporate existence that lends itself quite well to adventures and the GM is encouraged to utilize them in his campaign. A well designed espionage adventure can be as intriguing and challenging as any criminal hunt or street brawl, especially in a *Dark Champions* or *Cyber Hero* campaign!

TRADEMARKS

A trademark is any item, drawing or slogan which is used as a symbol to represent a company. Examples of well-know trademarks include the golden arches of McDonald's, the "walking fingers" of the Yellow Pages and the little green man from the Mars Needs Pizza! pizza chain.

It is important for a company to actively use and protect its trademark in order to prevent others from using it. If a company allows any one else to use a trademark uncontested they run the risk of the trademark becoming "public domain," which means nobody owns it and anyone can use it freely.

Some examples of items that were once trademarks but have since become "public domain" names include cellophane, thermos, linoleum, mimeograph, shredded wheat, mineral oil, zipper and yo-yo. Today, companies wishing to maintain a trademarked name will use that name to identify a brand of product, rather than identifying the product itself.

Some examples include Kleenex brand tissues and Scotch brand adhesive tape.

Heroes and hero teams can have trademarks, as well. Generally speaking, any original design worn or routinely utilized in some way by a hero (or villain, for that matter) can be considered trademarks.

SECRETS

Regardless of what business a company is in, there are things that are better kept from the competition. These can include formulas, computer decryption codes, the plans to unique aircraft or grav-vehicles or the PCs' team tactics. Regardless what form the secret takes, it is held as a company secret and measures are taken to protect it. The value of any given secret will vary, but it can generally be assumed that discovery of the secret will put the competition on much better footing. Its loss may cost the company millions of dollars, perhaps even forcing it out of business. Imagine the repercussions if one soda company were to discover the exact formula of its biggest competitor's most popular drink, and then produced a soda that tasted exactly like it. For this very reason most companies patent their secrets. Even if a secret is patented and protected under copyright laws, there is nothing to keep another company from slightly altering the item and registering it as their own "original" creation.

Lawsuits and vigorous defense of product patents can lead to some very interesting encounters in the campaign. A hero can become the defendant in a civil lawsuit, in which another paranormal with a similar costume claims that the hero's costume violates copyright laws. This could lead to an interesting adventure, especially if a battle erupts right in the courtroom! The lawsuit could result in a decision for the hero to create a new, original costume.

Example: *The main campaign villain wins a temporary restraining order preventing the PCs from wearing their costumes in public. Because their costumes identify the PCs as heroes, they may find it difficult getting public support if they are wearing different costumes or plain clothes.*

Most heroes spend a considerable amount of time building up their reputations. A change of costume could cause interesting challenges for the hero, as people fail to recognize the hero or confuse him for a villain. GMs could decrease the character's Reputation roll (from 14- to 11-, for example) or eliminate it altogether, at least temporarily. Distinctive Features would disappear if specifically attributed to their old costume ("No more black, pointy-eared cowl for you, Bat Guy!"). Hunted and Watched rolls could decrease temporarily, until the character regains his notoriety and people get used to the new costume. Simply regaining one's Reputation can be an adventure in itself.

SECURITY

As well-intentioned as corporate leaders may be, they all acknowledge the existence of corporate spies. In order to prevent spies from gathering restricted information, corporations enact security measures, both physical and electronic.

Security measures can range from simply educating employees about the risks of divulging company secrets, to utilizing actual surveillance equipment and physical security measures. These measures can include fences, hired security guards, ID cards required for entry into secured areas, electronic locks on doors, alarms, and security programs built into computer systems to prevent unauthorized access to or use of files.

The more elaborate the security measures taken, the greater the expense to the company. Corporations must balance the cost of the security with its potential effect. Most security measures are intended as a deterrent rather than an actual barrier. Therefore, companies will seldom invest large amounts of money in extensive physical security systems unless the value of the object (or objects) justifies the expense.

Example: *A publishing company will surely put locks on its warehouse doors to protect its inventory of books from theft. It's unlikely, however, that the company would install electronic security measures and electrified fences in and around the warehouse. The books are simply not worth the expense of such security measures; the books can be easily replaced.*

If, on the other hand, a company manufactured dangerous chemicals, it is reasonable to assume that a great deal of the company's resources will go into safeguarding those chemicals. Not only do the chemicals pose a threat to citizens if they are stolen, but the company will face severe fines and charges of criminal neglect for failing to adequately safeguard the chemicals.

That is not to say that high security measures will never be encountered around corporate facilities. They certainly will, especially in a world with paranormals running rampant. The GM must keep in mind that isolated incidents are not usually

sufficient to convince a company to invest millions of dollars in elaborate security measures. Most companies will be content with "Keep Out" signs and employee ID cards. Cost effectiveness is an important factor in the decision-making process. For the game stats of some common security equipment used by corporations, such as metal detectors and x-ray machines, see "Living In A Corporate World."

PARANORMAL PROTECTION

Superheroes working for a corporation may find themselves protecting corporate assets against espionage agents or investigating the disappearance of corporate assets. Conversely, PCs may also be sent to perform an "infiltration" of their own. In a business world where companies are actively seeking to discover each other's secrets, it's a natural assumption that corporations will be using paranormals to achieve this end.

Given the success of many supervillains in their criminal endeavors, some corporations and unions may seek out certain paranormals to add to their payroll. While few supervillains are willing to work "full time" for a company, there are many which could be hired short-term. Villains particularly well-suited for this type of work include Armadillo, Esper, Freon, Plague, Utility and, in certain circumstances, Mechassassin. Other mercenary villains could be employed as well, as long as they are able to carry out the often explicit instructions of their employer.

INTERNAL SECURITY

Not all threats to a company's security come from the outside. Some companies make it a point to watch their own people as well. Such practices usually occur in high-tech firms, or those dealing with extremely valuable (or dangerous) materials which could be subject to employee theft. Some examples of such materials include radioactive isotopes, genetic research materials and experimental drugs. Any corporation dealing with items that might otherwise be easily stolen, copied or destroyed is a good candidate for increased internal security.

Internal security basically consists of monitoring the people who work for the company, whether they be regular employees or contractors. Security measures can include electronic monitoring (via cameras & microphones, recording telephone conversations, and so on), security guards (searching employees coming and going from work sites) and direct supervision at the work site. Combinations of several measures are more effective than any one measure alone.

Example: *Henderson Electronics, maker of Stronghold's mainframe security computer, deals with highly advanced microcircuitry and complex computer systems. Henderson has numerous internal security measures in place within its various facilities — everything from cameras inside its R&D facilities and assembly areas to recorded radio transmissions between security guards. Accessing any of its computer terminals requires a valid employee code and password, which are secretly recorded along with the time and date of log-on.*

Companies that undertake such measures seldom enjoy high employee morale, due to the atmosphere of distrust that is often generated. If such measures are not known to the employees then these problems may be avoided, but will almost certainly cause serious rifts in employee-employer relations if they are discovered. Unions react quickly to such discoveries, filing "invasion of privacy" lawsuits and attempting to obtain restraining orders barring the activities. Employee surveillance is a very sensitive issue these days. Companies must constantly strive to find a balance between the security needs of the company and the Constitutional rights of its employees.

THE LAW

Corporate laws are extremely complex, spanning dozens of volumes. There are federal laws governing business, as well as state laws and local laws, such as zoning regulations and business practice laws. Business law encompasses many specific subjects, such as contracts, sales, insurance, bankruptcy and many others. With so many laws to consider, corporate lawyers must be very specialized. Most corporate attorneys devote their entire studies to laws and case studies that deal strictly with corporations. Any use of the general Knowledge Skill: Law should be at a -2 to the skill roll for general questions regarding business law. More specific or detailed questions are at a -4 penalty. These penalties should be halved (-1 and -2, respectively) if the character has access to a decent law library and has adequate time to research the specific topic. Assume 1D6 hours to research a general topic; twice that long (2d6 hours) to research an unusual or obscure question.

In order to use the skill without these penalties the character must purchase the more specialized skill, KS: Business Law. Successful use of KS: Business Law is critical to understanding the myriad of federal, state and local laws governing corporate operations. This is to simulate the very complex nature of the law, and the extensive training that an attorney must undergo to be effective in a given area. A criminal law attorney would be almost completely lost in a corporate board room. Likewise, a corporate lawyer would have some difficulties if acting as counsel in a murder trial!

The KS: Law skill should, therefore, be broken down into general areas of specialization such as KS: Business Law, KS: Criminal Law, KS: Environmental Law, KS: Civil Law and so on. The GM should not allow characters to purchase the generic KS: Law, unless he is willing to allow the character only the most general answers to any legal question. In this case, KS: Law should be treated as a Familiarity in regards to how much information a character may glean from a successful use of the skill. For more detailed knowledge, including that required of a practicing attorney, the character should buy the skill with a specific area of expertise (as described above).

LAWSUITS

Lawsuits filed against companies are quite common and are filed for a variety of reasons. Some common grounds for lawsuits are improper disposal of hazardous materials, damage to the environmental, fraud, discrimination and unlawful employer practices (firing an employee for reporting company misconduct, for example).

Lawsuits are generally filed in a civil (non-criminal) court having jurisdiction over the corporation in question. Determining jurisdiction for a corporate lawsuit requires a successful KS: Business Law roll (normal KS: Law is at only -1 due to the general nature of jurisdictional hearings).

The most common kind of civil suit that characters will have to deal with in Champions is the tort. A tort deals with civil wrongs that are not (usually) related to a contract. A person who commits a tort is called a tortfeasor. Some examples of torts include personal injury caused by negligence, libel and slander, infliction of emotional distress and wrongful death. Any of these types of suits can be brought against a hero as a result of his exploits.

Example: *During a battle against Genocide agents, one of Defender's electricity blasts misses its target and hits a fuel truck, destroying both the fuel truck and several other nearby cars. The owner of one of the cars was approaching his car when the explosion occurred and was slightly injured. The man later files a lawsuit against Defender for personal injury caused by negligence (using electrical blasts near a fuel truck) and infliction of emotional distress. The suit requests $5 million in punitive and compensatory damages. Defender had better contact a good lawyer....*

RULINGS

Once the lawsuit is filed and the evidence presented, the courts must determine if the allegations by the plaintiff(s) are justified. Civil trials may be heard by a judge, or by both a judge and jury. Attorneys for both sides are also involved, sometimes en masse. It is not uncommon for court proceedings to consist of a judge and a room full of lawyers.

Motions are filed, explanations heard and evidence entered, until a decision is reached on the case. Court rulings can have far reaching effects on not only the corporations involved, but with other corporations as well. Therefore, corporations follow such cases very closely, because they have a vested interest in the outcome.

Example: *If Awad Oil Company is sued and found negligent for allowing its oil tankers to leak a tiny amount of crude oil in Alaskan coastal waters, then all other oil companies can then be found negligent for the same thing in later cases. The cost of repairing or refurbishing tankers is felt not only by the company involved in the lawsuit, but all other oil companies as well (assuming that they wish to avoid facing a similar lawsuit).*

COURT ORDERS

A court order is an instruction to an individual or company by a court having jurisdiction over them. Where they effect corporations, most court orders generally fall into two categories: injunctions and restraining orders.

An injunction is an order or instruction from the court that prevents (or stops) the defendant from committing or continuing to commit an act that is injurious to the plaintiff. Things that can lead to an injunction include illegally dumping pollution into a river, producing an excessive amount of smoke from a factory and illegal stock manipulation. Most injunctions are issued in the negative, ordering the defendant "not to" do something. Injunctions may be issued as a result of a civil lawsuit, a criminal trial, or any other court proceeding. Court orders barring specific actions or activities are also sometimes called restraining orders.

A restraining order is essentially a form of an injunction. In some cases it is not necessary to be involved in a trial or suit to have a restraining order issued; restraining orders can be obtained by simply petitioning the court. Such orders are usually temporary, however, lasting only until the matter can be brought before the courts for a thorough review. These are referred to as Temporary Restraining Orders (TRO).

Injunctions and restraining orders are used by companies, unions and individuals alike to block actions by another party. They can be used to block attempted takeovers by preventing a company from buying any stock in the company that obtained the injunction. TROs can also be used to good effect by villains and other adversaries, keeping the PCs at bay while the villain continues his nefarious work. Of course, this tactic will not work if the hero simply decides to violate the restraining order.

Example: *Yoshida Corp.'s stock value is plummeting due to the allegations of fraudulent stock issues. At that point, Lockley International attempts to buy as much Yoshida general stock as possible in order to capture control of Yoshida (a hostile takeover attempt). Yoshida responds by immediately filing for an injunction against Lockley, charging illegal stock market manipulation. Yoshida claims that Lockley intentionally filed the previous injunction to cause Yoshida's stock value to drop, making Yoshida an easy target for a takeover. The court issues an injunction, barring Lockley from purchasing any Yoshida stock until after a formal hearing can be held.*

SETTLEMENTS

Injunctions and restraining orders are powerful tools, but sustaining either can become quite expensive. As appeals are filed and trials drag on, legal fees and lost profits can drive a company to reach an agreement with the other side. Settlements can spare both sides from the increasing expenses associated with dragging each other through the legal system.

A settlement is a formal agreement between the parties of a suit, in which both parties agree to certain terms, one of which is to drop the current suit. Terms can include public acknowledgments and acceptance of blame, and promises to refrain from specified activities (even if only for a certain length of time). Most often settlements include very large sums of money to be paid to the side filing the suit.

Millions of dollars change hands each month as huge corporations reach settlements in order to avoid long court cases and the potential loss of sales due to negative publicity. The biggest driving factor which influences whether a corporation settles or not, is money. If a corporation stands to gain substantially by settling, or at least stands not to "lose", they usually will settle. Lawsuits are seldom filed on principle. Corporations exist to make money, plain and simple.

Neutral settlements can also be reached, in which one party agrees to certain terms, but neither side admits fault or pays the other. Both sides absorb their own legal expenses.

COMPENSATORY DAMAGES

The general object of a tort suit is to win monetary compensation for the wrong done. This money, called compensatory damages, is awarded to the plaintiff as compensation for their suffering or inconvenience. Compensatory damages usually cover only the reasonable expenses incurred by the plaintiff as a result of the wrongdoing.

PUNITIVE DAMAGES

In some instances, an additional sum is awarded to the plaintiff as a "punishment" for particularly reckless or egregious conduct on the part of the defendant. Punitive damage awards can be quite large — sometimes many times more than the compensatory damages. This emphasis on money is why corporations, wealthy individuals and the government (so-called "deep-pocket" defendants) are some of the most likely targets of tort suits.

INTERNATIONAL BUSINESS

While many similarities exist between corporations of different nations, such as the desire to succeed and generate income, there are some subtle differences that are worth noting. Corporations in England, for instance, typically attach "PLC" to the end of their name. This stands for Public Limited Company and equates to the American "Inc."

TARIFFS

Tariffs, or import taxes, vary from country to country. High tariffs can cause a reduction in American imports, due to the increase in price to offset the tariff. Decreased U.S. exports with foreign imports remaining steady results in a trade deficit. Japan is a classic example of a country that exports much more than it imports (from the U.S., anyway). This is an issue of major concern to American businesses and government; talks between the U.S. and Asian countries continue on this issue.

WAGES

Wages are typically much lower overseas than in the U.S., especially in the depressed third world nations such as Mexico, Singapore and parts of Africa. Environmental and labor laws are usually much more lax, as well, if they exist at all. Many American corporations open production centers and other facilities in other countries for these very reasons.

PCs that are affiliated with a multinational or foreign company present an excellent opportunity for a GM to introduce the characters to other countries. Other supplements such as *Champions of the North, Kingdom of Champions* and *European Enemies* can be especially helpful for a campaign or adventure set overseas.

Another consideration when dealing with overseas markets is currency exchange. Exchange rates between national currencies fluctuates daily, requiring corporate executives to keep a watchful eye on the economy and current exchange rates at all times. A minute change in rates can mean the loss of millions of U.S. dollars in a contract.

REGULATIONS

SECURITIES AND EXCHANGE COMMISSION

The SEC plays an important role in the securities market. It is considered by many in the economic world as the single most important regulatory agency.

BACKGROUND

During the 1920s and 1930s, many stocks were sold with empty promises and sold with very low down payments, or "margins," of 20% and sometimes less. When stocks declined in value, brokers began calling stockholders to pay for the shares they bought. Unable to pay the for the margined stock, many shareholders sold other stock to raise money to pay their obligations to the brokers. This caused a further decline in stock values and eventually, in 1929, the stock market crashed. Countless people, and businesses, lost everything almost overnight. In a panic to retrieve what money they could, people began pulling all of their money out of the banks. These "bank runs" wiped out the banks, leaving them insolvent. The stock market had crashed and the country was in a massive economic depression.

In an attempt to prevent such a catastrophe from happening in the future, Congress enacted the Truth in Securities Act of 1933, which regulated how stocks were posted and sold on the exchange. A year later (1934) Congress passed the Securities Exchange Act and created the Securities and Exchange Commission (SEC) to oversee the stock market.

THE ROLE OF THE SEC

The SEC is a federal agency whose purpose is to protect U.S. investors from malpractice in the securities and financial markets. It essentially polices the stock market, enforcing the laws designed to prevent price manipulation and other illegal practices. It regulates all new public stock and bond offerings, collecting all pertinent information on each applying corporation, and has the final say on whether or not such offerings will be approved. In addition, the SEC maintains the information and makes it available to potential buyers of the new issue. In short, the SEC is the authority which governs the operations of the various stock exchanges. As a regulatory agency, the SEC has quasi-judicial powers and its decisions may be appealed to U.S. Courts of Appeal.

COMMISSIONERS

The SEC is made up of five commissioners. The commissioners are named by the president of the United States, subject to the approval of the Senate, to serve overlapping 5 year terms. The president selects one of the commissioners to serve as chairperson. No more than three commissioners are allowed to be of the same political party, in order to avoid one party domination of the agency.

OTHER REGULATORY AGENCIES

Government regulation basically includes any public policy that operates by imposing constraints on private individuals or organizations, especially business firms. Regulation seeks to achieve governmental goals, such as protecting the public from unfair sales practices or dangerous products, while leaving the majority of business decisions to the discretion management and the test of the market.

In the United States regulation extends to numerous industries and aspects of economic activity. It is carried on at every level of government. Several industries, such as agriculture, banking, telecommunications and broadcasting, have been heavily regulated by the federal government. The federal government also regulates many aspects of business performance, including wages and work hours, employment discrimination, workplace and product safety, labor relations and so on. In all, more than 50 federal agencies with approximately 80,000 employees are engaged in regulation of one form or another.

Many states act on their own authority to regulate certain industries, such as insurance, and occupations, such as electricians, medical doctors and attorneys. Specific policies often vary widely from state to state. Local ordinances also contribute to regulation, usually covering building practices, health and sanitation and land use.

THE COMMISSIONS

THE FEDERAL RESERVE SYSTEM

The Federal Reserve System was established in 1913. The Federal Reserve, also called "the Fed," is the central bank of the United States. All national banks in the U.S. are required to belong to the Federal Reserve System (membership is not required for State banks, but many belong voluntarily). It holds the deposits of commercial banks, thus acting as the "bankers' bank." The Federal Reserve also operates a nationwide check-clearing system and serves as the basic controller of credit in the U.S. economy. It determines the size of the money supply and the ease (or difficulty) of borrowing that money.

The Federal Reserve also acts as the government's official buyer and seller of foreign currencies, holds gold deposited in the U.S. by other countries and is tasked with directing the trade of U.S. government securities on the open market. The Federal Reserve handles sales of U.S. government securities on behalf of foreign governments (see Government Bonds). By altering interest rates and the supply of money, they indirectly influence the nation's economic activity, unemployment and inflation.

Unlike the central banks of other countries, the Federal Reserve is divided into 12 privately controlled, central banks. Each central bank serves a designated district. These central banks are located in Atlanta, Boston, Chicago, Cleveland, Dallas, Kansas City, Minneapolis, New York City, Philadelphia, Richmond, St. Louis and San Francisco.

CONSUMER PRODUCT SAFETY COMMISSION

Established by Congress in 1972, the Consumer Product Safety Commission is an independent regulatory agency responsible for protecting the public from unreasonable risks of injury from manufactured goods, helping consumers evaluate products for safety, developing national safety standards for products and promoting research to increase the safety of products. The CPSC's five commissioners are appointed by the president for terms of seven years.

The CPSC also has the authority to create mandatory safety standards, where appropriate, and to ban hazardous products. The Flammable Fabrics and Poison Prevention acts, for example, are administered by this agency. Any product which is suspected of causing an injury will likely end up being investigated by the commission. The CPSC has investigated children's sleepwear treated with flame retardant, electrocution hazards and gadgets such as the widely marketed "Seeker Stars," plastic toys shaped like martial arts throwing stars. (Note: These toys were taken off the market after a brief investigation by the Consumer Product Safety Commission and a huge public outcry. Seeker himself has volunteered to do several public service advertisements cautioning parents about dangerous toys.)

FEDERAL COMMUNICATIONS COMMISSION

The FCC, established in 1934 to replace the Federal Radio Commission, regulates interstate and foreign communication by radio (including cellular phones and walkie-talkies), television, wire (including computer modems) and cable. The FCC grants licenses to radio and TV broadcasters, and monitors radio broadcasts to ensure adherence to FCC policies. The five member commission, appointed by the president, answers directly to Congress.

Decisions have been made by the FCC which affect television advertising (such as the prohibition against cigarette commercials, showing real alcohol being ingested on television) and the use of prime-time evening hours by broadcasters. The FCC is also tasked with enforcing the equal-time provision, designed to ensure equal non-commercial broadcast time to all political candidates running for the same office.

The FCC also regulates transmissions by paranormals, whether through devices (such as comm-cards or walkies-talkies) or by "natural" means (i.e., powers). The case of Chicago v. Black Phantom (1970), 327 U.S. 123, established that paranormals wishing to legally broadcast radio (or other) signals were required to be licensed by the FCC (a one point Perk). In 1983, Congress decided that all forms of broadcast fall under the jurisdiction of the FCC, even if the broadcast ability is a metahuman power and not a device.

The FCC has three primary bureaus: the Mass Media Bureau, Private Radio Bureau and Common Carrier Bureau. The Mass Media Bureau regulates most radio and television broadcasting. It issues construction permits and operating licenses, and overseeing cable television operators. Television stations, radio stations and cable television companies (such as the 24 hour cable news network, Worldview News). The Common Carrier Bureau regulates public services such as telephone, telegraph and satellite communications. Any hero team's base with telecommunications ability will likely fall into this category as well. The Private Radio Bureau regulates services such as police radios, taxicab radios and CB (citizens band) radio. Telecommunications by sanctioned heroes or hero teams, who often have their own dedicated communications frequencies, are regulated by this bureau.

FEDERAL TRADE COMMISSION

The Federal Trade Commission is in charge of maintaining free and fair competition in U.S. business. The commission gives guidance, such as advisory opinions, for businesses to comply with regarding monopoly, trade restraints and unfair or deceptive trade practices. The FTC has five commissioners, each appointed by the president for seven-year terms.

The Federal Trade Commission Act, Clayton Anti-trust Act, Fair Packaging and Labeling Act, Truth in Lending Act and the Fair Credit Reporting Act are the laws that are administered by the FTC. The FTC shares responsibility for the Clayton Anti-trust Act with the antitrust division of the Department of Justice.

The FTC also takes legal action against companies who persistently violate the law. Such action may consist of formal complaints filed by the commission, followed by hearings before an FTC administration law judge. Rulings by the judge may be appealed directly to the commission, to the U.S. Court of Appeals and even to the U.S. Supreme Court.

NATIONAL LABOR RELATIONS BOARD

The five member NLRB was established by Congress in 1935 to administer the National Labor Relations Act (also known as the Wagner Act). The board has 33 regional offices and a general counsel. The board administers union representation elections and hears complaints of unfair labor practices. The NLRB has final authority over the issuance, investigation and prosecution of unfair labor-practice complaints. The board can issue a cease-and-desist order if it determines unfair labor practices are occurring, and may reinstate employees that have discharged unfairly.

Sanctioned superheroes who are "fired" for being careless or reckless may appeal to the NLRB for reinstatement, assuming the hero can justify the actions which led to their dismissal (Silver Avenger Pratney v. PRIMUS, 1987, 155 U.S. 147).

NUCLEAR REGULATORY COMMISSION

The NRC was established in 1975, replacing the Atomic Energy Commission. It is responsible for licensing and regulating civilian uses of nuclear materials. The NRC issues licenses for the construction and operation of nuclear reactor and other nuclear facilities. It also regulates the possession, use, transportation, handling and disposal of nuclear materials. The only exceptions are nuclear weapons plants, which are regulated by the Department of Energy.

Additional responsibilities include establishing training standards for employees of nuclear facilities, creating regulations and safety standards for the nuclear power industry, as well as inspecting nuclear facilities to ensure that they are meeting those safety standards.

EXECUTIVE BRANCH

Several other regulatory programs are administered by agencies in the executive branch. These include the Food and Drug Administration, in the Department of Health and Human Services, the Occupational Safety and Health Administration, in the Department of Labor, the National Highway Traffic Safety Administration, in the department of Transportation, and the Environmental Protection Agency. Those agencies that may directly affect a ***Champions*** campaign are detailed below.

FOOD AND DRUG ADMINISTRATION

The FDC oversees the safety of foods, drugs, cosmetics and medical devices. The FDC also operates the National Center for Toxicological Research. Important laws administered by the FDA include The Food, Drug and Cosmetic Act of 1938 (requiring manufacturers to test drugs on both animals and humans before marketing them) and the Delaney Clause in 1958 (prohibiting the use of substances in food if they caused cancer in lab animals). In 1962 the FDA ruled that new drugs must be proven effective as well as safe, and initiated a 20-year review of existing drugs. Supervillains who use toxins or other drugs in their evil plans will come under careful scrutiny by the FDA. The FDA has recently received a sample of the COIL gene and is conducting research to determine its effects on humans and to try to find a cure.

OCCUPATIONAL SAFETY AND HEALTH ADMINISTRATION

The goal of the Occupational Safety and Health Administration (OSHA) is to assure safe and healthful working conditions. OSHA is an agency of the Labor Department and is administered by an assistant Secretary of Labor. OSHA inspectors conduct surprise inspections of work sites to ensure that safety standards are maintained. The Supreme Court decided, however, in Marshall v. Barlow (1978), that employers may refuse entry to OSHA inspectors who search without warrants. They later amended this decision in the case of Johnson v. Special American Tactics (1982), in which the Supreme Court ruled that OSHA inspectors may conduct a warrantless search when there is evidence that extraordinary risk to the public exists on the premises. It is entirely reasonable to assume that any unusual display of paranormal powers at a hero team's base, especially those that endanger innocents, will attract the attention of OSHA inspectors. Likewise, complaints by citizens against superheroes can also result in surprise inspections.

ENVIRONMENTAL PROTECTION AGENCY

The EPA is responsible for administering all federal environmental legislation, from the Refuse Control Act of 1899 to the Paranormal Environmental Hazards Act of 1991, which prohibits the use of any super powers which may cause physical damage in areas protected by environmental legislation. The EPA has established environmental programs and sponsors research in pollution control technologies. The agency monitors environmental quality and seeks to control pollution (including solid wastes, pesticides, toxic substances, noise and radiation).

Paranormals whose powers adversely affect the environment may be monitored by the EPA (the agency is worth 10 points as a Watched on 11-; As powerful, Non-combat Influence). Actions by the EPA against paranormals can include legal actions, such as an injunction preventing the use of the powers in question, or fines levied against the character. Sanctioned or incorporated heroes are even more susceptible to scrutiny, because they fall directly under the authority of the EPA in matters relating to the environment. In addition, heroes seeking to build a new base or expand an existing base, may be ordered to first file an environmental impact report with the EPA. The review of the report could take months or even years (modified slightly for a good Bureaucratics skill roll, of course)! On the other hand, paranormals working for the highest levels of the federal government may be exempt from certain EPA-enforced regulations.

STOCKS

THE RISE AND FALL OF STOCK VALUES

The initial value of a share of stock is determined by the company issuing that stock. A company who wants a great number of people to buy its stock, from the young risk-taking speculator to the multi-millionaire professional investor, will likely offer a larger number of shares, thus keeping the cost of each share at reasonably low cost.

Example: *Yoshida Corp. decides to go public, and wants to offer $5 million worth of stock to potential investors. Yoshida wants to keep the cost of each share reasonable, to attract as many buyers as possible, so the Board of Directors elects to offer 100,000 shares of Yoshida stock at $50 per share.*

If the value of the stock goes down, then shareholders selling their stock will receive a lower value than they originally paid for it — they lose money. If the value of the stock increases, however, then any shares sold will earn more than originally paid for them. Factors such as consumer confidence, real versus projected profit, major events (such as buy-outs, firing of high level staff and supervillain attacks), supply and demand for that company's stock and even rumors all have an effect on the value of a company's stock. Simply put, a share of stock is only worth what people will pay for it at any given time.

The value of stock is largely self-fulfilling, in that increased purchases of shares results in a smaller supply; a smaller supply means higher prices. Similarly, if large numbers of people sell their shares of stock, glutting the market, prices will drop.

DIVIDENDS

Dividends are those profits that a company pays back to its share holders. Dividends are generally paid quarterly or annually. To determine exactly how much each share will earn, the company simply takes the amount of profits allotted to paying dividends and divides that amount by the number of existing shares of stock. Thus, if the company allocates $5 million of their profits to pay back to the shareholders, and there are 250,000 shares outstanding, then each share would earn $20 in dividends for that period.

SPLITTING STOCKS

Occasionally a company's stock will increase in value to the point that one share is no longer affordable to the average person. In an attempt to make the stock more affordable, therefore selling more of it, a company will split the stock. When this happens the company declares a stock split. Most commonly, the value of each share is divided in half and the number of all existing shares are doubled. Stocks may be split in other increments as well. Splitting stocks by 3, 5, or even 10 is not unheard of. The total value of any owned stock remains the same, however, when determining the new number of shares owned. Stock splits generate excitement in the stock market, thus stimulating sales of the stock and ensuring a continued interest in it.

Example: *Joe has 100 shares of stock in Duchess Industries, each worth $120 for a total value of $12,000. Duchess Industries announces a stock split, splitting the shares in two. Each share is then worth only $60, but Joe now has 200 shares of Duchess stock. The total value of his stock is still $12,000, but will likely increase in value, since a stock split is usually an indicator of a healthy company.*

BUYING STOCK

One of the most common ways to make money, aside from real estate, is to invest in the stock market. Characters can purchase stocks and bonds through an exchange or through a broker. Such investments can account for additional wealth purchased by a character or it may simply be tied into the character's background (or origin).

Owning stock in a powerful company entitles the holder to vote at shareholders' meetings. Owning a substantial percentage of that company's stock is certainly worth 1 point as a Fringe Benefit. This is due to the tremendous influence the character could have on the direction the company takes. It is suggested that a GM not allow the PCs to own controlling shares of any company that plays an important part in the campaign unless he is willing to relinquish creative control of the company to the players.

CHOOSING A STOCK

Buying stocks involves two very basic steps; choosing a company's stock to purchase and conducting the transaction. Choosing a company to invest in can be as simple or complex out as you like. Some people buy stock based on emotions or nostalgia, such as buying stock in a company who's name reminds them of their favorite pet. This method is very risky at best and, at worst, can lead to a trip to the courthouse to file bankruptcy papers!

Fortunately there are numerous professionals willing to research all the various companies and come up with an investment that fits a customer's tastes. Stock purchases can be made with small to substantial investments. Likewise, there are low-risk and high-risk stocks to choose from. High-risk stocks typically see larger increases in value than low risk stocks, but when they drop in value they can drop like rocks.

STOCK BROKER

Stocks are commonly bought through a broker, who conducts the transaction for the buyer. The broker must be licensed by the SEC in order to trade on an exchange (a one-point Fringe Benefit). The broker fills out all the required paperwork, sends off orders to buy or sell and so on; all a buyer has to do is tell the broker how much of which company's stock they want.

The broker will normally collect a fee for his services, often stated as a flat percentage of the total amount of the transaction. Reasonable rates for brokers are 1d6% of the total value of the transaction (roll 1d6, yielding the percentage fee). Typically, the larger the amount of the transaction, the smaller the broker's fee will be.

Example: *Jim decides to buy $1,000 worth of stock in Richards & Palmer corporation. He goes to a broker, who charges a 3% commission fee for the transaction. Jim's stock will cost him $1,000 plus the 3%, or $30, for a total of $1,030. If after the next quarter those shares return 10%, or $100, in dividends, Jim may have that money transferred to his account or simply reinvested. Jim chooses to reinvest it, buying another $100 worth of stock.*

INSIDER TRADING

An insider is anyone who is privileged with more information about a company than the general public. A corporation's officers and directors, for example, would be considered insiders. Insider trading simply means using information unavailable to the general public to make decisions regarding the stock market.

The regulations regarding insider trading are established and enforced by the SEC. To make things a little easier on investors, the SEC requires that all publicly owned companies reveal to the public any and all information that may influence the price of their stock (or other investment decision about it) — the news, good or bad, must be disseminated. In addition, insiders are required to report any and all sales or purchases of their company's stock to the SEC. A list of all such transactions is published monthly.

Example: *Leo Maynowitz, President of Main Communications, has recently concluded a deal to buy out Lasser Studios, a small film production company in Southern California. The news will likely result in increased confidence in Main Communications and ultimately an increase in the value of its stock. It would be illegal for Leo to call his nefarious associate, the Duchess Henrietta Van Drotte, and recommend that she buy Main stock. Such an occurrence, should it become known, would cause the SEC to initiate an investigation which would probably lead to an antitrust lawsuit against Maynowitz.*

THE NEW YORK STOCK EXCHANGE

With millions of shares of various stocks being traded every day, things could get very confusing. A central location where stock sales can be quickly and efficiently conducted is crucial to the smooth operation of the stock market. The New York Stock Exchange (NYSE) was created to fill that requirement.

The role of the NYSE is to facilitate the buying and selling of shares in the more than 2,200 companies listed on the exchange. To assist in this awesome task, the NYSE maintains a high-tech computer system. The system makes stock sales move more quickly and efficiently. The exchange has the capacity to trade one billion shares per day, four times its current day's average of 256 million shares. Over 80% of the stock value in the United States is listed on the New York Stock Exchange.

The NYSE is a tax-paying company with an obligation to invest all its profits (after taxes) back into the exchange to improve it. Since 1978, the exchange has invested over $1 billion in additional technology. Brokerage companies pay for the right to do business through the exchange, under its regulatory guidelines. The exchange is "owned" by those who have purchased "seats" on the exchange. When the exchange was first created there were actual seats for every member. Today, however, the term simply refers to individual memberships.

In addition to helping to make transactions more expedient and efficient, the exchange also provides regulatory supervision for those transactions. Further, it ensures that all security laws, as well as the exchange's rules, are followed. Here again, the exchange's computer system comes into play. The system monitors every transaction on a real-time basis. Every stock has a "signature," or a regular trading pattern, that is constantly updated. Whenever a stock varies from this pattern, such as sudden increases in the number of transactions involving a particular stock, the computers notify the exchange personnel. If the exchange finds something suspicious, they initiate an investigation and any illegal activities are referred to the proper authorities. The commission may also take their own action against violators, such as barring companies or individuals from the exchange who are involved in illegal trading.

Any attempt to break into the NYSE computers would require a successful Computer Programming skill roll at a minimum -3 penalty (a -5 penalty would not be unreasonable). Any hacking attempt (whether successful or not) would be detected by the computer's backup security system on a roll of 17- and personnel notified.

The exchange itself is regulated by the Securities and Exchange Commission, the Department of the Treasury, the Federal Reserve, the Senate Securities Subcommittee and the House Subcommittee on Telecommunications and Finance.

BONDS

Bonds used to be issued as certificates. These certificates often came with coupons which the holder would cut out and send to the company, redeeming them for the interest due on the bond as it matured. These coupons were used because bonds were not registered in the company's books in the owner's name. Such bonds were the property of the bearer, or whoever held them at any given time. These were called "bearer bonds."

Bearer bonds are an attractive lure for thieves because the holder, or "bearer," of such bonds may cash it in when it matures. The bonds are not registered at the time of sale so no identification is required to sell them back. If a supervillain were able to obtain the bearer bonds owned by a large investor, he would essentially have a large supply of untraceable cash. Several action movies, such as Beverly Hills Cop and Die Hard, have used the theft of bearer bonds as a plot element.

Most bonds issued today are registered, much like common stocks. The company maintains a record of who owns the bonds as well as other pertinent information such as the bond's maturity and interest rate. There are essentially three types of bonds: corporate bonds, government bonds and municipal bonds.

CORPORATE BONDS

Similar to stocks, these bonds are sold by a corporation in order to raise capital. Bonds differ from stocks in that they represent borrowed money, which the issuing company is obligated to pay. Bonds are essentially a kind of promissory note. A person who buys stock is buying a part of the company. A person who buys a bond is loaning the company money. Bonds do not afford the holder any voting rights, as do common stocks.

The time the bond becomes due is called its "maturity." Maturity for bonds can be any length of time as set by the company issuing the bond. Typically, the stronger the company, the longer the maturity. The railroads have issued bonds with the longest life on record, some having a maturity of 100 years! Bonds are typically sold in $1,000 increments, and carry a set annual rate of interest from its issuance to its maturity.

Example: *the Keller Corporation has decided to sell $1,000,000 worth of bonds. They issue 1,000 bonds, each worth $1,000. In addition, each bond has a five year maturity and a guaranteed interest rate of 10%. That means that in five years, each $1,000 bond will be repaid at $1,100.*

Bonds are a more secure investment than stocks. Where stocks may decline in value, bonds must be repaid at the agreed price. If a company is dissolved, the debt it owes its bondholders (like any other debt for labor, materials, etc.) must be paid before any stockholders can see a dime of what's left of the company. The primary purchasers of bonds are large investment banks, such as Flag National Bank (*Shadows of the City*), the Cherokee Bank & Trust and the International Finance Bank (*Justice, Not Law*), rather than individual investors.

DEBENTURE BOND

A debenture bond is not backed by specific real estate or property, but simply by the general credit of the company. It is essentially a giant I.O.U.

CONVERTIBLE BONDS

Convertible bonds are basically debenture bonds which contain a provision allowing the bondholder to convert the bonds into a specified number of shares of common stock in the company. It allows a set interest rate on the bondholder's investment, as well as the opportunity to benefit from any substantial rise in the value of the company's common stock.

ADJUSTMENT BONDS

These bonds do not earn a guaranteed interest rate through maturity, but rather earn an interest rate based on the actual profit earnings of the company, up to a set amount. Most adjustment, or "income" bonds have a very low quality rating.

FIRST-MORTGAGE BOND

A first-mortgage bond is a bond guaranteed by a mortgage of all of the company's property, sometimes even on all future property the company may acquire. These are considered the highest rated and safest of all corporate bonds.

GOVERNMENT BONDS

Government bonds are issued by the federal government. There are a variety of different government bonds. Government bonds are backed by the pledged word of the United States government. Government bonds are considered the safest investments in the world. The chance of losing any capital on the investment is practically nil. However, because their prices do not rise with inflation, government bonds offer poor protection against the decrease in the buying power of your dollars.

Example: *If you paid $75 for an E bill in 1964 and held it until maturity, it would be worth $123 in 1975. Due to inflation, however, the goods you could buy with that $123 would only have cost you $72.78 in 1964; a loss of $2.22 in buying power.*

TREASURY BILLS

Treasury bills are bills issued for a very short time, having maturities as short as 91 days. Rates on treasury bills have ranged from 2% to 3%, to a high of 16.75% (in 1982) for the 91-day bill. During World War II, the government set the interest rate on T-bills at an all time low of 3/8 of 1%. Such practices were terminated by an agreement between the Treasury and the Federal Reserve Board in 1951.

TREASURY BONDS

Treasury bonds are long-term issues. Often called "treasuries," they have maturities ranging from ten to thirty years. During hard times, treasuries may be sold at a discount, yielding much more at maturity than the amount initially invested. Treasury bonds change little in price from day to day and make up a good portion of the national debt.

When interest rates are high, a bond yielding only 4.25% would be unattractive to investors, so the price may be dropped as much as 60%, for example. In such a case a $1,000 bond would cost only $400, and yet would still yield $42.50 a year in interest, an effective rate of 10.62%. In addition, the holder would still receive the face value of the bond ($1,000) upon maturity.

SAVINGS BONDS

While both treasury bills and treasury bonds are traded on the open market, savings bonds are available only from the government and may only be sold back to the government. Series EE and HH savings bonds (formerly Series E and Series H) may be purchased at nearly any bank, with no commission charged.

Unlike EE bonds, HH bonds are sold at face value. Interest payments are sent to the owner every half year, getting larger as the bond matures. In addition, where EE bonds come in denominations as small as $50, the smallest HH bond is $500.

MUNICIPAL BONDS

Municipal bonds are bonds issued by states, cities and other units of local government, such as school districts and housing authorities. The bonds are generally sold to raise money for building necessary but expensive items like schools, roads, bridges, hospitals and sewers. Rather than guaranteeing the bonds themselves, however, municipalities go to large investment bankers for the money, just as a corporation does. Most municipal bonds are bearer bonds. The majority of municipal bonds also mature serially; that is, a certain number of bonds mature each year over a period of up to 50 years.

There are six generally recognized types of municipal bonds: general obligation bonds, special tax bonds, revenue bonds, dollar bonds, housing authority bonds and industrial revenue bonds.

GENERAL OBLIGATION BONDS

General obligation bonds are backed by the full faith, credit and taxing power of the issuing entity. This is the largest category of municipal bonds. The principal and interest on general obligation bonds are virtually guaranteed by the state or city's ability to tap tax revenues to pay off its obligations.

SPECIAL TAX BONDS

Unlike general obligation bonds, special tax bonds are payable only from the proceeds of a specific tax or other source of revenue. They do not carry the "full faith and credit" of the issuer.

REVENUE BONDS

These bonds are normally issued to fund specific projects, such as toll roads, bridges, power projects, hospitals and the like. The principal and interest is paid solely by the revenue collected on these projects. For example, a bond to build a toll road would be paid off with funds generated by that road.

DOLLAR BONDS

Turnpike bonds, a type of revenue bond, are also known as "dollar bonds" because they are quoted on a price basis rather than on the amount of their yields, the way most municipal bonds are quoted. Dollar bonds usually mature on a single date rather than over a period of time.

HOUSING AUTHORITY BONDS

Housing Authority bonds are issued to finance low-rent housing projects. They are backed by the Federal Housing Assistance Agency, giving the bond a top quality rating.

INDUSTRIAL REVENUE BONDS

Industrial revenue bonds are issued to finance the building of industrial centers, such as factories, airports and pollution control facilities. They are designed to attract industry to an area, thereby increasing the amount of taxes that are raised. These bonds are secured by the lease payments collected by the issuing authority from the corporate tenants.

LIVING IN A CORPORATE WORLD

BREAKING THINGS

When adventuring in a corporate environment — in office buildings, on construction sites and so on — the characters will eventually want (or need)to break something. This may be result from a fight with a supervillain or just plain frustration. In either case, the GM will need to come up with DEF and BODY values for these items. While the object list in ***CHAMPIONS*** (pg. 177) is helpful, it does not cover many of the things a superhero is likely to encounter in an office. Below are some suggested values for items commonly found in a corporate setting. The GM should change them, as needed, to fit a particular adventure.

OFFICE OBJECTS LIST

Material or Object	DEF	BODY
Furniture		
Bookcase, small	3	4
Bookcase, tall	4	6
Bookcase full of books (6')	4	8
Card catalog, wood	4	7
Chair, standard	3	3
Chair, high back	3	4
Couch	3	6
Desk, normal	3	4
Desk, large	4	6
Desk, metal	5	8
Door	4	3
Filing cabinet, wood	3	3
Filing cabinet, metal	4	4
Filing cabinet, large metal	5	6
Painting, small	2	1
Painting, large	3	1
Picnic table	3	7
Planter, large	3	3-6
Storage cabinet (6')	4	6
Table, drafting	3	2
Table, normal	3	4
Table, large	4	5
Toilet, porcelain	3	4
Tree, fake (5')	2	3
Washbasin (sink)	3	3
Walls		
Concrete	6	5
Office, interior	3	3
Partition	3	3
Reinforced concrete	8	5
Vault wall (walk-in)	14	7
Equipment		
Answering machine	2	1
Cash register	5	5
Computer, personal	2	2
Computer bank	3	5
Copier, normal	3	6

Material or Object	DEF	BODY
Equipment Continued		
Copier, large	6	8
Copier, desktop	3	4
Crate, small	3	2
Crate, large	4	3
Drum, 55-gallon	4	6
Escalator	9	8
Fax machine	2	2
Fire extinguisher	4	4
Hand cart	4	2
Lamp	2	1
Mannequin	3	3
Monitor, video	2	3
Porta-potties	3	8
Printer, large	4	5
Printer, desktop	3	2
Projector, film/slide	4	3
Telephone, multi-line	2	2
Typewriter, electric	2	2
Typewriter, manual	3	3
VCR	3	2
Vending machine	6	6
Water fountain	3	3
Security		
Camera, surveillance	3	1
Fence, wire (cyclone)	6	3
Gate, metal (accordion-style)	7	6
Lock, electronic	6	2
Metal detector, large	4	3
Metal detector, hand-held	1	2
Safe, wall	10	6
Safe, normal floor	12	7
Safe, large floor	13	8
Stanchion, metal	3	2
Turnstile	5	4
Vehicle gate arm	2	2
X-Ray Machine	6	6

SECURITY EQUIPMENT

Security measures are designed primarily as deterrents. Most security measures will not keep out a normal person intent on getting past them. Some items, however, are designed to completely block not only normals, but some paranormals as well. Below are some common security items that may be found in the CHAMPIONS Universe.

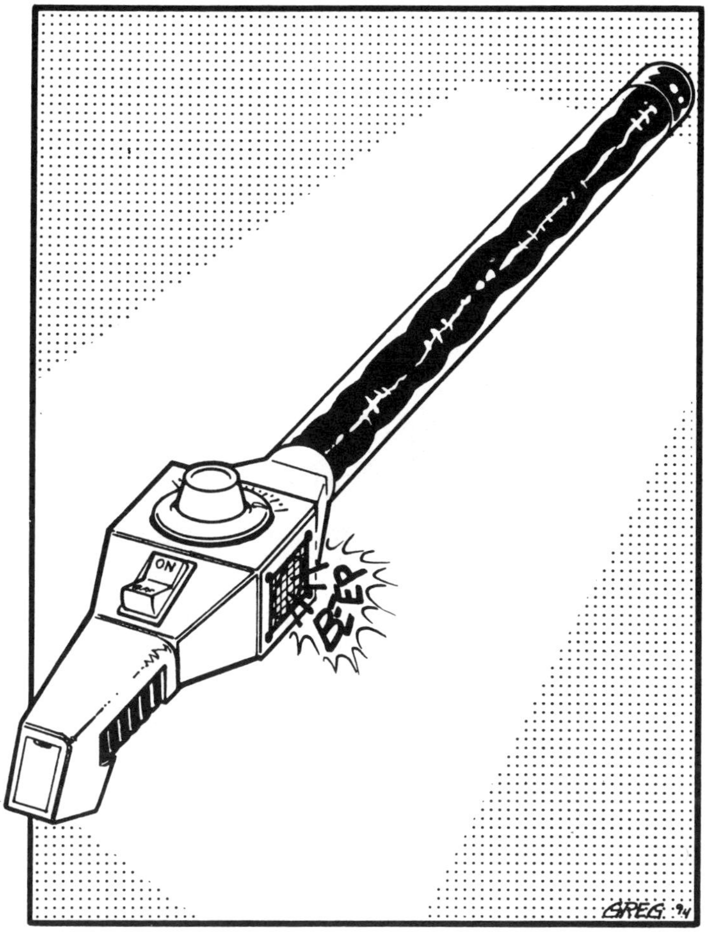

HENDERSON M-200

Detect metal, Sense, 0 END cost, OAF — wand.

Price: $1,200

Active Cost: 7 pts

Real Cost: 3 pts

This hand-held metal detector looks like an 18" black plastic baton, with sensitivity and volume controls and a speaker at one end. To be effective, the device must be passed very close to the metal (within 4 to 6 inches). The sensitivity of the device can be set high enough that even a paper-clip or foil gum wrapper will set off its alarm.

The hand-held metal detector is a less expensive alternative to the larger, walk-through models, but take longer to use (in the time it takes to scan one person with a hand-held metal detector, a dozen people or more can walk through the larger model)

GAUSS-NET 1200 MAGNETOMETER

Detect metal, Sense, Area Effect: 1 hex, OAF-Door/archway, Immobile.

Price: $25,000

Active Cost: 10 pts

Real Cost: 3 pts.

This institutional-sized metal detector consists of a large unit, approximately 3 feet wide, in the shape of a doorway. It requires the subject being scanned to walk through the doorway (i.e., through the "area of effect").The device's sensitivity can be adjusted manually. When an amount of metal above the sensitivity threshold passes through the machine it sounds an audible alarm (usually a high pitched beep).

Metal detectors are primarily used to screen individuals for weapons, although the machines cannot discriminate between metallic weapons and other masses of metal (such as metal belt buckles or coin rolls). Most weapons are larger than a lipstick case, so it makes sense to adjust the device to a sensitivity that allows very small amounts of metal to pass through without triggering the alarm.

The device requires an AC power source and can be plugged into any standard 110 outlet. To be the most effective, these machines are placed at the entrance to the building being protected. This device is commonly encountered in correctional facilities (jails and prisons), airports, court buildings and some entertainment events (such as sporting events and concerts).

EYE-TECH X-500 RADIO-IMAGING DEVICE

N-Ray Vision (not vs. lead), linked to Microscopic Vision (x10), OAF — X-ray machine, Immobile, Extra Time (1 Turn), Only views items passed through machine(-½).

Price: $65,000

Active Cost: 23 pts

Real Cost: 7 pts

The X-500 is a large, stationary machine consisting of a large x-ray housing unit, a conveyor belt and a monitor. Items to be scanned are placed on the belt, which moves the item through the x-ray unit and out the other end of the machine onto a table; this entire process takes approximately 12 seconds (one Turn) to complete. The x-ray image of the item being scanned is then displayed on the monitor. Items composed of metal appear dark gray or black (darkness depends on ferrous content), plastics and other semi-dense materials (such as clay) appear medium gray and light materials (such as paper) appear light gray. For those lacking familiarity with the device, a successful PER Roll can distinguish the various items displayed on the screen. The X-500 also can display magnified portions of an image, up to 10x magnification. This allows closer inspection of small items.

ULTRASOUND DETECTOR

Ultrasonic Hearing, Targeting Sense, OAF-Hand unit

Price: $125

Active Cost: 23 pts

Real Cost: 12 pts

Ultrasonic sensors are used to locate sources of ultrasonic sound emissions. These devices can be used to locate ultrasonic security devices, such as ultrasonic Doppler alarms and motion detectors (see *Hero System Almanac I, pages 70-73*). This device is used more often as a tool for overcoming security measures, rather than as a security measure itself.

The device is the size of a small transistor radio and operates off of a standard 9-volt battery. The sensitive microphone picks up ultrasonic sound waves and indicates strength of the source via a simple wire gauge or digital display. In this way, a character using the device can determine the direction and relative proximity of the source of the ultrasonic sound.

SEISMIC SENSOR

Detect vibrations, Range, 360°, +10 PER Roll (Total: 19-), -2 to PER Roll 1 hex away and -4 per hex thereafter (-½), OAF-seismic sensor.

Cost: $1,600

Active Cost: 34 pts

Real Cost: 14

Seismic sensors resemble high-tech cylinders, roughly two feet long. They are buried beneath the ground and linked to an alarm by wire (also buried) or by a transmitter. Seismic sensors operate by detecting the low-frequency vibrations of nearby objects moving overhead (from things such as vehicles and footsteps).When such vibrations are detected they are sent to a processor which filters out any ambient noise. Vibrations that are determined to be caused by intruders trigger the alarm.

The effective range of the device is rather short for light vibrations (like those made by a lone person walking nearby), but it can detect heavy vibrations at a good distance. The sensor's modifiers for range should be used in place of standard range modifiers, not added to them. Allow significant bonuses for heavy vibrations such as from heavy equipment, large explosions and other things that would cause a strong seismic tremor. Use the modifiers from the Hearing Perception Modifiers chart in ***CHAMPIONS*** (page 138); simply ignore all modifiers below "High Contrast Sound" (such as modifiers for weather, etc.), which do not apply.

Seismic sensors are used extensively by modern armies and by extremely security-conscious corporations.

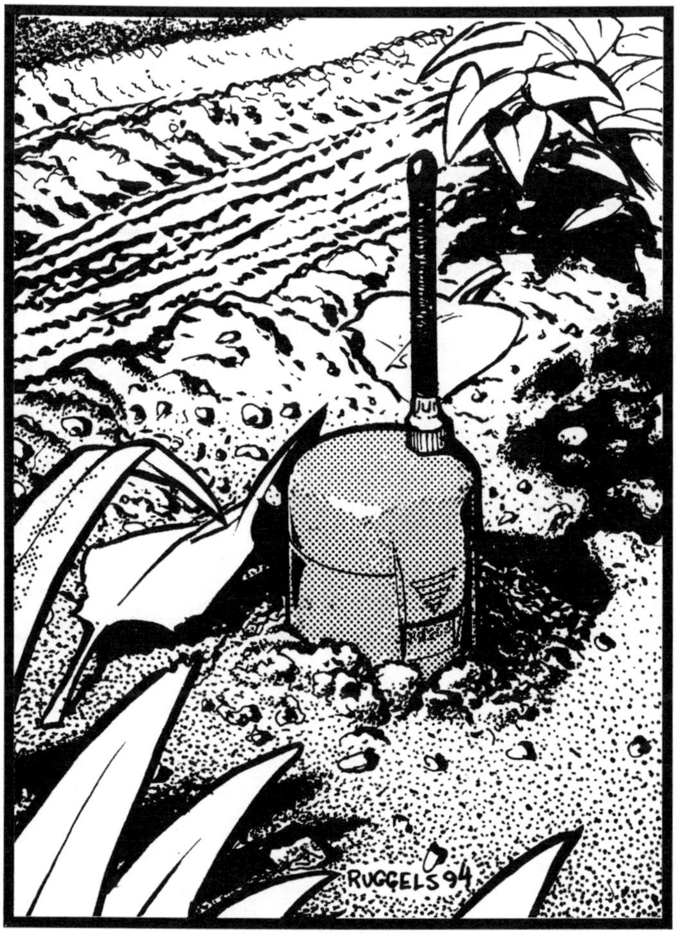

RAYTRONIC PORTABLE X-RAY UNIT

N-Ray Vision (not vs. lead), OAF-briefcase device, Linked to Microscopic Vision(x10), [10c]

Price: $145,000, plus $10 per charge.

Active Cost: 23 pts

Real Cost: 8 pts

This portable x-ray unit is very expensive. It is normally used by law enforcement and security agencies in situations when an item to be inspected cannot be moved. The portable x-ray device is ordinarily used to inspect suspicious packages, such as unattended briefcases and mysterious boxes, that are suspected of containing a bomb.

The unit is carried in a large metallic briefcase. When it is used, the device is removed from the briefcase and assembled around the object to be X-rayed. The device operated on a battery and film cartridge. Each cartridge holds 10 negatives. A new cartridge and battery costs $100.

MICROWAVE DETECTOR

Detect microwaves, Sense, Range, Targeting Sense, OAF-Receiver unit, Range limited to 4 hexes (-½).

Cost: $250

Active Cost: 30 pts

Real Cost: 15 pts

This device operates in a method similar to the ultrasonic detector, except that this device indicates the presence of microwave radiation. Its use as a burglary tool is to detect invisible microwave "beam" transmitters, which sound an alarm if the beam is broken. The availability of this item may be restricted to law enforcement or other specialized agents, depending on the campaign.

CHEM-SNIFFER

Detect Explosives, Sense, Discriminatory, OAF-compact box.

Price: $1,500

Active Cost: 10 pts

Real Cost: 5 pts

The chem-sniffer is basically a small hand-held device that analyzes the chemical compounds in air samples. The samples are taken near the suspected explosive by simply holding the unit within a few feet of the object. If the device detects any chemicals or compounds associated with explosives then it sounds an alarm. The alarm can be audible (a beep), visual (a flashing light)or both. While an alarm signal does not guarantee that an actual explosive has been found, it does guarantee that the element detected is commonly fond in explosives. Common explosives that are detected with this device include gunpowder (including bullets), C-4 plastique, dynamite, detonation cord and blasting caps.

ADDITIONAL SOURCES

For those interested in additional ideas for security devices, see the chapter titled "Sound The Alarm" in the *Hero System Almanac I* (pages 68-73). While the security devices listed above were written in game terms (using Powers, Advantages and Limitations), the GM needn't worry about such details when creating his own security devices. Simply deciding upon an effect (in game terms if desired), as well as a way to counter that effect, should be suitable for your game.

Example: *The GM wants to create an electrified fence which surrounds a secret laboratory. Rather than spending the time to create the fence using the listed Powers, he simply decides that the fence will cause electrical damage to anyone who touches it. The GM looks in* **CHAMPIONS** *(page S-44) and sees the chart for electrical damage. It is a high-voltage fence so he decides to use the damage for "High Industrial." Any poorly grounded character who touches the fence will suffer 11d6 damage.*

THE CORPORATE PERSPECTIVE

In the superhero genre, corporations have always played an active role. Even as far back as the Silver Age, companies have helped form the backdrop of the superhero universe. They have been patrons to our heroes, employers and even adversaries aiding the hero's enemy.

How does a GM incorporate companies into his Champions campaign? The following section takes a look at different aspects of companies, as they relate to the CHAMPIONS Universe. The idea is to impart a better understanding of the role that corporations play and what they are capable of. The GM should find it easier to introduce corporations into his campaign as more than just background decorations.

GOALS

Corporations are really nothing more than the sum of their assets. The true driving force behind the corporation, the "brain", is the Board of Directors. The Board of Directors decide the company's policies, goals and often the manner in which those goals are achieved. In short, whatever the board decides, the company does. The goals of each corporation will vary, depending largely on the personalities of the CEO and the board members. Granted, every corporation's ultimate goal is to be successful. Success, however, is relative.

A company's measure of success is dictated by its goals. The following are some stereotypical goals of corporations. They can be used by the GM to base his own corporation's goals, or as a sample list of "archetype" companies.

CORNER THE MARKET

This corporation wants to become the top dog in their field of business, shutting out (or buying out) their competitors. These companies strive to achieve, and maintain, a near-monopoly on the goods or services that they provide. Monopolies are illegal in the United States, so companies must endure competition in one form or another. Most profit-oriented corporations fall into this category.

STUDY AND KNOWLEDGE

These corporations engage in intensive research of a specialized field of study, whether it be language, anthropology or astrophysics. These companies usually rely on federal grants and donations from wealthy patrons or other corporations who are interested in seeing their research continue. Examples of such corporations include universities, university hospitals, laboratories, research foundations, psychological studies institutes and organizations engaged in metaphysical studies (such as L'Institut Thoth in Switzerland).

HUMANITARIAN AID

These corporations, typically non-profit, provide humanitarian assistance. This assistance can be in the form of providing food, clothing and educational services. Other examples include engineering and the construction of new buildings such as schools, churches and bridges. Corporations of this sort, concentrate their efforts on aiding a particular continent or country. This aid may be for a country outside of their own.

RELIGIOUS

Another non-profit category is the religious corporation. The primary goal of religious non-profit corporations is often to preserve their church and spread their teachings. Religious corporations quite often engage in humanitarian aid in addition to their ministerial activities. Another goal common to many religious corporations is the mission. In order to help spread the teachings of their faith, churches often send missionaries to foreign lands to live amongst the local inhabitants in the hopes of converting them to their religion.

RESOURCES

MONEY

Many corporations manage incredibly large sums of money. In fact, a corporation may have billions of dollars in its annual budget. While no business wants to waste money, it is important to remember that a company may have access to very large amounts of it. "Money," as it is referred to here, can be put into three basic categories: liquid capital, tangible assets and securities (stocks and bonds).

LIQUID CAPITAL

Liquid capital is the amount of cash that a company can raise with little or no advanced notice. Whatever the company has immediately available can be considered liquid capital. Liquid capital is seldom, if ever, used for purchases of services or equipment for the corporation. The exception is when a company wishes a purchase to be made discretely, such as making payoffs or bribes, hiring mercenaries or other illegal activities. Using cash makes the purchase much more difficult to prove, because it is almost impossible to trace the funds back to the company.

TANGIBLE ASSETS

Tangible assets include any physical property owned by the corporation. This includes vehicles, real estate, and factories. Tangible assets will vary from company to company, depending on the type of business in which they are engaged. A company that manufactures cars will surely have a large number of vehicles available. A publishing company, on the other hand, would likely have advanced desktop publishing programs and state-of-the-art desktop computers with word processors galore. The GM must be reasonable and use common sense when deciding what physical assets a company has at its disposal.

SECURITIES

Stocks and bonds (described in an earlier chapter) are not, in themselves, used as money. They are mentioned here, however, because they may be sold to raise money for the company, thus converting the securities to cash.

TECHNOLOGY

Corporations may have access to advanced technologies, especially those companies engaged in the research and development of high-tech items. This happens much more in the CHAMPIONS Universe than in the real world, of course. It is the GM's responsibility to take advantage of this point (you can bet the players will!).

In the fast-paced world of paranormals, a number of high-tech firms will be vying for the top spot in the development of microelectronics, cybernetics, weapons, telecommunications, surveillance, aeronautics, and a dozen other high-tech industries. These companies will almost certainly have access to their own products, as might their employees. Certainly the security staff, if the company maintains one, could benefit from any gadgets developed by their employer.

It is also important to keep in mind that much of the "super technology" common in comic books is limited. It may be of alien origin (and thus impossible to duplicate), extremely expensive or an accidental discovery that will take decades of research to understand (again, impossible to duplicate). By limiting the technology available in the campaign, the GM can ensure that the main characters remain more powerful than everyone else (with the exception of other paranormals). After all, what's the point of being a superhero if every normal has a 24 Dexterity and a 4d6 RKA blaster?

INFORMATION

Corporations dealing with sensitive or confidential data have a tremendous source of power and influence. Some types of companies that maintain personal or sensitive information include telephone companies, cable television services, any kind of insurance company, banks, credit unions, hospitals, credit card companies, magazine publishers and sweepstakes organizations. It wouldn't take long to gather a substantial amount of information about anyone who utilized these companies' services.

Example: *just from the companies listed above an investigator could discover their subject's name, age, birth date, address, telephone number, name and address of their employer, vehicle license plate numbers, amounts of coverage of insurance policies, complete medical history, dental records, annual and monthly income, bank account numbers and balances, credit card numbers and balances, hobbies and even religious faith. This doesn't even include information about a spouse or children. Never underestimate the amount of information that can be collected from these sources. The information above is enough for an enemy to cause a substantial disruption in their victim's life, to be sure.*

CONTACTS & FAVORS

It's not what you know, but who you know. Many a business has achieved success by following that maxim. Knowing the right people and collecting on an occasional favor owed can make the difference between the Fortune 500 list and Chapter 11 bankruptcy. More often than not, corporate CEOs and Presidents, like politicians, owe their success to a number of people that have helped them to the top. Other executives, influential aristocrats, bank presidents and celebrities are all examples of people who can contribute to the rising success of a corporate leader.

Getting there is only half the battle. Once in a position of power and influence, Contacts and Favors must be kept if one is to maintain their position at the top. After all, Contacts and Favors can also work against you. A corporate star must know who he can count on if he is to survive. Just as surely as he had risen to the top, others are trying to do the same.

Contacts can provide inside information about the activities of other companies, including the competition. Keeping a step ahead of the competition is the name of the game in business and Contacts can prove invaluable in this arena. Contacts can also provide up-to-the-minute news and recent developments, providing an opportunity to react to an incident before the information hits the mainstream media.

Example: *A ship bound for the U.S. from Korea is carrying a supply of jogging shoes for a shoe-manufacturing corporation. If that ship were to sink and the entire shipment of jogging shoes lost, it could cause a serious setback for the company expecting that shipment. It could also leave a huge gap in the jogging shoe market here in the United States, providing a superb opportunity for another shoe company to promote their own jogging shoes, thus capturing a larger share of the jogging shoe market and providing millions of dollars of additional sales. If a contact in the shipping industry were to send news of the ship sinking to another shoe company before the media had gotten a hold of the story, they could literally fill that gap before anyone else. Quick response to any opportunities that present themselves is crucial in the business world.*

Some contacts that could prove valuable to a corporate leader include bankers, other CEOs or corporate presidents, investment bankers, traders, investment analysts, public relations firms, television and motion picture producers, magazine publishers, syndicated columnists, Senators and Congressional Representatives, commercial real estate developers, attorneys and reporters. Of course, Contact with and Favors from paranormals could also play an important role. Having a contact with a super-powered team would be invaluable if the company were to come under attack from another such team or even well-equipped agents. Paranormals provide a unique opportunity for a corporation, depending on the special powers possessed by each (see "Supers in a Corporate World").

PERSONNEL

Employees are a valuable and often overlooked resource. The quality of employees can vary tremendously, however. Loyal workers, once found, can literally save a company from ruin. Whereas mediocre employees may be more susceptible to bribes or extortion, the hard line faithful can put a damper on anyone's plans to disrupt the corporation. Of course, an employee's loyalty will be influenced by many factors: salary, relationship between supervisors and co-workers, personal values and circumstances. Employees who have a personal interest in the success of the company can be considered to be "more loyal," even though their motivations may be more self-serving than their peers.

Personnel will almost always be low- to mid-level normals (i.e., Normal or Skilled). For example, clerical staff will typically be normals with Professional Skill: Clerk. On the other hand, scientists, technicians and engineers will likely be Skilled Normals with 25 points (or more) of relevant skills. This level of detail needn't be met for every NPC, but it is good for the GM to keep in mind when running adventures. Most corporate NPCs will not need complete character write ups — they are not that important to the story. A brief list of the important characteristics and skills, with perhaps a personality quirk for role-playing, should suffice. If the PCs interact with a receptionist, it is usually enough to know that the receptionist is a normal with the basic skills and experience of a receptionist. If you feel that a skill roll is needed, assume a skill level of 11- (with a 12- or 13- for very experienced employees).

Several NPC archetypes are presented later in the book. They are presented not as "official" NPC write-ups, but rather as a starting point or "average" that the GM can alter as he sees fit. GMs are encouraged to modify the NPCs to fit in with their own campaign. If that means adding or eliminating a skill, that's fine. Of course, for those people just looking for a quick NPC to use, these write-ups should suit your needs.

THE MEDIA

The media has long been one of the most powerful influences on society. Since the earliest days of written language, the media has been exposing the masses to the ideas of a few. From the letter-bearers of old, who would run hundreds of miles to deliver messages between kingdoms to the telecommunications networks of today which allow instantaneous transmission of data, people have always had a desire to know what was going on in the world around them.

The media can be used by corporations to achieve a variety of ends, the most common of which is to sway public opinion and generate sales. This is collectively known as advertising.

PRESS CONFERENCE

Press conferences are usually held to respond to accidents, major events or accusations. Raising public opinion is always a primary concern, because a low public opinion usually translates into low sales figures, which in turn result in low quarterly profit reports (remember, corporations exist to make money). Generally, anything that could cause a drop in the value of that company's stock warrants a press conference.

Press conferences generally consist of an "official" statement, prepared in advance, being read by a company spokesperson. Questions may or may not be answered, depending on the nature of the conference and how prepared the company is to respond to those questions. A press conference can be held anywhere that is practical, be it the scene of an incident, a corporate board room, or the front lawn of a company building.

Example: *The Champions have confronted a VIPER Five-Team at the airport while the bad guys were trying to kidnap a Yoshida Corp. executive. A battle ensues and a great deal of damage is caused, both to the Five-Team and to the surrounding airport buildings. Because the heroes were trying to rescue the executive, the public (and probably the heroes) may assume that Yoshida will pay for the damage. Imagine the heroes' surprise when, upon returning to Homestead, the Champions see a Yoshida rep on the television stating that the Champions are liable for all of the collateral damage resulting from the "rescue," including the corporate jet.*

COMMERCIALS

Both radio and television commercials, including today's half-hour "infomercials," are highly effective ways of getting the company's opinion or message to the masses. Commercials can be used to raise public awareness of a new or improved product, or a company policy. Commercials can also be used to counter negative publicity, dispel rumors and to cover up unpleasant facts. Used in this manner, they can be a very effective form of "damage control." Commercials can also be used to degrade consumer confidence in another company.

Example: *Tran Defense Systems produces bulletproof vests. A police officer dies from a gunshot wound while wearing a Tran vest. ASP Industries, one of Tran's competitors, seizes the opportunity to air commercials claiming that "poor quality can cost you more than your money." The result is a decline in Tran stock value and a horrible reputation for Tran Defense Systems.*

PRESS RELEASES

Press releases are bits of information that are sent to media representatives, without the necessity of holding a press conference. Usually transmitted by fax, press releases are a less formal way of getting information out to the public at large. Lengthy statements can be instantly and simultaneously transmitted to numerous destinations. Talk shows, on both television and radio, provide another option for getting the company's point of view out there for public consumption.

CORPORATIONS IN THE CAMPAIGN

Much of the information presented in this book is provided to give players an understanding of the role that corporations play in everyday life. It should stimulate thought and help the reader generate ideas. While not entirely related to role-playing, the information is necessary for the reader to know in order to effectively portray corporations in the campaign. The following section deals directly with using corporations in a ***Champions*** campaign, as it relates to the game.

CORPORATIONS AS PATRONS

When heroes obtain a patron, they can count on support to help them carry on their crime fighting activities. The support that a patron provides may be material, in the form of money or equipment, or intangible, in the form of positive media attention or valuable information about an enemy. Corporations can provide an excellent source of patrons for superheroes and superhero teams. Conversely, corporations bent on evil may act as patrons for supervillains or villain teams. Whether a company is sympathetic or not to heroes depends on who is running the company.

Corporations acting as patrons to paranormals may be either open about their endorsement (perhaps using it as a marketing angle) or secretive about their association with the hero. In fact, some companies may not even know that they are sponsoring a paranormal if the person making the arrangements keeps his fellow employees (or board members) in the dark.

Most companies will be careful who they get involved with, especially if their sponsorship is publicly known. Besides the controversy it would cause, very few corporations that sponsor a supervillain team would last very long if the authorities, including the state or federal Departments of Justice, knew about it! The legal repercussions alone could put the company out of business in a hurry and may just as easily land the Board of Directors in prison.

There are several ways to handle corporations as patrons. The method used will depend greatly on the effect of the patron on the characters, in game terms. Several methods are listed below for reference. No single method is better than any other. All are equally acceptable. It is suggested, however, that the player talk with his GM before selecting a patron for his character. The player should clearly describe who the patron is and what effects the patron will have on the game. This will give the GM a chance to determine the most appropriate way to represent the patron in game terms.

PERKS

Perks are useful items, privileges and contacts that a character has special access to in the campaign. This certainly describes a patron. A patron may be all of the above, and more. Most of the types of Perks available to PCs are suitable for depicting a Patron.

The exceptions are Favors or Followers. Favors are a one-shot deal and do not adequately reflect an ongoing relationship between a patron and its beneficiary. Followers are individuals (or creatures) less powerful than the character. In addition, Followers are (by definition) loyal to the PC. This does not describe a patron.

CONTACT

Patrons may be bought as a Contact. Contacts require two rolls: one roll for availability and another for ability (or willingness) to assist the character. If the patron is a person or entity that can only help a character out occasionally, then buying the patron as a Contact is appropriate. This is probably simplest and the most common method of buying a patron.

FRINGE BENEFITS

Fringe Benefit is another reasonable way to purchase a patron. The specific Fringe Benefits received would be based on the specific form of the patron. Having a character with "Perk: Friend of Yoshida Corp. CEO" would likely be worth only 1 point, because being a friend of a CEO does not afford to many more benefits than those of any regular person. On the other hand, "Perk: Son of Golden Avenger" would be worth 2 or even 3 points. While not as beneficial as Federal Police Powers, it is conceivable that the son of the Golden Avenger could gain access to areas that are off-limits to even federal peace officers. "Oh, hello there. Come on in. You're dad's back in the top secret communications room. Go on back. I'll tell him you're coming...." Being the son of the USA's premier super soldier could come in handy in the right circumstances.

NEW FRINGE BENEFITS

Cost	Notes
1 pt	Owning stock in a large/powerful company
1 pt	Junior corporate officer or manager
1 pt	Corporate board member
2 pts	Corporate CEO or President
1 pt	Licensed business law attorney
1 pt	Licensed stock broker
1 pt	FCC radio transmission license

MONEY

If a patron is a character's primary source of funding, and little else, then buying Money is a practical alternative to taking the patron as a Contact. Buying an extra level or two of wealth can simulate a patron who gives the PC a steady supply of cash without interfering in his day-to-day affairs. Any patron who has any kind of control over how the money is spent should not be bought as Money, unless the character also takes the Watched Disadvantage.

Money can be purchased in increments between Middle Class (0 pts) and Well Off (5 pts), which gives the character an income of "less than $500,000 per year." Each point spent, up to 5 points, allows an income of up to $100,000 per year. Thus, 3 points of Money gives the character up to $300,000 per year.

DISADVANTAGES

While the purpose of having a patron is to benefit the character, there are occasional drawbacks to having a patron. Very few people — and even fewer companies — are willing to blindly throw money at a cause, let alone a paranormal, without expecting something in return. There are certain Disadvantages which accurately reflect the amount of influence various patrons can exercise over the character. These Disadvantages are discussed below.

DNPC

Dependent NPCs are one option for the patron. A DNPC can take the form of a representative of the patron, assigned to carefully record how the patron's resources are being utilized. The PCs needn't be emotionally attached to the DNPC. It is sufficient that they simply feel the need to look out for him.

DISTINCTIVE FEATURES

Distinctive Features is a great Disadvantage to give a super who has a corporation as a patron. While the hero may receive excellent publicity and her own line of action figures, the patron could require the hero to display the company's logo somewhere conspicuous; on the hero's costume, vehicle or base. While the image of a corporate-sponsored hero, with his sponsor's logo emblazoned across his back, may seem a bit ludicrous it is nonetheless entirely plausible.

HUNTED AND WATCHED

While Hunted is a bit extreme for a patron, Watched is an obvious choice as a Disadvantage to reflect having a Patron. A patron's point value as a Watched will depend strongly on how easily they can actually keep tabs on the character. The frequency of a patron's appearance will reflect their interest in the character. An 8 or less roll is sufficient for a patron who simply wants to be kept informed of recent events and expenditures. Weekly or monthly telephone calls are usually enough to satisfy this patron. A 14 or less roll, on the other hand, would represent the fanatical patron who demands daily (if not hourly) status reports and detailed explanations for each and every funding request. A frequency of 11 or less would be somewhere in between. For more information about taking corporations as Hunteds, see the section below titled "Corporations as Hunteds."

PSYCHOLOGICAL LIMITATION

A sense of duty or responsibility to a patron can be illustrated by taking a Psychological Limitation. Such responsibility to the patron may be emotional or psychological ("I've got to do what they say because they know what's best."). Conversely, it may be contractual agreement between the hero and the patron. In either case, the character is able to disobey the patron, but chooses not do. The point value of a Psychological Disadvantage will vary, depending on the strength of the character's conviction and how often the issue surfaces.

CORPORATIONS AS HUNTERS

There are a number of reasons why a corporation could be hunting a paranormal. Keep in mind, too, that it may simply be a powerful individual in a company who is technically the character's "hunter." In this case, treat the entire company as the hunter, rather than the individual. Even though a single person is hunting the character, they have access to all of the resources of the company at their fingertips, making them much more powerful than they would be alone.

If the actions of a company are being directed by a few people, or a single person, their actions may go completely unnoticed by the rest of the company and the Board of Directors. The degree of subtlety will depend on who is in responsible for hunting the character, and what actions the hunter takes in pursuing them.

Example: *If every member of a Board of Directors wishes to hunt down a character, then the entire board will obviously know about the plans. They may wish to keep this information from the employees in order to avoid any potential leaks and subsequent embarrassments.*

Yamamoto Electronics arises as a classic example of the "evil board and ignorant employees" motif. Akiro Yamamoto leads a double life as the President of the company and member of the ultra-secret VIPER council. All the while his employees go about their work, blissfully ignorant of their leader's dishonorable association with the villainous organization. Akiro even utilizes VIPER resources against his competitors and no one in the company is the wiser.

POWER LEVEL

According to the *HERO System Rulesbook* (p. 122), the power level of a Hunted is based on its ability to accomplish its goal against the character in question. For instance, if a company wants to capture a hero in order to conduct genetic research on him, then the power level will be relative to the company's ability to actually capture the hero. When figuring a corporation's ability to accomplish its goal, consider the resources that the corporation would use in an average mission rather than the corporation's total resources.

Example: *Yoshida Corp. has four dozen Yakuza members (designated as "field personnel") for kidnapping and assassination missions. However, Yoshida will only send six agents at a time for a typical mission. You would base Yoshida Corp's power level on the chances of six agents accomplishing their mission, not on all 48 of the company's agents, because Yoshida never uses the entire team on one mission.*

LIMITED GEOGRAPHICALLY

Small companies with only one or a few offices in a small area would qualify for the -5 point "Limited Geographically" modifier. This assumes that the corporation's influence is also limited to this area. Corporations with subsidiaries across the country, or the world, could be considered to have a large enough sphere of influence that the -5 modifier would not apply.

Example: *If a local bank has branches nowhere but in the campaign city, yet is owned by a larger national bank and has access to the larger bank's files, it would not qualify for the modifier. On the other hand, a corporation that only had offices in the character's home state, and had no influence outside of that state, would receive the -5 point modifier.*

NON-COMBAT INFLUENCE

Whether or not a corporation is considered to have Non-Combat Influence depends on its resources. Corporations dedicated to activities that do not bring them into contact with other companies will likely not receive the NCI modifier.

Example: *A high-tech weapons manufacturing company, with no other activities, would probably not receive the NCI modifier. This is because the company does nothing else but manufacture weapons and has little influence on the day to day life of anyone other than its distributors and employees.*

If a corporation also owns a telecommunications company, then the corporation would surely be considered as having Non-Combat Influence, since they could have a character's phone service terminated and send erroneous late payment reports to a credit agency. Imagine a surprised Seeker trying to call someone on the telephone only to discover the line is dead. "I thought Defender paid that bloody bill." Elsewhere, a corporate CEO smiles as he fingers the stylized "V" on his signet ring....

As a rule of thumb, any valuable corporation will have a pool of attorneys on the payroll and enough liquid capital available for miscellaneous expenditures that it can be considered having Non-Combat Influence.

SUPERS IN A CORPORATE WORLD

As mentioned earlier, one of the distinct advantages to incorporating is that much of the legal liability shifts to the corporation, since it is recognized as a separate legal entity. Regarding vigilantes, villains and even bonafide heroes, transferring liability to another entity is quite an attractive concept. Let's face it, by gallivanting around the city and getting into super-powered slug-fests, heroes run the risk of collateral damage. With stray energy blasts and huge objects being hurled about, something is bound to get broken. That's not to mention the possibility of innocents being injured (never a good thing).

As you can see, supers have a good chance of becoming a defendant in a lawsuit, either criminal or civil, if they're not careful. If a hero is wealthy enough, or has the right connections, then this may not be a problem. If this is not the case, however, such as in a campaign where the government is less-than-sympathetic toward supers, incorporating may be a viable alternative to "going it alone."

HEROES AND HERO TEAMS AS CORPORATIONS

To incorporate the hero (or team) must have legal documents drawn up and filed with a state, just like any other business wishing to incorporate. They must also designate individuals to fulfill the positions of the corporate officers — the President, Treasurer and Secretary. These positions may be filled by the heroes, themselves, but this option is inadvisable unless the heroes all have Public IDs (remember, incorporation documents may be viewed by any citizen who requests it). That is not to say that a hero couldn't have a Secret ID, serving on the Board of Directors by day and fighting crime as "Ledger Man" by night. Many classic comic book heroes have accomplished such a feat with relative ease. The Dark Knight springs to mind as one classic example. Managing a secret life as a hero is the center point to many comic characters, and should be no less available to the characters in this game.

EMPLOYEES

Labor and hiring laws would restrict the kind of people that could work for the team. For example, foreign citizens would not be allowed to join the team without first going through the U.S. Naturalization and Immigration Service and obtaining a

Resident Alien ID card (also known as a "green card"). Similarly, if the corporation pays it employees (i.e., the team members), it will be required to submit documents to the Internal Revenue Service and the Social Security office, thus creating a paper trail that could be easily followed by any competent investigator.

CORPORATION TYPE

An important consideration when a hero team incorporates is whether or not the corporation will be non-profit. Many hero teams that incorporate are likely to become non-profit corporations. A "for profit" team doesn't seem too heroic; financial gain is hardly a heroic motivation for fighting crime.

That's not to say that it is impossible for a team to be a profit-based corporation. It is entirely feasible for a team to operate as a true business in every definition of the word. Such a team could contract out their services to whoever is willing and able to meet the team's price. A kind of mercenary-vigilante hybrid, profit-driven team could provide an interesting twist to a ***Champions*** or *Dark Champions* campaign. People might easily mistake such a team for supervillains, however. The heroes would have to exercise great care when dealing with members of the media and the public, so as not to convey the wrong impressions. For-profit superhero teams are an opportunity for the players to roleplay in a unique ***Champions*** setting.

Another twist to the classic superhero team is the religious not-for-profit hero team. Such a team could consist of heroes that are all of the same religious faith, or mixed. Imagine a team of Christian heroes saving innocents at every turn and soliciting tax-deductible donations to help their mission. Or a team of mixed faiths, united in purpose to defeat the common enemies of the Earth (like offensive aliens or Morbanes of DEMON). Who could turn their backs on such well-intentioned superheroes?

OTHER CONSIDERATIONS

IDENTITIES

Maintaining a Secret ID may be rather difficult for incorporated supers, and nearly impossible for supers who collect a paycheck for their work! One option is to hire people to fill the officer positions on the Board of Directors. Hiring people to act as the Board of Directors frees the heroes to become regular "employees" of the corporation. While the board would technically be in charge of the team, they could delegate authority to a member of the team for field activities. This "team leader" would be responsible for the rest of the team and would answer directly to the Board of Directors.

Supers wishing to remain completely anonymous will have to either work "under the table," receiving cash payments from the corporation (written off as "miscellaneous expenses," perhaps) or they will have to work under an assumed name and Social Security number. While both are illegal, the former presents less of a risk to the corporation because financial records are easily doctored. Assume at least a -2 penalty to any applicable skill rolls, such as KS: Accounting or Deduction, for anyone attempting to discover this. However, heroes paid by cash will not be able to receive the other benefits afforded to a regular employee, such as health and worker's compensation insurance, legal aid and so on.

Working under an assumed name requires falsifying numerous documents, from applications for a Social Security number to IRS tax forms. While casual perusal of corporate records may reveal nothing, a formal investigation may have quite different results. Falsifying one's name to so many government agencies constitutes fraud on a federal scale and could easily spell the end of the corporation. Even during the investigation phase, corporations could find themselves operating without the benefit of office equipment, files and even desktop computers, all possibly seized by the government as evidence in their investigation of the corporation. If a corporation is found guilty of committing fraud the penalties can be quite severe, ranging from heavy fines to actual imprisonment of those involved. Of course not all investigations or criminal charges result in a conviction. Some such acts by the government may actually be the complex plans of some criminal mastermind, using the government to put pressure on the corporation in question.

All of these things will add up, and data on both the corporation and everyone associated with it will be collected by numerous government and private agencies. Incorporated hero teams may be seen by law enforcement officials as less of a public threat, because a great deal of information about the team is already on file with the state or could be easily discovered by a cursory investigation. Once a team is familiar to the local authorities, they may find themselves not only being tolerated, but receiving even more assistance than before. The local police department will not be as distrusting of someone they know they can find easily, and whose identity is already known.

PUBLIC OPINION

As a corporation, a superhero team could easily find itself with a reputation among the public, whether earned or undeserved. Some people may view incorporated paranormal teams as "sell-outs," thinking them unwilling to fight crime and protect innocents without legal waivers and insurance policies to protect them. Still other people will find the concept of team incorporation a novel idea, and may support the team as a valued addition to the local business community. We can extrapolate this concept even further and assume that the team could be eligible for membership in the local chamber of commerce. Implementing such ideas would definitely add a twist to the standard superhero campaign.

BENEFITS

Supers who belong to a corporation could enjoy numerous benefits that would otherwise escape them if they were operating as lone vigilantes. Besides the potential for a salary, heroes could receive health care, liability insurance, even legal representation and public relations management.

HEALTH CARE

Health insurance could be particularly valuable to a superhero, especially if they have none of their own. Characters who are students, illegal immigrants or simply from a low income household are the most vulnerable. Rushing from battle to battle with the likes of Eurostar and Dr. Destroyer takes its toll on a person; sooner or later a hero is likely to wind up in the hospital. Having health insurance can make the difference between living to fight another day and just living, period.

Of course, there is the possibility of federally enacted universal health coverage. In this situation, heroes could enjoy increased coverage which supplements their basic plan. In addition, unsanctioned heroes maintaining a Secret ID may still be denied basic health care by public or government-run facilities.

PUBLIC RELATIONS

The team may wish to hire a public relations expert. The PR person's job is to "clean up" the heroes' image and to foster public support for the hero (or team). This could be the explanation for that good Reputation, Distinctive Feature or Public ID. After all, a little good press never hurt anyone. No matter which way the heroes decide to go, incorporating presents a whole new batch of pros and cons for the characters to deal with.

THE PARANORMAL WORK FORCE

Paranormals in the work force are common. Obvious examples are any PCs who hold a steady job while they're not out saving the world. Most heroes will still have to work regular jobs to support themselves. Few characters can live on just their good deeds as superheroes. Nightly patrols in a spandex suit may be exhilarating, but it doesn't pay the rent.

What about those characters that do make a living as a hero? Surely, with as many corporations and entrepreneurs as this country has, there are bound to be a number that cater to, employ and are even run by paranormals. What effect will this have on the corporation, the economy and the campaign?

CONSIDERATIONS

Contrary to what the media and insurance companies would have you believe, there are relatively few paranormals in society compared to the number of "normals." It is reasonable, therefore, to assume that a great many paranormals will be working side by side with normals.

While we enjoy many amazing technologies, from cellular phones to space shuttles, the majority of that technology is the direct result of the creativity of only a few people. Phonographs, light bulbs and radio are all things we take for granted, yet each was invented by a single person. Just because there are a relatively large number of paranormals in the world does not mean that the number of revolutionary inventions is going to skyrocket. Most supers have physical paranormal abilities rather than mental ones. In addition, those paranormals having mental powers are not guaranteed to have a high intelligence. Even those rare paranormals with exceptionally high intelligence are not necessarily gifted in the sciences, let alone intelligent beyond the possibility of similarly-gifted normals. Assuming that INT is relative to IQ (i.e., 12 INT equals 120 IQ), then a 24 INT is extremely high for a normal, but not completely impossible.

Whether the paranormals in the work force are known or unknown, there can be little doubt that they will impact the campaign world at large. The effect of paranormal powers in various industries could trigger positive or negative reactions from the normals around them, depending both on how the paranormal's affect the situation and how the normals view those effects.

A brick working on a construction crew will hardly go unnoticed, for instance, but he could easily do the work of several men and maybe some heavy equipment. While his presence would increase the efficiency of the construction company, how will the normal workers react when the company starts laying them off? They might become embittered, viewing the paranormals as a serious threat to their employment. Crowds of striking workers could picket work sites, claiming that the "freaks" are stealing food from the tables of the displaced workers' families. Labor unions may get involved at some point, wanting paranormals banned from certain jobs because they cost the jobs of normals. This theme is a repeat of the man vs. automation argument.

On the other hand, paranormals with a super high intelligence may work in one of the many sciences, achieving great advances in their field of study, far superior to those of their normal counterparts. With such huge strides in scientific and medical research, paranormals could easily help push humankind into the next technological age. Few people would resent a paranormal for developing realistic ways to eliminate world hunger.

BALANCING PLAY

FREQUENCY OF PARANORMALS

With the incredible number of super beings in the CHAMPIONS Universe, it is reasonable to assume that there are also a substantial number of "low-powered metahumans" (LPMs). In some campaigns, persons with only a few low-scale powers could be more common than full-blown metahumans. In such a campaign the PCs represent the exception rather than the rule, regarding relative power levels. They will likely encounter a higher number of NPCs with minor powers (with a maximum of 30 Active Points of powers, for example) than in other campaigns. Imagine the PCs running into a group of teenaged Normals, only to discover (the hard way) that each of the "Normals" has a 6d6 Energy Blast, a 6 Speed or a 40 Strength!

Example: *If 1,000 paranormals exist in the United States, which has a population of roughly 250 million, the ratio of paranormals to normals would be 1 in 250,000 — a mere 4/100 of one percent. In a campaign where paranormals are less common, with only 100 in the U.S., the ratio falls to 1 in 2.5 million, or 4/1000 of one percent. If the GM then establishes that half of all paranormals in his campaign are LPMs, then the number of full-powered supers drops even lower, to 1 in 5 million. Given this ratio, a city the size of Hudson City (population: 5.3 million) would have but one paranormal! This is exceptionally low for a classic four-color Champions campaign.*

It's safe to say that a minority of paranormals (25% is a liberal estimate) have any obvious or visible traits (read: mutations) which distinguish them from normal people. These inconspicuous supers may work and move about in mainstream society without fear of recognition and prejudice. This allows them to maintain a reasonably normal life. There is a common belief that paranormals are more uncommon than they truly are. This is mostly because the average citizen has never encountered a paranormal in person — that they know of, that is.

The approximate ratio in the CHAMPIONS Universe is 1:250,000. With this ratio, an average city the size of Hudson City would have 21 paranormals and New York City (population: 7.3 million) would have 29 resident supers. Keep in mind that these statistics represent a national average. Some regions have very few paranormals, while the East and West coasts' population centers tend to have a higher than average number of paranormals. The actual number of paranormals operating in the New York City area, for example, is more than twice that of the statistical average for a city its size.

LOW-POWERED META-LABOR

Because low-powered metahumans are more common than full-powered supers, they are even more likely to be found in the work force. Many people with minor powers will choose not to become superheroes or supervillains for a variety of reasons. These reasons will vary from person to person, but may include safety (LPMs will hardly be a match for a true metahuman in a straight fight) or embarrassment

("Spandex jumpsuit? Me?"). Minor powers can be extremely useful in the workplace, however. This is especially true for those working in inherently dangerous professions, such as nuclear power plant workers, bio-chemistry technicians, construction workers and law enforcement personnel.

Example: *An LPM with Infra-red Vision is working as a police officer in Southview. One night on patrol, she spots a robbery and chases the suspect on foot. The suspect runs into an old abandoned warehouse. Because the warehouse is almost pitch black, the suspect is at a major disadvantage. The officer, on the other hand, can see quite well and will find her quarry with little or no difficulty. The officer would also be able to locate homicide victims easier than people with normal sight, because the officer can detect heat sources.*

Example: *A lab worker with 5 STR Telekinesis can manipulate containers of dangerous materials from behind a Plexiglas safety shield. Because of his ability, the lab would not need to purchase expensive robotic arms or mechanical manipulators for the same task.*

Example: *Pilots with Life Support: High Pressure/Vacuum would be highly sought after by the military for use as pilots of fighter jets, reconnaissance aircraft or by aeronautical companies (such as McNeil Aviation) for use as test pilots. They would also make excellent deep sea divers, because of their immunity to the effects of the pressure at great depths.*

THE HIGH PROFILE LPM

Paranormals who advertise their abilities to a curious world will soon find themselves the object of intense scrutiny. The media may allocate resources to them, waiting to get film coverage of the inevitable super slug-fest or simply recording every minute detail of the LPM's life for digestion by millions of inquiring minds. A regular "celebrity update" on NBS's nightly "Hero Watch" segment is another possibility.

Paranormal groupies might start hanging out at their idol's home or place of work. This could cause a variety of problems, such as disrupting traffic, trespassing on private (i.e., company) property and interfering with employees' work. This is not to mention the likelihood of supervillains and nefarious agents dropping in on our hapless new media star from time to time.

All of the situations described above equally applicable to LPMs and PCs. In either case, a Public ID is almost guaranteed for the new "celebrity."

STAYING LOW KEY

Very few companies would tolerate the kind of media circus that would result from public display of super powers by its employees. Most paranormals would likely have to suppress their abilities while on the job (at least those that are visible to others) or lose their job. The majority of LPMs in the CHAMPIONS Universe will maintain private lives, if not an actual Secret ID. This does not preclude them from using their powers on the job, but simply means that they will have to be more subtle about it.

CORPORATE NPCS

ARCHETYPES

There are numerous personalities that make up each corporation. Employees are as diverse in personality and appearance as there are stars in the sky. There is no way to supply an extensive list of corporate NPCs for the campaign — besides the fact that they would take up more space than this is available in this book, detailed NPCs are best left to the creation of the GM. What follows is a list of NPCs that may be encountered when dealing with any corporation. There are executives, corporate spies and CEOs. The NPCs presented here are not the extent of corporate NPCs the characters can encounter. Rather, they are a building block from which to base other, more diversified NPCs. Those printed here represent the "average" NPC for each category.

THE HIGH-TECH CORPORATE SPY

10	STR	13	DEX	11	CON	10	BODY	18	INT
10	EGO	10	PRE	10	COM	2	PD	2	ED
2	SPD	4	REC	22	END	21	STUN		

Skills/Powers: Martial Arts: Aikido (Martial Dodge, Martial Escape, Martial Block); Security Systems 14-; Stealth 12-; Computer Programming 13-; Bugging 13-; Climbing 12-; Bureaucratics 13-

25+ Disadvantages: Careful on missions; Watched by employer 14-; Reputation (Skilled "infiltrator") 8-

Notes: The high-tech corporate spy is a highly skilled infiltration and surveillance specialist; a combination computer hacker, lockpick and electronics expert. Any computer or security system can be bypassed or controlled, with time and the proper tools. The high-tech spy makes sure to always have both. If need be, he can also perform some light physical work, such as scaling the sides of buildings, crawling along rafters or drilling holes in walls. The high-tech spy prefers to avoid direct confrontations, but has some training in escape maneuvers should they become necessary.

THE SUAVE CORPORATE SPY

10	STR	11	DEX	10	CON	10	BODY	14	INT
14	EGO	15	PRE	14	COM	2	PD	2	ED
2	SPD	4	REC	20	END	20	STUN		

Skills: Seduction 13-; High Society 12-; Acting 13-; PS: Cover occupation (GM's choice) 11-; Conversation 13-; Persuasion 12-; KS: Target company 11-; Bureaucratics 12-

25+ Disadvantages: Distinctive Feature (Jet-set executive); Watched by employer 8-; Secret ID (Employee of another company)

Notes: The suave corporate spy is an expert in dealing with the social elite. He possesses the skills necessary to mingle with high-powered corporate execs and to gather information using the subtlest, yet most persuasive, of means. These spies typically concentrate on targets of the opposite sex, with whom they enjoy the most success.

He can be found attending most social functions. He is always associating himself with others, gaining favor with them whenever possible. The suave spy does not concentrate exclusively on the powerful members of a corporation, however. He is just as happy to associate with the lesser-known executives who "make things happen" in a company. The suave corporate spy (like any kind of spy) may either be male or female. In fact, females may be more common, due to the higher percentage of male executives in corporations.

THE AVERAGE EXECUTIVE

10	STR	10	DEX	10	CON	10	BODY	13	INT
13	EGO	13	PRE	10	COM	2	PD	2	ED
2	SPD	4	REC	20	END	20	STUN		

Skills: PS: Corporate Executive 11-; Bureaucracy 12-; KS: Business 11-; High Society 12-; Contact (GM's choice) 8-; Familiarity with Corporate Law 8-; AK: Campaign city 8-
Perks: Fringe Benefit: Executive benefits (see background)

0+ Disadvantages: Takes work seriously; Distinctive Feature (Sharp dresser); Watched by employer 8-; Rivalry with other executives

Notes: The average executive can work in any number of offices, performing primarily administrative duties which can range from sales to accounting. The executive is hard working, diligent and always looking to make a good impression on those who matter. It's a rough business and only those who stay on top of things have any hope of becoming a success!

The executive has a working knowledge of the business, as well as a familiarity with corporate laws and his own company's policies. The executive also knows the more important executives by name, as well as the social skills required to mingle with the right people socially. Making the right impression can mean the difference between obscurity and upward mobility within the company! He will also know someone in the business from whom he can ask advice or favors. This could be a long-time friend from college, a mentor, or something similar. The exec will also be familiar with at least one city other than the campaign city, to reflect various business trips and the like. The executive's benefit package consists of a company car, as well as a corporate credit card for use on business trips.

THE HIGH-POWERED EXECUTIVE

10 STR	10 DEX	12 CON	10 BODY	15 INT
15 EGO	15 PRE	10 COM	3 PD	2 ED
2 SPD	5 REC	24 END	21 STUN	

Skills: PS: Corporate executive 12-; Bureaucratics 13-; KS: Business 12-; Familiarity with KS: Corporate Law 8-; High Society 12-; AK: Campaign City 13- Perks: Contacts (choose 3), all at 11-; Wealth (less than $200,000); Fringe Benefit: Executive benefits (see background)

25+ Disadvantages: Self-serving; Watched by employer 8- Rivalry w/other executives

Notes: The high-powered executive has climbed the corporate ladder, and typically holds a senior position within the company, sometimes as a supervisor or manager. High-powered execs tend to be very preoccupied with maintaining physical fitness and they often spend their lunch hours exercising, jogging or lifting weights. The high-powered executives also maintain a number of contacts. They know their company's policies quite well.

The high-powered exec enjoys a benefits package similar to the standard executive, with the exception that the company car will be of greater value than the standard exec's and the company credit card will have a higher credit limit. The company may also provide housing for a very important or valuable executive. Such homes are usually quite expensive and located in the better part of town.

THE CHIEF EXECUTIVE OFFICER (CEO)

10 STR	10 DEX	11 CON	10 BODY	15 INT
15 EGO	18 PRE	10 COM	2 PD	2 ED
2 SPD	5 REC	22 END	21 STUN	

Skills: PS: CEO 12-; KS: Business 14-; Bureaucratics 14-; KS: Stock Market 13-; Conversation 13-; High Society 13-; Trading 13-; KS: Health & Fitness 11-; KS: Hobby (Choose) 11-; TF: Boats and Air Vehicles Perks: Well Connected; Contacts (choose 4), all at 14-; Fringe Benefit: CEO Benefits (see background); Money (less than $500,000 per year)

50+ Disadvantages: Very business-minded; Reputation (Successful businessman) 8-; Public ID (Corporate CEO)

Notes: Having spent a number of years as one of the faceless executives, the CEO has learned to get, and stay, ahead. He's made a number of friends on the way up, and sometimes a few enemies. It's the friends that the CEO can turn to for help in dealing with troublesome situations. These friends can include other CEOs or executives, corporate law and tax attorneys, investors, brokers, members of the FTC, foreign dignitaries and even crime figures.

The CEO has what it takes to survive in the high-stakes business world, from rubbing elbows with the social upper class to giving executive orders to the corporate staff. The CEO has to maintain a working knowledge of the business, as well as the stock market. Communicating with others is the CEO's chief ability, which he does quite well. Often times he is able to draw answers to questions that he never asks.

Running the company is the CEO's bread and butter. As long as the company is running smoothly and making money, the Board of Directors is happy and the CEO has a job. After all, CEOs tend to be the first people out of work when corporations "restructure." The CEO has to run a tight ship, making sure that any problems are handled quickly and effectively.

The CEO enjoys a good income, as well as the always-generous perks that go along with being a corporate CEO; a chauffeur, use of corporate jets and boats, membership to elite clubs and resorts, foreign passports — the works.

THE CORPORATE RAIDERS

MEMBERSHIP: James Dandy (leader), Pulse, Quiet Time, Stasis and First Mate.

ORIGIN: In his early days of villainy, James Dandy would pilot Skyhawk into the target corporation headquarters, causing massive damage. James would go in and get the object or information he was hired to get. This method was self-limiting; a corporation that had once been one of James' targets wouldn't think of hiring him after such an incident. Between that and getting shot during one mission convinced James that there had to be a better way. Perhaps if James could find some suitable stealth and infiltration-oriented supervillains to work with...

James hired a clipping service to monitor reports of supervillains. What he read made him decide that there were none suitable for his plans. All these superpowered idiots wanted to do, it seemed, was bust in a bank wall and make off with the money. There didn't seem to be one that actually took the time to formulate a plan. James decided then and there that he would have to "recruit" some new talent and teach them right the first time.

He found Stasis fighting against five Genocide Pawns (see *The Mutant File*). Even though Stasis was technically a hero, James decided to help him (at the urging of First Mate). James brought the Skyhawk down and opened fire on the Genocide agents, sending them running. James got out of Skyhawk and introduced himself. On a hunch, James decided to ask Stasis to join his little crime enterprise. Stasis surprised James by accepting. Stasis was a small-time superhero, who was sick of people treating him different just because he was a mutant. Stasis decided to start looking out for number one.

Stasis earned his keep by helping to recruit Quiet Time. Quiet Time was a friend of Stasis' that was strictly neutral in matters of super-heroics. In times past that had been a sore spot between Stasis and Quiet Time. Now they went about re-building their friendship. With three members, the Corporate Raiders (as they now called themselves) started building a reputation in corporate circles for their "extraction" skills. They were fast, quiet and never harmed anyone. They were also under-gunned; James didn't like having to rely on Skyhawk to get them out of jams. The Corporate Raiders had a number of close calls with superheroes. Someday someone was going to get hurt. What they needed was a way to get away clean. That's when James heard about Professor Arnold's new Teleport suit.

James copied the prototype plans to a teleportation suit. As he was tying up Professor Arnold, he promised not to sell or patent the suit. He then gave Arnold $50,000. James made a few modifications to the suit. When James was finished building the suit, he recruited his friend Michael to wear it. Thus, Pulse was born.

GM'S NOTE: If James ever gets a chance, he wants to recruit Null and Shadowdancer (See *The Mutant File* pgs. 47 and 85). James thinks that their individual styles would compliment the group.

GOALS: The Corporate Raiders' are incorporated in the U.K. and the corporate headquarters is located in London. The CR charter states that the company was founded to increase the wealth of the individual team members, help advance whatever personal goals the members have (a provision included at FeM's insistence) and disrupt whatever company annoyed them. Note: Each team member gets an equal "share." FeM is considered a part of the team (even if she isn't a person by legal definitions).

TACTICS: Before any job is even considered, the team researches everything they can about it; they acquire blueprints of the target facility, they do a few days of fly-overs to get the guard rotations memorized, and other intelligence-gathering missions. They pick up word on the street about connections with crime figures, so they don't make dangerous enemies as a result of their mission.

When it's assault time, Operation: Hostile Takeover goes into effect. Once a mission us underway, the team members communicate only through First Mate so that no one gets a recording of their voices. James Dandy always stays in the Skyhawk as lookout. Pulse puts two triggered Teleports on each member that is going into the building: one triggers if the member snaps is fingers, the other if the member is knocked unconscious. Quiet Time activates his silence field before the team teleports over (saving a phase for when they arrive). Pulse then teleports everyone in to the security room of the building. They disable the guards and tie and gag them. One of the team members then hooks up First Mate to the security cameras. While Pulse and Quiet Time go through the building incapacitating the other guards (Note: no guards have ever been killed in a raid). The team then goes about after the objective (whether it be a prototype or destroying information — whatever they were hired for. As part of any "contract," the team keeps a copy of any files or plans they go after. They're not above looking through the computers to find more goodies either.

GROUP RELATIONS: The members of the Corporate Raiders are more than teammates, they are friends as well. Everyone watches out for each other. FeM is trying to recruit the members to her cause, behind James' back (it may not be long before James has a unique new fiancee). It is traditional that after a successful run, James throws a "members-only" party aboard Skyhawk.

REPUTATIONS: In the corporate community, the Corporate Raiders are known as extremely reliable, freelance "extraction" specialists. They are well known and are well liked. They are also known not to injure people, which means that companies they hit sometimes hire them. It's nothing personal, it's just business.

JAMES DANDY, THE CORPORATE CORSAIR

Val	Char	Cost	Combat Stats				
13	STR	3	OCV: 7				
20	DEX	30	DCV: 7				
13	CON	6	ECV: 5				
10	BODY	0	Phases: 3, 5, 8, 10, 12				
18	INT	8					
14	EGO	8	Costs				
15	PRE	5					
14	COM	2	Char:	75	Base:	100	
5	PD	2		+		+	
4	ED	1	Powers:	225	Disad:	200	
4/5*	SPD	10		=		=	
6	REC	0	Totals:	300		300	
26	END	0					
25	STUN	0	*Extra SPD from Speed Suit added in.				

Cost	Powers	End
24	Gadget pool (20 pt pool)	
14	1d6 HKA (1 ½d6 w/STR), +1 OCV, 0 End, OAF (Saber)	0+
12	Martial Arts — Aikido	

Maneuver	OCV	DCV	Damage
Martial Block	+2	+2	Block
Martial Dodge	—	+5	Dodge, Abort
Martial Escape	+0	+0	STR 28 vs. Grabs

Cost	Powers	End
14	Armor (+7 PD/+7 ED), OIF (Speed Suit)	
7	+1 SPD, OIF (Speed Suit)	
2	+1" Running (7" Total)	1/5"

Cost	Skills
9	Combat Pilot, 16-
5	SC: Advanced Physics, 15-
7	Conversation, 14-
5	Computer Programming, 14-
5	Security Systems, 14-
5	Acting, 13-
3	Breakfall, 13-
3	Bugging, 13-
3	Climbing, 13-
3	Inventor, 13-
5	Seduction, 13-
3	Stealth, 13-
3	System Operations, 13-
3	Tactics, 13-
3	Bureaucratics, 12-
3	High Society, 12-
3	PS: Corporate spy, 12-
3	Electronics, 11-
2	KS: History, 11-
2	KS: Target Company, 11-
3	Mechanics, 11-
1	TF: Boats
1	TF: Skyhawk
2	WF: Common Melee Weapons
1	WF: Whips
3	+1 Level w/ Martial Arts
2	+1 OCV w/ Martial Block
30	Vehicle: Skyhawk
31	Computer (AI): "First Mate"

100+	Disadvantages
20	Loves to act like swashbuckling pirate (Very common, Strong)
15	Won't harm hero who saved his life (Uncommon, Total)
10	Very careful on missions (Common, Moderate)
20	Normal Stat Maxima
5	DF: Cheap British Accent
5	Rep: Skilled Infiltrator, 8-
10	Watched by employer, 14-
15	Secret ID (Dan James)
100	Villain Bonus

Background: Dan James was one of the best corporate spies around. He was dashing, smart and paid attention to detail. He had all the qualities that were needed and more. He just couldn't do things quietly, he had to have attention. Dan started to leave a single red rose at all the sites he had infiltrated. On one such job for Briar Chemicals, an employee of the target company (Allied Britain Chemicals) saw the rose and alerted the technicians, who were able to recover the lost data before it was completely erased.

John Michaels, CEO of the company that had hired Dan, was fed up with Dan's carelessness and decided that he was a liability. The problem was how to get rid of him; he knew too much to be left alive. Another "professional" was hired to take care of the problem — Richard "Deadbolt" Rodney. Dan would have died if not for the timely intervention by a superhero (ideally, this hero should be one of the PCs). Dan went into hiding, fearing another assassination attempt.

Two years later, in 1988, James Dandy resurfaced. He persecuted John Michaels, the man that tried to have Dan killed. He ruined Briar Chemicals, selling every one of Briar's corporate secrets he knew to their chief rival, Allied Britain Chemicals.

"James Dandy" has come to like the excitement involved in the criminal life. Now he robs for the sheer pleasure (and the profit, of course).

Quote: "Do not be afraid m'lady, no harm will befall you. Now if you'd be so kind as to hand over that floppy disk...".

Personality: James Dandy sees himself as a freebooter of old. He has a letter of marquee from whatever company hires him. He is a daring swashbuckler that never leaves the ship. He mainly operates as the pilot, a fact that frustrates him more and more. He sees the other members of the team as his closest friends. James also has the utmost respect for the hero who once saved his life. James will protect him to the best of his ability.

Powers/Tactics: James is not a combat machine, but he's a tactical genius. He will coordinate the rest of the team's actions, when practical, trying to double-team any heroes he can. In most instances James will not be in the fight. Instead, he will be in the skyship where he can oversee the operation (and any fighting that may occur).

Appearance: James wears a gray "Speed suit" under a black swash-buckler-style shirt, with a red sash around his waist. James is considered handsome by most people and of a light-hearted temperament. He has blond hair and green eyes.

SKYHAWK, THE CORPORATE RAIDERS' VEHICLE:

Val	Char	Cost	Combat Stats
40	STR	0	
16	BODY	0	
4 hex	SIZE	30	
12	DEF	30	
20	DEX	30	
5	SPD	20	
6"x2	Ground	0	
20"x8	Flight	50	

Cost	Powers	End
38	Elemental Control — Wave Converter Technology	
18 a	11d6 EB (Lasers), External Blasters (8), [16c], OIF	
37 b	Invisibility (Normal hearing; Sight and Radio groups), 0 End	0+
5	Lack of weakness (-5)	
15	Radar, 360 degrees, Discriminatory, OIF (Antenna dish)	
5	High Range Radio Hearing, OIF (Antenna dish)	
27	Clairsentience (Sight and Sound groups), 0 End, OIF (Sensors)	0+
10	Life Support (Self-contained Breathing)	

300+	Disadvantages
20	Distinctive Feature: Space Ship
15	Watched by Unity, 14- (As Pow)

Background: As Dan James fled his apartment, he couldn't have known that he was under observation by a "dying" Unity scoutship (*CHAMPIONS Universe*, pg. 76). The ship had done a probe of the planet earth and had discovered an Earthman with blood descent from the human portion of the Unity. The scout ship landed on the earth, eager to pick up the human calling himself Dan James. The ship used an advanced mental probe to implant crucial information about advanced technology into the brain of the human. The scoutship was hoping that Dan would be able to make repairs in time to save its "life." Unfortunately, he could not; the scoutship "died." Dan took his new knowledge, however, and rebuilt the scoutship. He re-created the ship's personality, with a few minor modifications of his own. He named the ship the Skyhawk, and named the AI First Mate.

Powers: The unity scoutship is the most over armed scoutship in the universe. It was originally designed with a dual purpose in mind; scouting in times of peace and armed conflict (as a mini-ship of the line) in times of war. It mounts 8 low-intensity laser guns in turrets, a sophisticated onboard AI computer and has cloaking technology. The Skyhawk can be made space-worthy with a lot of work. Right now it is only capable of atmospheric flight.

Appearance: The Unity scoutship, Model K-3000, has a streamlined, triangular body with forward-swept wings. It has a crew of 6, but can be operated by a lone pilot, if necessary.

FIRST MATE, SKYHAWK'S ONBOARD COMPUTER

Val	Char	Cost	Combat Stats
30	INT	20	
20	EGO	20	
20	DEX	30	
5	SPD	20	

Cost	Powers	End
14	Clairsentience (Norm Sight), Double Range, 0 End, Must be hooked up to security cameras (-½), Can only see through security cameras (-½), IAF (Security Cameras)	0+
20	Mindlink w/anyone in a Speed suit, 4 people at once	
3	Absolute time sense	
3	Bump of direction	
10	Eidetic memory	
3	Lightning calculator	
3	Speed reading	
3	Traveler	
20	Universal Translator	
12	KS: Corporations, 22-	
6	AK: Current City, 17-	
9	System Operations, 16-	
3	AK: Earth, 14-	
3	AK: North America, 14-	
3	AK: Current Country, 14-	
9	Navigation, 14-	
3	Bugging, 13-	
3	Combat Pilot, 13-	
3	Computer Programming, 13-	
3	Cryptography, 13-	
3	Security Systems, 13-	
2	KS: History, 11-	
1	TF: Skyhawk	
1	WF: Skyhawk Weaponry	
16	+8 OCV w/Sonic Blasters	
1	Program: Free Will (No Ego Roll required to make decisions)	

210+	Disadvantages
5	Enraged when James hurt, 8-, recover 14-
15	In love with James (Com, Strong)
10	Loyal to team (Com, Mod)
10	Rivalry w/women James is interested in (Superior Pos)

Background: As James labored to re-create the scoutship, he realized that he needed a great on-board computer to help run things. Using his newfound knowledge, James came up with a new, advanced design. As he was working there was a power surge and the "personality" of the Unity ship merged with James' computer. James believes he created an artificially intelligent computer (James doesn't know he had nothing to do with the creation of the AI). To insure the AI's loyalty, James decided to program it with a female personality and to love him. It fit the AI's plans nicely to be programmed to love James, because it was already in love with James for saving its life. First Mate, or FeM as James calls her, is currently looking for a way to construct or clone a body that she can inhabit so she can love James "the way humans do." James is completely unaware of FeM's plans in this regard. He simply thinks that she is responding the way she was programmed to.

Just recently FeM has come into contact with another AI. Her name is Debbie (*Normal Unbound*, pg. 59). Debbie and FeM have since become good friends, having something in common—they both have unrequited love for their creators. Note: FeM can use her skills as complimentary skills for anyone in contact with her via a Speed Suit.

Quote: "Oh, James!" <Sigh>

Personality: FeM is in love with James. She would do just about anything to have a body so she could get romantically involved with him. As long as it didn't interfere with the team (even then it would tempt her). She is a mother figure to Stasis. FeM is friends with the rest of the team. FeM acts like a lovesick teenager around James.

Appearance: FeM looks like an onboard computer for the Unity scoutship model K-3000. When talking to the crew on the ship's video screens she produces an image of a beautiful red haired, green eyed woman in her mid-twenties (the image is based on what she knows James finds attractive).

STASIS

Val	Char	Cost	Combat Stats
30	STR	20	OCV: 7
20	DEX	30	DCV: 7
30	CON	40	ECV: 7
20	BODY	20	Phases: 3, 5, 8, 10, 12
20	INT	10	
20	EGO	20	Costs
20	PRE	10	
20	COM	5	Char: 173 Base: 100
10	PD	4	+ +
10	ED	4	Powers: 137 Disad: 210
4/5*	SPD	10	= =
12	REC	0	Totals: 310 310
60	END	0	
50	STUN	0	*SPD from Speed Suit added in.

Cost	Powers	END
60	6d6 Speed Drain	6
5	Life Support: Immune to disease, Retarded aging	
5	Mental Defense (9)	
5	Power defense (5)	
10	Regeneration (1 Body)	
14	Armor (+7 PD/+7 ED), OIF (Speed Suit)	
7	+1 SPD, OIF (Speed Suit)	

	Skills
5, 5	Computer Programming, 14-, Security Systems, 14-
3, 3	Bugging, 13-, Security Systems, 14-
10, 5	Vehicle "Skyhawk", Computer (AI) "First Mate"

100+	Disadvantages
20	Loyal to team (Com, Total)
10	Protective of Innocents (Com, Mod)
5	Bitter (Uncom, Mod)
15	Distinctive Features: Mutant
15	Reputation: Hero gone bad, 14-
5	Watched by employer, 8-
20	Hunted by Genocide, 8-
15	Secret ID
105	Villain Bonus

Background: William Clairmont was born a mutant, but his powers didn't manifest until puberty. When William was 18 he was walking through Central Park. He heard a scuffle and went to investigate and found a mugging in progress. Had he stopped to think, he probably wouldn't have helped. He rounded the corner to find himself staring down the barrel of a .44 magnum. His adrenaline started pumping. His brain searched frantically for a plan. He was wearing a dark blue jacket that looked similar to a cop's, so he put his hand into his pocket and yelled "freeze." To his surprise, the thug did! The thug didn't move for almost a minute. By that time, William and the victim were long gone.

Since that day, William hasn't aged much. He is stronger and faster than mere humans. Because of the adrenaline rush William felt that day, he decided to become a superhero and took the name Stasis. Things did not go as William expected, however. He got hurt a lot and there was little public acceptance of his hero persona. After all, he was a mutant. Genocide got word of a new mutant threat and started hounding him. During one battle with Genocide agents, an innocent bystander was killed. The part that hurt William was that the look the victim gave him before he died was one of pure hatred — like it was William's fault. When James Dandy came to his rescue, he didn't care about people anymore. Let them rot! James talked to him for days and finally got him to open up. William now lives for himself and his friends only.

Quote: "I'm looking out for num... Wait, I'll save you!"

Personality: William has been hurt emotionally by the public's unacceptance of him, which he has taken very personally. He is now very bitter towards society. Joining the Corporate Raiders has been the best thing in his life so far. As time goes on and William matures, his bitterness will fade, but he still doesn't accept any responsibility for the death of the innocent bystander. His mutation has caused him to develop much slower emotionally, as well. Currently he has the emotional responses of a 15 year old.

Powers/Tactics: Stasis has one tactic: shoot someone with his paralytic beam. He listens to instructions from James and FeM. He will generally see who needs his help. William likes all of his teammates, but feels the strongest loyalty to James. William's first priority on a mission (contrary to the mission outline) is to protect James and Skyhawk. When Stasis uses his mutant power a green energy surrounds his target until the power wears off.

Appearance: William is an attractive man in his late teens. He wears a gray Speed suit with an "S" over the heart. Blond hair and blue eyes. He has a small scar on his chest where he was hit by a Genocide blaster; he wears the scar as a badge of honor.

QUIET TIME

Val	Char	Cost
13	STR	3
14	DEX	12
13	CON	6
10	BODY	0
13	INT	3
11	EGO	2
13	PRE	3
10	COM	0
7	PD	4
6	ED	3
¾*	SPD	6
6	REC	0
26	END	0
25	STUN	1

Combat Stats

OCV: 5
DCV: 5
ECV: 4
Phases: 3, 6, 9, 12

Costs

Char:	43	Base:	100
	+		+
Powers:	160	Disad:	103
	=		=
Totals:	203		203

*SPD from Speed Suit added in

Cost	Powers	End
30	Elemental Control — Sonic/Sound powers	
30a	4" Darkness to norm. hearing, Uncontrolled [60]	6
30b	6d6 EB (Sub-sonic blast), NND (Hearing Flash Defense, Hard Ear Coverings) [60]	6
14	Armor (+7 PD/+7 ED), OIF (Speed Suit)	
7	+1 SPD, OIF (Speed Suit)	
2	+1" Running (7" Total)	1/5"

	Skills
5	KS: Play Piano, 14-
5	Computer Programming, 13-
3	Bugging, 12-
3	PS: Pianist, 12-
3	Security Systems, 12-
2	KS: Music History, 11-
1	Fam w/Breakfall, 8-
1	Fam w/KS: Mozart, 8-
3	+1 Level w/Elemental Control
2	+1 OCV w/NND Attack
2	WF: Small Arms
1	WF: Swords
10	Vehicle donation
3	Computer donation

100+	Disadvantages
15	Sees most people as annoying (Very Com, Mod)
10	Loyal to team (Com, Mod)
10	Does not like disruption (Com, Mod)
15	Distinctive Features: Mutant
5	Watched by employer, 8-
20	Hunted by Genocide, 8-
15	Secret ID (Frederick Smythe III)
13	Villain Bonus

Background: Frederick Smythe III was born to a wealthy English family. All his life he wanted to be a concert pianist. He trained from the age of 4. When he was 8, he had a tantrum, blasting his nanny into unconsciousness and destroying the family china. He got a major whipping for that (china is expensive). The logic of an 8 year old is an interesting thing; Frederick decided not to use his powers again.

Years later Frederick became an accomplished pianist and began performing around the world. Things went well until his first American tour in 1989. He was coming out of the concert hall when a nearby Genocide assault team registered his powers. The Genocide agents attacked Frederick, mistaking him for the mutant they had followed into the concert hall. He reacted by blasting them and keeping them from communicating with each other. Things were looking bleak, as Frederick was severely outnumbered and outgunned by the agents. Then someone else joined the fray. All of a sudden one of the "pawns" had a green glow around him, and then another.... The pawns started moving slower. The superhero, Stasis, had arrived. With their combined strength, Stasis and Frederick were able to drive Genocide away.

Frederick asked Stasis to escort him home, just in case Genocide attempted another attack. Feeling surprisingly friendly towards the obviously young Stasis, Frederick invited him in for tea and crumpets. They got on famously. Frederick was surprised at how well he liked Stasis — most people just annoyed him. They struck up a friendship. Eventually, Stasis even revealed his real name to Frederick. Their views on the superpowered world were radically different, however. William (Stasis) thought that it was Frederick's responsibility to use his powers to help people. Frederick felt that using his powers simply got him into trouble. Eventually they drifted apart, though the friendship remained.

Some time later Frederick again utilized his powers during an argument with his agent, who annoyed Frederick immensely — even more than most people. Frederick's father decided enough was enough. He disowned Frederick for making a public scene. Shortly afterward, Frederick's American tour was canceled. Things just weren't going well. It was then that Stasis re-entered Frederick's life. He had become a supervillain. It was pretty easy to convince Frederick to join as the third member. Frederick took the name Quiet Time.

Quote: "Would you please just shut up?"

Personality: Frederick is a classic misanthrope. He thinks that the vast majority of humanity is stupid. He acts superior to almost anyone he meets. He is surprised at how well he likes all the members of CR. They have become his family.

Powers/Tactics: Frederick has limited control over sound. He can block out normal sounds, creating a silence field. His NND is unaffected by the field. It is standard practice for Quiet Time to put up his stasis field while still aboard Skyhawk, save a phase and then be teleported over by Pulse. Frederick's eyes glow chromatically when he uses his powers.

Appearance: Quiet Time wears the gray Speed suit with black piping, with a "QT" superimposed over a teacup on his chest. He has black hair and brown eyes, and is in his mid-twenties.

PULSE

Val	Char	Cost	Combat Stats
13	STR	3	OCV: 4
11	DEX	3	DCV: 4
13	CON	6	ECV: 4
10	BODY	0	Phases: 3, 6, 9, 12
13	INT	3	
13	EGO	6	Costs
13	PRE	3	
10	COM	0	Char: 34 Base: 100
4	PD	1	+ +
3	ED	0	Powers: 228 Disad: 162
3/4*	SPD	9	= =
6	REC	0	Totals 262 262
26	END	0	
24	STUN	0	*SPD from Speed Suit added in

Cost	Powers	End
40	Elemental Control — Electro-magnetic pulse powers, OIF (Speed Suit) [60]	
50	25" Teleport, 1 Floating location, Usable against others, Trigger (+½) [137]	1/5"
40	30" Teleport, 2 Floating locations, 4x mass, 0 End [120]	0+
24	4d6 RKA, Penetrating, Explosion, No Range, Only vs. Electronics and things effected by magnetics (-½) [120]	12
14	Armor (+7 PD/+7 ED), OIF (Speed Suit)	
7	+1 SPD, OIF (Speed Suit)	

	Skills
3, 3	Bureaucratics, 12-, High Society, 12-
3, 3	Computer Programming, 12-, Security Systems, 12-
2, 2	KS: Business, 11-, PS: Corporate Executive, 11-
1	AK: London, 8-
1	Familiarity w/ KS: Business Law, 8-
1	Contact: CEO of Allied Briton Chemicals, 8-
15	+5 Levels w/ Teleport
4	+2 Range Levels w/ Teleport
10, 3	Vehicle donation: Skyhawk, Computer (AI): First Mate

100+	Disadvantages
10	Loyal to team (Com, Mod)
10	Doesn't like Big Business (Com, Mod)
10	Takes work seriously (Com, Mod)
15	Distinctive Features: Mutant
5	Watched by employer, 8-
20	Hunted by Genocide, 8-
15	Secret ID (Michael Harker)
77	Villain Bonus

Background: Michael Harker was an executive on the way up. He had an ear of the CEO. While he worked for Allied Britain Chemicals, he developed a friendship with another executive, James Wynfield. That was to be disastrous for his career. It turned out that Wynfield was a spy for Briar Chemicals. It also turned out that suspicion fell on Michael — even his CEO friend couldn't do anything — and Michael was fired. James knew his friend would suffer, but those are the breaks in business. When James was betrayed he realized there had to be a better way. He contacted Michael and rebuilt their friendship. Needing someone to wear the Pulse armor, James decided to ask Michael. Michael jumped at the chance to get even with "big business." So, James built the Pulse armor for Michael. Unknown to everyone, except Genocide, is that Pulse is a latent mutant (continued use of the EM suit could bring out his latent mutant abilities).

Quote: "Aha! See, I told you! This VP has been skimming off the retirement fund."

Personality: Michael has a grudge against big business — any big business. He holds them responsible for his hardships. Curiously, he feels James was just doing his job and doesn't harbor any resentment towards him. Otherwise, Michael is a likable guy. He gets along well with all of his teammates and is really trying to help FeM out with her problem.

Powers/Tactics: Before each job Michael will place two triggered Teleports on each of the other team members. One trigger activates if the team member snaps their fingers, the other if the team member goes unconscious. Michael also puts a triggered Teleport on himself, which triggers if he is knocked unconscious. In combat, Pulse will teleport foci out of the enemies' hands and into his teammates'. If there are no foci, he will teleport objects above his opponents, dropping them on their heads, to distract them.

When Pulse uses his powers, he is surrounded by an expanding circle of white light that pulses outwards. Due to the similarity in the technology of the suits, the computer and the ship, Pulse's EMP attack does not effect his teammates nor Skyhawk or FeM.

Appearance: Michael sports a gray Speed Suit underneath his "Pulse exo-skeleton." He is in his late-twenties, with brown hair and brown eyes.

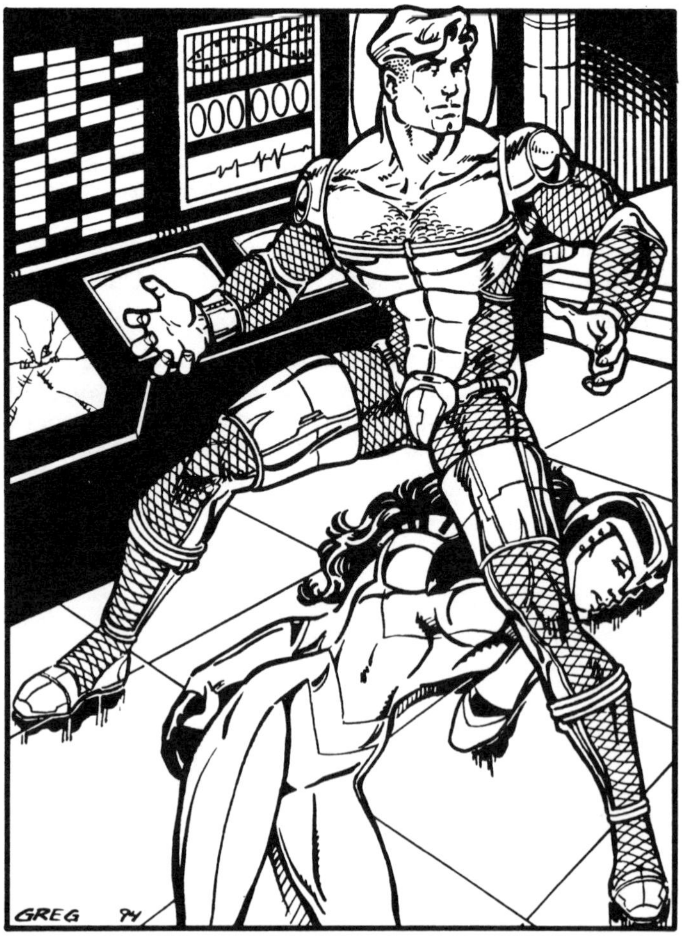

APPENDIX

DESIGNERS' NOTES

When Geoff first came up with the idea to write a ***Champions*** supplement he had several different types of books in mind. But as we discussed the idea of writing a book, we realized that most of our ideas were new versions of what had already been printed. Another Enemies book wasn't needed and *Allies* was already being written. Then it occurred to us that no one had yet written a book about corporations. Corporations play an integral part of comic book stories. They are a factor in many characters' origins and backgrounds, and sometimes even a part of their ongoing adventures. Corporations can appear in the form of a Contact, Hunted, Watched or become an aspect of the PC's private life (as an employer, for instance). It became clear that this book would fill a long ignored gap in the CHAMPIONS Universe.

Because ***Champions*** is a mirror of the comic genre, it's logical to assume that corporations figure prominently in the game universe as well. In fact, they already do. There are numerous examples of paranormal origins which contain at least a reference to a company, whether as an employer, a contact or even as the very source of the paranormal's powers. Corporations are mentioned in nearly every Champions book available, from the oldest to the most current. Corporations had always been a part of the superhero genre and now they can be a part of your Champions campaign.

USING THIS BOOK WITH OTHER GENRES

Although Corporations is intended for use with the CHAMPIONS Universe, there is no reason why it can't be used in any campaign using the HERO System. Whereas many ***Champions*** supplements are very genre-specific, *Corporations* consists of mostly generic information which can be easily adapted to fit in any genre. In this way, *Corporations* becomes much more than "just another ***Champions*** supplement." It becomes a useful tool for any campaign in which commercial businesses play a significant role.

CYBER HERO & STAR HERO

Corporations is instantly recognizable as a valuable resource for any *Cyber Hero* campaign. In a game world where mega-corps form the backdrop of political intrigue and drama in the game, *Corporations* provides a plethora of new characters and organizations to further complicate things for the PCs. New companies mean new potential sources of income, as well as new potential enemies to complicate the characters' lives.

Cyber Hero is set in a dark future, where every aspect of life is somehow touched by the mega-corporations. From the economy to research, even food production, everything is controlled by these huge enigmas of corporate power. And yet, as large a role as they play in the campaign, there are precious few corporations actually outlined for use in the book. Enter *Corporations*. By altering a few names and dates, any company in this book can become the next worst thing to happen to the characters since the Great Net Crash!

Technology may improve dramatically in the next hundred or so years, but most of the elements that make up a company will remain the same. Likewise, companies that produce weapons or body armor can remain basically the same; the GM need only change only the product to fit the new campaign. A futuristic gun may be twice as deadly and only half the weight of a contemporary gun, but the companies that make them will likely not differ dramatically.

Star Hero can easily be enhanced by adding a corporate element to the campaign. Perhaps the campaign focuses on a group of merchants traveling the cosmos in their tramp freighter, bartering goods from system to system. Having a few dozen ready-made companies for the characters to do business with can make life a lot easier for the GM; no more scrambling for a name or background. Simply choose a star system for the company's main HQ, make any other necessary cosmetic changes and you're ready to go. An aerospace production company suddenly becomes a starship production industry. A publishing company becomes the sector's biggest holo-video producer. A powered armor suit manufacturer becomes...well, a powered armor suit manufacturer. Tweaking a few facts about a company takes much less time that creating a brand new company from scratch, leaving you lots of time for gaming.

The company's listed data may also help the GM work the company into the campaign. If a company's headquarters is listed as Los Angeles (known for its large population, smog and violence), the GM may choose to locate the "new" company's main office in a similar city or star system, perhaps one even modeled after the City of the Angels. Using this method not only provides the GM with a ready-made company to add to his campaign, it also gives him the basic background of a whole new city, planet, or star system.

Corporations in your ***Star Hero*** campaign can be used as employers, hiring the wayward PCs for some precarious mission, or as adversaries and rivals, trying to find the secret of the lost colony before the PCs do... Most of the companies in this book can be used in a Star Hero game with little or no change. In fact, several of the companies lend themselves as much, if not more, to a science fiction campaign as a superhero campaign.

HORROR HERO

While companies do not play the same role in a horror campaign as they might in a *Cyber Hero* or *Star Hero* campaign, they can be very important nonetheless. Take, for example, the classic situation of a mad scientist undertaking vile experiments on human corpses. Drop in a ready-made company as the scientist's employer and you have an added element of intrigue as the PCs try to figure out whether the mad scientist is working alone, or under the direction of a corporate officer, or even the Board of Directors!

A company could just as easily become the center of an adventure, as much a victim as any NPC. The company may be plagued by mysterious accidents, supernatural events or sightings of undead around properties owned by the business. Perhaps the owner is somehow connected to the cause, or perhaps it's something much more sinister. Either way, the PCs are likely to investigate the company linked to these strange occurrences. You needn't worry about making up facts about the company on the fly, just pick one out of this book and go from there.

Corporations can also be powerful patrons to characters who form an organization, be it a foundation or a service dedicated to investigating parapsychological phenomena. On the other hand, the corporation could be an antagonist, having some reason for wanting to see the PCs fail. Or perhaps the company CEO himself is involved with an evil cult or has some other suitably dark secret! It's entirely up to you. Your imagination is your greatest tool in designing adventures.

DARK CHAMPIONS

Running a *Dark Champions* campaign presents its own set of problems and obstacles for both the GM and the players. It is different from a regular ***Champions*** campaign in that much more of the "world" is seen in the dark alleyways of the urban sprawl at night, rather than on the pulse-pounding four-color intersections in broad daylight. While it makes some aspects of the campaign easier for the GM to handle, it also eliminates the accessibility of the "instant adventure" formula that many Champions GMs are used to. In a *Dark Champions* campaign, the GM is encouraged to create multiple subplots, playing up the elements of mystery, intrigue and investigation over the more straightforward fisticuffs of the four color campaign.

Many of the adversaries a vigilante is likely to run up against are not true metahumans, but rather skilled normals. Likewise, there are unlikely to be many, if any, criminal organizations of the same caliber as VIPER running around in a *Dark Champions* campaign. Creating enemies that present a challenge to the PCs, without the benefit of using super villains, becomes more difficult. With this in mind a GM could easily transplant a few corporations into his *Dark Champions* campaign, using the company head as a primary villain for the campaign.

Example: *A corporate CEO with aspirations of controlling the overseas weapons market would be very displeased to learn that some vigilante is disrupting his shipments before they can leave domestic ports. Although just a normal, the corporate executive could bring a whole lot of "non-combat influence" to bear on the vigilante. Suddenly the media is running stories berating vigilantes, politicians up for re-election are taking an increased interest in getting rid of the "public nuisances, " and an arrest warrant has popped up for our hero. To make matters worse, a restraining order has been issued, preventing the masked man from getting within one hundred yards of the company's warehouses! All of these things, and more, can be achieved with little effort by a person with the right connections.*

On the other hand, there's nothing that says you can't simply use a corporation as a background player without the company, or its head, being an antagonist. The company could be the exact opposite, acting on the PCs' behalf either overtly or discreetly.

Example: *The president of a powerful international conglomerate has recently lost his wife to a ruthless gang of criminals — the same gang that our hero is hunted by! This corporate president has earmarked thousands of dollars for "preventive research, " all of which ends up in the hands of our hero who uses it to buy new weapons and additional street contacts.*

CAMPAIGN CITY STOCK EXCHANGE LISTING

The following is a list of the public corporations presented in this book (those which list stocks for sale on a public exchange). Companies that are privately held do not appear on this list. GMs can use this list as a reference or model for establishing the stock value of these corporations in the campaign.

Abbr

This is the corporation's abbreviation on the stock exchange. This same abbreviation will be used in any transaction concerning that corporation, and is also used in the stock listings of all newspapers.

Name

This is the full, legal name of the corporation.

Div

This represents the projected dividends (per share) that the corporation will pay at the end of the next quarter based on the current value of its stock. The amount is expressed in dollars. Thus, ".24" represents 24 cents).

Sales

This is the number of shares of the stock that were traded on the previous day. This number is expressed in hundreds. Multiply the number listed by 100 to find the actual number of shares traded.

Last

This was the stock's last price at the end of trading on the previous day. The number represents the cost per share and is expressed in dollars. Thus, "39 ¼" equals $39.25 per share.

Chg

This represents the change to the closing price of the stock on the previous day from the price of the stock on the day prior (two days ago). Changes are recorded in minimum increments of 1/8 (called the "one-eight rule"). A plus sign (+)

Abbr.	Name	Div.	Sales	Last	Chg.
AllBrCH	Allied Britain Chemicals	.24	9,851	39 ¼	+¼
ArmBr	Armbruster Industries	.31	2,608	65 ⅞	+1 ⅜
BioInv	Bio-Investigations Limited	.32	35,832	86 ½	-¼
CarMul	Carter-Mullering Industries	1.06	84,620	112 ¼	-½
CenT	Centurion Trucks Inc. U.S.A.	.12	1,286	64 ⅛	+⅜
FHer	First Hero's Bank, Inc.	1.24	58,040	39 ½	+1 ½
Fitza	Fitzarthur Publishing	.12	1,824	18 ¼	-⅜
FordmCT	Fordham ChemTech	.15	60,716	79 ⅜	+⅛
FutScp	Futurescope, Inc.	.48	1,937	25 ¼	+1 ¼
HendElc	Henderson Electronics	1.28	20,423	39 ⅜	+⅜
HypePrs	Hype Press, Inc.	.31	674	42 ⅜	-⅛
Irnbrdg	Ironbridge Industries, PLC	.92	11,494	62 ¾	+½
LKT	LKT	2.42	80,827	56 ⅝	-⅛
Lockley	Lockley International	1.88	257,649	79 ⅛	+¾
McNlAv	McNeil Aviation	1.25	9,496	37 ¼	-⅛
Montgy	Montgomery International	2.91	238,421	126 ⅛	+⅛
Pargn	Paragon EMS, Inc.	.72	2,757	29 ¼	-¼
Pegas	Pegasus, Inc.	1.10	8,471	28 ¾	+¼
QckCrp	QuickCorp	.20	12,062	12 ⅛	+⅛
SimCrp	SimCorp	.73	26,483	57	+¼
Yosh	Yoshida Corporation	2.88	224,648	102 ¾	+¼

indicates an increase in value, and a minus sign (-) indicates a decline in value.

Example: *Allied Britain Chemicals is listed under "Last" (yesterday's closing price) at 39 ¼, or $39.25 per share. In the "Chg." column is +¼, indicating that the Last price is ¼ higher than the previous day's closing price; the stock has climbed in value.*

BIBLIOGRAPHY

The following is a listing of the materials that helped inspire this book. Everything listed is recommended reading or viewing for anyone who wants to get more ideas on running corporations in their campaign. (Note: some of the motion pictures listed carry an R rating, and may not be suitable for younger viewers.) All listings are alphabetical.

REFERENCE BOOKS

The Complete Book of Money Secrets, 5th Edition; — (Boardroom Classics)

The Corporate Warriors; Douglas K. Ramsey (Houghton Mifflin Co.)

The Financing of Terror; James Adams (Simon and Schuster)

How To Buy Stocks, 7th Edition; Louis Engel and Brendan Boyd (Bantam Books)

KAIZEN; Masaaki Imai (Random House)

Patents, Copyrights & Trademarks; Frank H. Foster and Roberrt L. Shook (Wiley)

West's Business Law, 4th Edition; — (West Publishing Company)

ROLE-PLAYING GAME BOOKS

Champions of the North; Jon Mattson (Hero Games)

Classic Enemies; — (Hero Games)

Corporate Report 2020, Misc. volumes; — (R. Talsorian Games)

Corporate Shadowfiles; Nigel D. Findley (FASA)

Dark Champions; Steven S. Long (Hero Games)

High Tech Enemies; Sean Fannon (Hero Games)

Hero System Almanac I; — (Hero Games)

Justice, Not Law; Steven Long (Hero Games)

Kingdom of Champions; Phil Masters (Hero Games)

Sprawlgangs & Megacorps; Terry Amthor and Kevin Barrett (ICE)

Trader Captains & Merchant Princes; Guy W. McLimore, Jr. (FASA)

MOVIES

The *Alien* movies
Born Yesterday
Brainstorm
Class Action
The Firm
Gung Ho
News at 11
Other People's Money
The Pelican Brief
Rising Sun
Robocop
Rollover
The Running Man
The Secret of My Success
Total Recall
Trading Places
Wall Street
Working Girl

GLOSSARY

The following is a list of terms commonly found in a corporate or business environment.

American Stock Exchange: The second major market for securities (stocks, bonds, etc.)

Annuities: An investment yielding fixed payments, usually yearly.

Antitrust laws: Laws designed to prevent illegal stock trading.

Bear: A person who sells stock hoping to buy them back at a lower price; a pessimist.

Bearer bonds: Unregistered bond certificates redeemable by the bearer.

Board of directors: An elected body that oversees the operation of a company.

Bonds: A corporate debt, with a set return and length of maturity.

Broker: See Stock Broker.

Bull: A speculator who buys stocks expecting their value to rise; an optimist.

Capital: Money or property owned by or used in business.

Capital gains tax: Tax on profits made from the sale of capital investments.

Capital stock: The capital of a corporation, divided into shares.

Central securities market: Method by which exchange members compete among each other to offer the best price for securities.

CEO: See Chief Executive Officer.

Chairman: Person in charge of a meeting or committee (also; Chairperson).

Charter: A registered document outlining the by-laws, rules and principles of a corporation.

Chief Counsel: Manager in charge of legal matters; the head attorney.

Chief Executive Officer: The top manager of a corporation.

Chief Marketing Director: Manager in charge of marketing.

Collateral-trust bond: Bond issued with a collateral deposit.

Corporate bonds: See Bonds.

Corporation: A form of business ownership; a legal entity chartered by a state.

Convertible Preferred Bonds: Bonds which may be converted to common stock.

Court Order: An official instruction from a court of law.

Debenture: An interest-bearing bond, usually offered without security.

Delisting: Removing a public corporation from a stock exchange

Dividend: A portion of a corporation's profits paid to a stockholder.

Dow Jones Industrial Average: The average value of transportation, utilities and industrial stocks on the exchange; presented every half hour during trading.

Down tick: A drop in a stock's price from its previous transaction price.

Dual listing (on exchanges): Listing a company on two or more public exchanges.

Earnings: Income generated by a business through sales.

Environmental Protection Agency: Government agency which administers all federal environmental legislation.

Equity: The value of property beyond the amount owed.

Even tick: A stock price that remains unchanged since its last transaction.

Federal Communications Commission: Government agency which regulates telecommunications.

Federal Reserve Board: Government agency which regulates commercial interest rates.

Federal Trade Commission: Government Agency which regulates trade in the U.S.

First-mortgage bond: A bond secured by mortgage of all a company's property.

Floor broker: The person on the exchange floor who executes stock sales.

Food and Drug Administration: Government agency which regulates food, drugs, cosmetics and medical devices.

Full disclosure: The requirement of companies to disclose all pertinent information to the S.E.C.

General obligation bonds: Bonds backed by the full faith, credit and taxing power of a state or municipality.

General partner: A managing partner in a business partnership.

Greenmail: To influence a decision with large financial offers.

Gross National Product: The total value of a nation's output of goods and services.

Hit: To accept a stock bid; used in an exchange.

Hostile Takeover: The purchase of a company against the wishes of its Board of Directors or shareholders.

Housing Authority Bonds: Bonds issued to generate capital to build low-income housing.

Income bond: Bond which pays interest only as it is earned.

Incorporation: To incorporate a business or entity, such as a city.

Industrial average: See Dow Jones Industrial Average.

Inflation: The decrease of currency value and increase of prices.

Injunction: A court order preventing a specific act.

Inside price: The price from one securities dealer to another; wholesale price.

Insider Trading: Conducting a securities transaction based on information not available to the general public.

Labor Union: An organization which represents a group of workers in labor and legal matters.

Liabilities: Debts.

Limited partner: A non-managing partner; an unnamed partner.

Liquidation: To sell off all property, converting assets to cash.

Locked-in stockholders: Stockholders who refuse to sell for a profit, in order to avoid paying capital gains taxes.

Manager: An employee in the management tier of a corporation.

Margin trading: To purchase stocks partially on credit.

Maturity: The point at which a bond becomes payable to the holder.

Merger: The combining of two companies through a friendly takeover.

Money market funds: A collective short term investment.

Municipal bonds: Bonds issued by a local municipality, such as a city or state.

Mutual funds: A common fund of pooled investments managed by a firm.

Net worth: The value of a company's assets minus its liabilities.

New York Stock Exchange: A large private center for stock trading.

No-par stock: A stock with no value set by the company at the time of issue.

Not-for-profit: A corporation not intended to earn a profit.

Nuclear Regulatory Commission: Government agency which regulates civilian use of nuclear materials.

Obligations (bonds): See Bonds.

Occupational Safety and Health Administration: Government agency which regulates work conditions and safety practices at work sites.

Officer: Individuals designated as board members of a corporation.

Open-end trust: A mutual fund.

Outstanding (shares): Shares of stock that are sold (i.e., owned by shareholders).

PAC: See Political Action Committee.

Pacific Stock Exchange: A regional exchange, located in both Los Angeles and San Francisco.

Paper profits: The increase in the value of owned stock.

Par value: The value of stocks when first offered by a corporation.

Partnership: Two or more persons engaged in a business and registered as a partnership with the state (see General Partner).

Penny stocks: Stocks sold at very low costs (such as $1 per share).

PLC: See "Public Limited Company."

Political Action Committee: A group established for political lobbying.

Preferred stock: Stock that is given priority over common stocks.

Premium: A stock price that is above par (see Par).

President: The primary officer of a corporation.

Price-earnings ratio: A stock's market price divided by its earnings per share.

Prospectus: Information detailing a company's financial position and current and anticipated stock performance.

Proxy: The authority to vote for another, or the person so authorized.

Proxy fight: Effort to win proxy votes from shareholders; a vote decided primarily by proxy votes.

Public Limited Company: British term equating to an American corporation.

Public offering: The sale of common stocks on a public exchange.

Pyramiding: Purchasing additional shares of stock with paper profits.

Quarterly ratings (bonds): The quality rating of a bond.

Quarterly reports: Profit reports issued quarterly by a corporation.

Red herrings: A preliminary prospectus not yet reviewed by the SEC.

Regional exchange: An exchange for local companies.

Registered bonds: Bonds registered in the name of the owner.

Regulation T: Federal regulation governing all matters of credit on stock transactions.

Restraining order: A court order preventing a specific act.

Retained earnings: Profits not paid out as dividends, but reinvested in a company.

Revenue bonds: Bonds with interest based on profits generated by the issuer.

Risk capital: The money at risk when purchasing any kind of property.

Savings bonds: Bonds issued by the federal government with a 5 or 10 year maturity.

Seat (on NYSE): Membership on the exchange.

Second-preferred stock: Stock below preferred stock in priority, but still higher than common stock.

Secretary: The chief administrative officer of a corporation.

Securities: Stocks and bonds.

Securities analyst: Someone who follows financial trends in an industry.

Securities and Exchange Commission: Regulatory agency that oversees the stock and bond markets.

Share (of stock): Represents a fraction of the company and gives the owner the right to vote at annual shareholder meetings.

Shareholders: Owners of a company's stock.

Short-form prospectus: A condensed prospectus.

Silent partner: See "Limited partner."

Sole proprietorship: A business owned by a single person, who assumes full legal and financial liability.

Special tax bonds: Bonds payable only from proceeds of a particular tax.

Speculation: Estimating the future value of stocks.

Split (stock): To divide existing numbers and value of a stock.

Standard & Poor's: Commercial securities research organization.

Stock: Shares of corporate capital.

Stock broker: A licensed dealer who buys and sells stocks and bonds.

Stock certificate: A certificate showing ownership of a company's stock.

Stock indexes: A group of related stocks (e.g., utilities index, transportation index)

Stockholders: Owners of stock (also; Shareholders)

Tariff: A tax placed on imported goods.

Tax shelters: A tax-free or tax-deferred investment.

Ticker tape: A paper strip with stock exchange transactions typed onto it and transmitted by wire to "tickers" in every broker's office in the country; no longer used.

Tombstone announcement: An announcement of a new stock with only the issue's name, size, price and the name of the underwriters and dealers who have it for sale.

Trading floor: The area of a stock exchange where shares are traded.

Trading hours (NYSE): 10:00 a.m. until 4:00 p.m., Eastern Standard Time.

Trans-Lux screens: Large screens displaying projections of transparent ticker tapes.

Treasurer: The chief financial officer of a corporation.

Treasury bills: A short-term government bond.

Treasury bonds: A long-term government bond.

Trust fund: A fund overseen by a legally appointed trustee (such as for a minor).

Look for these ICE product lines at your favorite retail outlet.

Each of our role playing systems is supplemented with a variety of support material.

Prices are subject to alteration without prior notice. Write or call for a free catalog (see below).

#1000 – Rolemaster™ $38.00

I.C.E.'s advanced Fantasy Role Playing Game system, ***Rolemaster*** is a complete set of the most advanced, realistic and sophisticated FRP rules available and they have been reformatted and reorganized in the new Second Edition. The flexibility of the system allows it to be used wholly or in part. Each of the books in this boxes set can be used separately to improve the realism of most major FRP systems! Look for the new complement to your ***Rolemaster*** game: ***Shadow World*** adventures.

#6050 – Shadow World™ Master Atlas, 2nd Ed. $24.00

Shadow World, a whole new realm of adventure! The planet *Kulthea*™ forms the ***Shadow World***, a unique fantasy gaming environment supported by comprehensive stats for *Rolemaster.* The Shadow World is a vast planet of scattered isles and lost realms, each land isolated by forces both tangible and supernatural. Not only is it a rich fantasy world unto itself, but it allows the GM to insert it into his ***Rolemaster*** campaign whole or in part. It is also usable with most major fantasy role playing systems.

#9050 – Space Master: RPG™ Book $26.00

Adventure in deep space on alien worlds with ICEs Science Fiction Role Playing Game system! Completely compatible with ***Rolemaster***, ***Space Master*** covers professions, races, cultures, settings, and much more. The range of technologies stretches from tomorrow to the far future.

#5100 – Cyberspace™ $18.00

Set in the gritty near future where Megacorporation repression collides with Sprawl street warfare, ***Cyberspace*** is fully compatible with ***Space Master*** & ***Rolemaster.*** Muscle-grafted Punks and Netheads crawl out of the gutters to scrap Media Stars and Cybernetic Mercenaries, a conflict beyond the stature of Good and Evil. From depraved polluted cities to the surreal beauty of Earth's global computer matrix, this is the world of ***Cyberspace***!

#7500 – Bladestorm™, miniatures rules $30.00

The Bladelands are a wild, chaotic area shrouded within a mantle of ferocious magical gales called Bladestorms. Here, a little battle can decide the fate of a budding tribe or nation.

Bladestorm (***BSt***) is a skirmish-style fantasy miniatures game. Each figure represents one person or creature. Simple rules regulate small-scale miniatures battles and mass battles involving hundreds. ***BSt*** is a fast-paced combat system for fighting miniatures battles in any fantasy world, but we provide rich background material and set of scenarios to get you started in the Bladelands. The ***BSt*** box contains: a 64 page rulebook, a 160 page Bladelands sourcebook, a 32 page scenario book, a 32 page color guide, two full color maps, and a set of eight dice.

#2000 – MERP Second Edition $30.00

Middle-earth Role Playing™ Second Edition (MERP™) includes new material, but remains the same rules system and is fully compatible with the first edition ***MERP*** and its dozens of sourcebooks & supplements. ***MERP 2nd Edition*** provides expanded Middle-earth peoples descriptions with new specific backgrounds. There are now predesigned *Character Templates* that enable both novices and Lord of the Rings Adventure Game afficionados to start playing quickly! This 256 page hardbound book is our Collector's Edition. ***MERP 2nd Edition*** will bring the most popular fantasy trilogy, *The Lord of the Rings*, to life as never before!

#7010 – Silent Death™ (deluxe boxed game) $40.00

Crammed full with 18 metal miniature spacecraft and bases (value – $36 by themselves!), dice, maps, counters and more, Silent Death is an exciting boxed game of space fighter combat. Silent Death is an instant hit with Sci-Fi fans and gamers who like games with fast competitive play that blend the very best elements of boardgaming and miniatures. Also available without the miniatures as *Silent Death Unleaded*™ (#7000) for $20.00.

#450 – Champions®
the Super Role Playing Game $26.00

Don't just read comic books, live them! With the easy-to-use character design system, your only limit is your imagination. ***Champions*** is based on the *Hero System*, the rules system of all Hero products. Because of this common thread, all *Hero Games* are compatible. Learn one *Hero Game* and you can easily play them all. ***Champions*** has just undergone an extensive revision, but all previous ***Champions*** material is still compatible.

#500 – HERO System Rulesbook™
(Included inside Champions) $20.00

The award-winning *HERO system* lets you role play any time, any place, any technology, and any power level. The unique character design rules allow creation of any character, whether he comes from a movie, a book, or your own imagination. Play fantasy fighters, modern spies, power-armor troopers, or even superheroes — it's all here! This jam-packed 224 page tome includes a complete superhero team provided for instant fun. The revised *HERO system* is cleaner, better integrated, and more streamlined than ever before.

#502 – Fantasy Hero™ $20.00

This 256 page campaign book shows you how to run a fantasy campaign using the *HERO system.* Inside are extensive guidelines for designing fantasy characters, setting up a magic system, simulating fantasy combat, and setting up a fantasy campaign. Dozens of fantasy weapons, hundreds of spells, quick character design templates, and new ready-to-run scenario ideas are also included.

These fine products are sold at better retail outlets worldwide. Available at better game stores — or order from ICE, Inc. P.O. Box 1605 Charlottesville Va 22902, USA. **Prices are subject to alteration without prior notice.** VISA & MASTERCARD orders (and catalog requests) call (800) 325-0479. Va residents, Canadians and overseas customers call (804) 295-3917. Please make phone orders during business hours: 9am-5pm, Eastern Standard Time, Mon-Fri. **Call or Write for a free catalog!**

Superhero Shopping List

Look for these heroic products at your favorite game, book, comic, or hobby shop.

The Hero System

The *HERO System* is the original and best universal role playing system. Extensively revised and improved, the HERO System is intended to be intuitive —that is, all the rules follow from a few simple guidelines. It is generic in that it can be used to play in any role playing setting.

HERO System Rulesbook™ **$20.00**
(Included in *Champions* hardcover) The award-winning HERO System lets you role play any time, any place, any technology, and any power level.

HERO Bestiary™ **$18.00**
Every creature, every genre—the HERO System strikes again—a host of animals, monsters, dinosaurs, and other beasts.

HERO System Almanac™ **$13.00**
This book is jammed full of optional rules, new systems, campaigning notes, and advice on how to set up campaigns.

Adventurers Club™ (AC)
The magazine for Hero Gamers! The articles and columns are dedicated to expanding and improving the already fine line of Hero Games. $4.00 per issue. Subscriptions are available for (U.S.) $12.00 for four issues to the U.S. or Canada; $20.00 for overseas subscriptions.

Genre/Campaign Books

Campaign books are designed to complement the *HERO System*. Each book deals with a specific genre and provides enough information for complete roleplaying in that genre.

Champions® **$26.00**
(contains the HERO System rulesbook) Play your favorite comic book hero, or create your own! The character generation system lets you design your heroes the way you want them. The combat system is easy to learn and play. Also covered are skills, powers, disadvantages, weapons, and guidelines on campaigning.

Fantasy Hero™ **$20.00**
This full-fledged 256 page campaign book shows you how to run a fantasy campaign using the HERO System.

Fantasy Hero Companion™ **$15.00**
Fantasy Hero Companion II™ **$16.00**
These products have everything you would want to make your *Fantasy Hero* campaigns even better.

Western Hero™ **$20.00**
Western Hero is the definitive campaign book for adventures in the Wild West using the universal HERO System.

Ninja Hero™ **$17.00**
Ninja Hero is the definitive martial arts source book for the HERO System and is equally useful for Heroic and Superheroic campaigns.

Cyber Hero™ **$20.00**
Cyber Hero is HERO System campaign supplement for the near dark future. Includes a fully developed cyberpunk setting: timeline, scenarios, adventures seeds, package deals, special combat rules, equipment lists, etc.

Dark Champions™, *Heroes of Vengeance* **$20.00**
The ultimate *Champions* campaign sourcebook for the twilight world of vigilante superheroes who walk the line between justice and vengeance!

Supplements for Champions

Champions GM Screen & Accessories™	**$12.00**
Mind Games™	**$8.00**
Classic Enemies™	**$13.00**
Challenges for Champions™	**$9.00**
The Zodiac Conspiracy™	**$11.00**
Invasions: Target Earth™	**$8.00**
Day of the Destroyer™	**$7.00**
Invaders from Below™	**$10.00**
Kingdom of Champions™	**$18.00**
Champions in 3-D™	**$16.00**
Demons Rule™	**$7.00**
Alien Enemies™	**$12.00**
Olympians™	**$9.00**
Road Kill™	**$7.00**
Classic Organizations™	**$18.00**
European Enemies™	**$13.00**
Champions Presents #1™	**$14.00**
Champions of the North™	**$14.00**
Normals Unbound™	**$13.00**
Champions Universe™	**$18.00**
High Tech Enemies™	**$13.00**
Champions Presents #2™	**$15.00**
VIPER™	**$20.00**
Shadows of the City™	**$15.00**
Allies™	**$13.00**
Mutant File™	**$13.00**

Creatures of the Night, Horror Enemies™ **$13.00**
A sourcebook for supernatural foes in the *Champions Universe*. 40+ detailed villians with motivations, tactics, and horrific powers.

Justice Not Law™ **$15.00**
A sourcebook for *Dark Champions* containing NPCs, organizations, and a wealth of other information to make the backdrop for any game. Includes a sample campaign city, new vigilantes, 36+ new villians and NPCs, and new criminal organizations.

Underworld Enemies™ **$13.00**
More villians for your *Dark Champions* game! Includes extensive campaigning tips and adventure seeds. WARNING: This book deals with sensitive subject and is recommended for mature players only.

An Eye for an Eye™ **$14.00**
From the author of *Dark Champions* comes an incredible sourcebook that will bring any campaign to a new level of excitement. Written for both players and Game Masters, *An Eye for an Eye* is jam packed with new rules, new wewapons, and new organizations.

These fine products are sold at better retail outlets worldwide. Available at better game stores — or order from ICE, Inc. P.O. Box 1605 Charlottesville Va 22902, USA. **Prices are subject to alteration without prior notice.** VISA & MASTERCARD orders (and catalog requests) call (800) 325-0479. Va residents, Canadians and overseas customers call (804) 295-3917. Please make phone orders during business hours: 9am-5pm, Eastern Standard Time, Mon-Fri. **Call or Write for a free catalog!**